The Competition Solution

The Competition Solution

The Bipartisan Secret behind American Prosperity

Paul A. London

The AEI Press

Publisher for the American Enterprise Institute

WASHINGTON, D.C.

Available in the United States from the AEI Press, c/o Client Distribution Services, 193 Edwards Drive, Jackson, TN 38301. To order, call toll free: 1-800-343-4499. Distributed outside the United States by arrangement with Eurospan, 3 Henrietta Street, London WC2E 8LU, England.

Library of Congress Cataloging-in-Publication Data

London, Paul A.
    The competition solution : the bipartisan secret behind American prosperity / Paul A. London.
        p. cm.
    Includes bibliographical references and index.
    ISBN 0-8447-4204-X (hardcover : alk. paper)
1. Competition—United States. 2. United States—Economic conditions—2001- 3. United States—Economic conditions—20th century. 4. United States—Politics and government—2001- 5. United States—Politics and government—20th century. I. Title.

    HF1414.L665 2005
    338.6'048'0973—dc22

                                                                    2004023183

10 09 08 07 06 05   2 3 4 5 6 7

Printed in the United States of America

Contents

Introduction

I take my stand absolutely, where every progressive ought to take his stand, on the proposition that private monopoly is indefensible and intolerable.

—Woodrow Wilson[1]

The American economy of the 1990s was the envy of the world. More than 20 million jobs were created, investment and productivity soared, and the fear of inflation that had haunted policymakers for forty years almost disappeared. The key question is why.

The resurgent economy was glorious in part because it came after a dismal beginning. The decade began with unemployment rising above 7 percent, the painful level that had prevailed for long stretches during the 1970s and '80s. Worse, most economists believed that joblessness could not drop much below 6 percent without reigniting inflation.

From 1992 until 1994, the economy improved, but the mood of the country remained sour. It was seen as a "jobless recovery"—although in fact the unemployment rate was falling fairly quickly. Then, almost miraculously, by mid-decade the American economy became sunshine itself. The whole country surged, while once-feared economic challengers, Japan and Europe, were stagnant and stumbling. By the latter part of the decade, unemployment had dropped to 4 percent, its lowest level in over thirty years, yawning budget deficits had turned into surpluses, and inflation seemed to be a thing of the past.[2]

The 2001 recession was painful, particularly in contrast to what had gone before: The boom years had been so good that even a relatively modest recession hurt badly. The tech-centered speculation in stocks started to collapse in early 2000. When the terrorist attacks on September 11, 2001, shocked the economy again, corporate profits dropped dramatically, investment fell off sharply, job growth stopped, and job losses accelerated. Unemployment rose from 4 percent in 2000 to a peak of 6.3 percent in June 2003 before edging slowly back down to 5.4 percent by mid-2004.[3]

The contraction of employment in manufacturing was especially sharp because the growth of consumer demand slowed while productivity kept rising. When productivity improves during periods of slow growth, fewer people are needed to produce the goods and services that are being consumed. High technology, telecommunications, and finance—the hottest sectors of the economy during the 1990s—took especially big hits in the first years of the new millennium.

Investors and retirees felt the pain, especially those who had believed that the high-tech boom would last forever and had ignored warnings to diversify their portfolios. The Dow Jones Industrial Average dropped from 11,500 in spring 2001 to a low of about 7,200 in fall 2002. While the Dow in 2003 regained much of the ground it had lost—and is over 10,000 as this book goes to press—the memory of the meltdown remains sobering.

The U.S. economy in 2003 and 2004 has been growing faster than most other advanced economies, despite a much more uncertain world, so the persistence of unemployment at a level that is well above what it was in 1999 and 2000 should not be too discouraging. Rather than believing that the economic performance of the 1990s is out of reach, we should understand why the economy was so good then—and what we can do to recapture the magic.

What made the record-breaking economy of the 1990s possible? Who created it—and how? Treasury Secretary Robert Rubin suggested in 1998 that the factors involved were many and varied, and that economic historians would still be identifying them decades from now.[4] Were the causes really so complex and unknowable? I believe not. This book argues that the answers to these questions are both clearly understandable and quite different from what most economists and political pundits have been saying. Most of these commentators, regardless of politics, give too much weight to policies that had relatively little to do with the success of the 1990s, while giving too little credit to the real causes.

A quick review of several of the most popular explanations for growth and prosperity is in order. The "supply-side" argument has been particularly popular with many conservatives, such as Dick Armey, a former professor of economics, who retired as majority leader of the House of Representatives in 2003. This perspective is very influential among Republicans in Congress and the George W. Bush administration.[5] For this group, low taxes, especially on interest, dividends, capital gains, and inheritance, are crucial to growth because they are sources of capital investment. The supply-siders believe that tax cuts enacted by President Ronald Reagan in the 1980s (like the so-called Kennedy tax cut enacted under Lyndon Johnson in the 1960s) led to surging investment and are the key to prosperity. They argue that the rebound from the 2001 recession is due to the tax cuts championed by President Bush and enacted in 2001, 2002, and 2003.

Another broad group looks to the Federal Reserve and its long-serving chairman, Alan Greenspan, for economic leadership.[6] This group is less influential than it was when inflation was a nagging problem in the 1970s and '80s. Its adherents, however, revere Greenspan and believe that the conquest of inflation and the prosperity of the 1980s and 1990s were principally the result of wise monetary policies pursued by Paul Volcker from 1979 to 1986, and by Greenspan, his successor.

A third group of economists, many of whom worked with the Clinton administration, have their own explanation for the booming 1990s. For decades, Democrats were seen as the party of government spending and budget deficits, hostile to business. In part to combat these perceptions, Democrats recently have emphasized that private investment surged and deficits turned into surpluses under Clinton. They argue that this was due to Clinton's willingness in 1993 to raise taxes on upper-income taxpayers and restrain the growth of some government programs, which led to lower interest rates and encouraged the record-breaking surge in investment. To stimulate the economy in 2004, they would raise taxes on more affluent Americans, reduce the deficit, and encourage investment in the United States while preserving some tax cuts for lower- and middle-income taxpayers.

A fourth group of analysts believes that the prosperity was the result of new technology. In this view, productivity surged during the 1990s because investments in new technology made over previous years began to pay off. In other words, prosperity had little to do with particular policies or approaches, but was largely a nonpolitical, technical phenomenon.

These summaries greatly simplify more complex ideas, of course, but they capture the most important points. Despite large apparent differences, all have an essential common core: They stress broad policies that affect the whole economy—macroeconomics as economists call it—rather than policies that affect specific sectors and industries—microeconomics.

This book takes a different tack. I believe that policy decisions during the last thirty years that increased competition in individual sectors and industries are the most important forces behind America's prosperity. The secret of the 1990s and the substantial recovery from the 2001 recession lies not in broad policies relating to taxes and money supply but in more than two decades of bipartisan policymaking affecting specific industries, which ultimately made competition in these sectors far more intense. This fundamental approach to the economy—the promotion of competition in industry after industry—was more important than taxes, monetary policy, or even technology in making the prosperity of the 1990s possible.

Of course, sensible tax and monetary policies are important, as are efforts to keep government spending within bounds and to use tax money wisely. And new technology did, indeed, make a significant contribution. But it is impossible to understand why the American economy was so good in the 1990s—and why America did better than other countries—without understanding the role that more intense competition played. American industries as varied as automobiles, steel, telephones, airlines, trucking, finance, and retailing were far more dynamic than they had been in the 1960s and 1970s because of more vigorous competition within them, not because American tax and monetary policies or technology were better than those of other countries.

And there is a surprising political dimension to this story as well: Competition in industry after industry became more intense despite the strenuous efforts by powerful business and labor interests to limit it. These established interests wanted political leaders and the government to help them keep new competitors out, but by and large, they failed. The "special interests" threatened and begged, but they lost, and the country prospered as a result.

That is the surprising story of this book: hard political fights over the last thirty years were crucial to our success. The battles were often confusing, but in case after case, competition triumphed. Improving our performance will depend more on future efforts to expand competition in areas like health care and education, which are holding the economy back today, than on tax arrangements and changes in interest rates, which do little to make poorly performing industries more dynamic and successful.

What kinds of policies are important? Our recent experiences offer clear guidance:

- The auto industry and the rest of American manufacturing would never have modernized had it not been for trade policies that encouraged both competition from imports and greater foreign investment in the United States. Such policies will be just as important in the future, and the fights will be fierce.

- Key industries like transportation, communications, and energy were fundamentally changed by legal, regulatory, and legislative decisions that increased competition. These industries would never have changed if political battles had not been won by the advocates of greater competition. Clearly, similar policies encouraging price competition and new competitive entrants in other sectors of the economy will be vital to prosperity in the future.

- Strong enforcement of antitrust laws starting as early as the 1950s and '60s also helped increase competition in manufacturing, the regulated industries, financial markets, and retailing and opened these areas to new entrepreneurial firms. Antitrust lawsuits, for example, led to the end of fixed brokerage rates, opening up financial markets, helped new entrants break the AT&T monopoly, and made it impossible for established retailers to keep new competitors out. Antitrust will have to play a similar role in the future to maintain these gains and to create similar ones in sectors where competition is still weak.

In sum, a variety of policies and political decisions affecting specific sectors of the economy forced American businesses to compete more vigorously in the 1990s than they had earlier. This changed the way business had to be done in the United States, encouraged investment that increased productivity, and made low unemployment possible without triggering inflation. These policies were the key to prosperity. These fundamental changes also made the American economy the envy of the world, and forced the Japanese and Europeans to follow this model. Neither America's overseas rivals nor Americans, who often overestimate the power of special interests, fully appreciate how successful the country's flexible political system was in making established interests do what they did not want to do—or how important this willingness to challenge entrenched interests will be in the future.

The failure of most analysts of the economy to give credit to the role of policies that forced businesses to compete is especially bizarre because the conviction that competition is the key to prosperity dates back to Adam Smith and his great work, *The Wealth of Nations*. It also is no exaggeration to say that America was built upon the idea of competition in politics, and that the Founders understood competition's importance in economics. The Founders made competition—the clash of "opposite and rival interests," as they called it—the keystone of the American system of government, and they knew it would be central to economic prosperity as well.[7] Their aim was to set limits on economic as well as political power, and they understood that checks and balances in governmental institutions had a key role to play in preventing the abuse of both.

The American consensus on competition persisted well into the twentieth century. President Theodore Roosevelt, a Republican, made "trust-busting" a cornerstone of his approach. Woodrow Wilson, Roosevelt's Democratic rival, also was a great champion of dynamic competition. He fought to lower the tariff walls that kept foreign competitors out of our markets, and for the passage of antitrust laws. His aim was to use both foreign and domestic competition to liberate the country from the "trusts"— monopolies, in modern terms—that he believed were strangling creative entrepreneurs. Like Adam Smith and the Founders, Wilson also understood that competition would have to be defended by governments against attacks by powerful interests. But the Great Depression and World

War II shifted America's focus from competition toward the powerful effects of monetary and tax policies. The ravages of the Depression made it seem as though capitalism and the competition associated with it had failed the country and drove economists to look for other ways to promote national wealth and well-being.

The procompetitive policy changes in specific sectors that made the 1990s possible suggest that another round of rethinking is at hand. The success of the policies that made competition more intense between the 1970s and the 1990s indicates that such policies are still central to prosperity, and indeed that no country, industry, or enterprise works well without them. It also tells us that government has an indispensable role to play in making sure that private interests check and balance each other.

This book centers on the battles that began in earnest in the 1970s to make competition more intense than it had become during the immediate postwar years. It recounts the courageous efforts by American presidents and political leaders of both parties to help new competitors challenge entrenched business and labor interests—the Big Three auto companies and the United Auto Workers; Big Steel and the steelworkers union; AT&T and the Communications Workers of America; the trucking companies and the Teamsters union; the major eastern banks and financial institutions; and even powerful retailing interests and their employees and sympathizers who wanted to keep new competitors out.

New American entrepreneurs needed—and found—support in different parts of the political system to challenge the establishments. Ken Iverson built Nucor Steel in states far away from the old steel heartland. Jack "the Giant-Killer" Goeken started MCI in a corner of Illinois, but needed legal help from Washington to protect him from Ma Bell. Fred Smith of Memphis, Tennessee, founded Federal Express and helped open airlines to competition with Washington allies on his side. Financier Michael Milken beat out the established Wall Street financial houses and essentially invented junk bonds; he, too, had help. And discounter Sam Walton built Wal-Mart from a base in rural Arkansas into one of the largest corporations in America, fighting a host of status quo interests at every level. These men changed the way we do business in America, but they had allies in government.

Another sea change in American business was the erosion of the power of America's labor unions, whose strongholds usually were in industries where competition was weak. Roy Siemiller, the president of the airline mechanics' union, beat President Johnson in the 1960s; but his union and others had lost power by the 1990s. They did not go without hard political fights, but the end result was that the industries that employed them grew faster, and consumers benefited.

There were political heroes—congressional leaders who held hearings, civil servants and regulators who listened and were persuaded that more competition would be good, and political appointees who told the powerful interests the bad news. They all worked with presidents in the 1970s, '80s, and '90s who took the political heat to make competition more intense. John Robson and Alfred Kahn at the old Civil Aeronautics Board led the fight (during the Ford and Carter administrations) to open air travel to competition. Republican Paul MacAvoy (working in Ford's White House) and Democrat Stu Eizenstat (in Carter's) both confronted the Teamsters in high dudgeon. And presidents Reagan, George H. W. Bush, and Clinton took political risks to face down powerful interests who wanted to limit competition.

In industry after industry, politicians and the American political system said no to the special interests that had seemed unassailable in the 1960s and '70s. By the 1990s, many of these battles were won—or at least, victory was in sight. Increased competition forced one sector of the economy after another to become more innovative, flexible, and productive. Competition in one area often led to competition in others. To thrive in this new environment, companies had to cut costs and prices, invest in new technologies, reallocate and reassign labor and capital, and become more efficient. Prosperity was the result.

These lessons are apparent when we look at what happened in each of these industries. If the past is any guide, they will repeat themselves. Political leaders will have to fight to maintain competition where it is strong now and to expand it in new areas, like education and health care, where it is still weak. Opposition to competition is always there, and new status quo interests will emerge and fight to handicap would-be competitors.

This book is organized to answer four basic questions. First: what happened? Chapter 1 compares two economies: the vibrant economy of the last decade, and the stagnant economy with high inflation and unemployment of the 1970s. How had key industries and sectors changed, and what did those changes mean?

Chapters 2 through 6 detail how the changes took place in auto manufacturing, steel, transportation and communications, finance, and retail. It is essential we recognize who pushed for more competition, who opposed it, and how it became so much more intense by the 1990s.

Chapter 7 asks two perplexing questions: Given that competition is the most important idea in the last two hundred years of economics, and political competition (checks and balances) the most important idea in American politics, why have economists focused more on monetary and tax policies in recent years? And why do so many Americans continue to cling to the populist and Marxist myth that the special interests get what they want in America, when it is so clear that many of the most powerful special interests of the 1970s were vanquished by the 1990s?

Chapter 8 pulls together these themes and looks to the future. How can we maintain the productive, competitive environment that existed in the 1990s in the face of new economic and political challenges, and how can we bring genuine competition to health care, education, and other areas where investment and change driven by it could give the economy a real lift?

This is a big story about economic change, but it is not a technical treatment filled with economic jargon. The important changes that made the 1990s possible are not hidden in complex mathematical equations. They are clear to see when we examine the history of these industries. This book shows that an informal, almost ad hoc, competitive policy was the key to prosperity in the 1990s. It opened up huge areas of the American economy, created thousands of new companies, and gave millions of Americans work and a bigger piece of the American dream. The question is, what can we learn from this experience that will expand prosperity in the future and how can we apply it not only to parts of the economy that could slide back, but to other sectors that are not yet modernized?

1

A Tale of Two Economies

In those sectors where both companies and unions possess substantial market power, the interplay of price and wage decisions could set off a movement toward a higher price level. . . . The Nation must rely on the good sense and public spirit of our business and labor leaders to hold the line on prices in 1962.

—John F. Kennedy[1]

If you talk to business executives they'll tell you they can't raise prices. . . . When executive after executive in industry after industry tells you the same thing in convincing detail, attention must be paid.

—Stephen B. Shepard[2]

Suspecting a Trap

Alan Blinder and the other White House economists who came into office with President Bill Clinton thought that the Republicans who preceded them might have set a trap. President George H. W. Bush's three-member Council of Economic Advisers projected in their last annual review in January 1993 that unemployment could fall to 5.3 percent by 1998, with a 3 percent inflation rate. Blinder suspected that this projection was too optimistic and was meant to make Clinton look bad. The Clinton economists thought that such low levels of unemployment and inflation were very unlikely, and they were sure—probably correctly—that the Republicans thought so as well.

Clinton's economists were more cautious in their projections. A year later, in the new administration's first *Economic Report of the President*, they projected that unemployment would fall to no lower than 5.5 percent in the next five years, with an inflation rate a bit worse than the 3 percent projected by Bush's economists.[3] The Democrats thought even their more cautious projections might be too optimistic, but they did not want to appear less hopeful than the Republicans had been.[4] In fact, both sides were far too pessimistic. The actual unemployment rate in 1998 was 4.5 percent, while inflation was 1.6 percent, about half what it was expected to be; unemployment was even lower in 1999 and 2000, with absolutely no increase in inflation.[5]

This anecdote underlines the most remarkable thing about the prosperity of the 1990s: The U.S. economy did far, far better than most economists had expected. Inflation had been the great fear of the previous thirty years, and economists affiliated with both parties, academics, and the Federal Reserve Bank believed that low unemployment risked bringing it back once again. In the 1990s, that did not happen, and the reasons why it did not are vitally important.

In 1993, economists seemed to be on safe ground when they said that low unemployment risked reigniting inflation. Their position was consistent with the forty-year-old work of A. W. Phillips, an Australian economist. Phillips had used data from Britain in the 1940s and '50s to demonstrate that inflation tended to rise as unemployment fell—a mathematical relationship that has become known as "the Phillips Curve." And it seemed to be true in America as well: Throughout the 1960s and '70s, any time unemployment fell to the neighborhood of 6 percent, inflation rose. There seemed to be little reason to doubt the continuing validity of this relationship.[6] Most economists of both political persuasions in the 1980s and '90s saw 6 percent (or something close to that) as a tripwire for inflation, and the Republicans' 5.3 percent projection for 1998 was—as Blinder understood—well past that danger point.

Blinder and his associates were part of a consensus in the economic profession that took a long time to change. In 1996, a full three years after Clinton and his economists came into office, the liberal economist and columnist Paul Krugman wrote an article in *The Economist* called "Stable Prices and Fast Growth: Just Say No"—a title that reflected the conventional wisdom. Krugman, who might have been expected to be sympathetic to the

Clintonians, said (in this article and others he penned during the same period) that growth faster than 2.5 percent and unemployment lower than 5.5 percent risked reigniting inflation, and he ridiculed the idea that it could be otherwise.[7]

Conservatives for the most part took the same position, and much was written about when the Fed would have to step in to slow the economy. Milton Friedman, the Nobel laureate and conservative hero, had talked about a "natural rate of unemployment"—a Phillips-like idea—in the 1960s.[8] Friedman's "natural rate" was whatever level of unemployment was consistent with stable wages and prices. Friedman did not know what that rate was, specifically, but said that efforts to push unemployment lower than that point would lead to inflation. In the mid-90s, most economists— conservative or liberal—believed that the Fed was taking a big risk letting unemployment fall to levels well below 5.5 to 6 percent.

For instance, N. Gregory Mankiw of Harvard, a conservative professor whom George W. Bush later appointed chairman of his Council of Economic Advisers, wrote on the subject of unemployment and inflation fifteen months after Krugman did, and sounded very much the same alarm. In a December 1997 article called, "Alan Greenspan's Tradeoff," he warned that the Fed could not push unemployment lower—it was then 4.7 percent— "without risking higher inflation."[9]

Pessimism about the economy among economists was shared by political commentators. In the early 1990s commentators on the right and left wrote extensively about the inability of the American political system to deal with the country's economic problems in large measure because special interests were believed to prevent it from doing so.

In 1986, David Stockman, Ronald Reagan's budget director, articulated one element of the "special interest" theme that remained popular for years: The economy was improving, but Stockman believed the $200 billion annual budget deficits were a sign of the prospect of American decline and a symptom of the power of special interests. Stockman had been frustrated in his efforts to attack "the politicians, interest groups, and organized constituencies which resolutely defended all the unaffordable largesse" that the government was handing out.[10] For him, the deficits were the measure of the power of the special interests and the inability of the American political system to deal with them.

Stockman had plenty of company in this belief over the next decade. In 1993, Kevin Phillips, a former Nixon strategist, published *Boiling Point: Democrats, Republicans, and the Decline of Middle-Class Prosperity*. He echoed Stockman's themes: The Washington establishment, including both parties, had betrayed the American middle class. In an earlier book, Phillips had written about a "developing national unease" and a "failure of government." In 1993, reflecting what the polls showed at the time, he spoke of "the rise of dangerous middle class frustration politics, much but not all of it related to the economy."[11]

The sense of political failure measured by perceived failures to deal with economic issues was at least as bipartisan as the belief that low unemployment would lead to inflation. Jonathan Rauch, a columnist now with the Brookings Institution, sounded much like Stockman and Phillips. In 1994 he published *Demosclerosis: The Silent Killer of American Government*. This much-acclaimed book (reissued in 1999 as *Government's End: Why Washington Stopped Working*) argued that powerful special interest groups had stripped the government of its ability to meet new challenges.[12]

With commentators on both Right and Left sounding the same theme, it is no wonder that Clinton's Council of Economic Advisers was suspicious in 1993. They saw optimistic employment projections being issued at a time when pessimism was the rule of the day. It had to be a trap. But if it was, it was a trap that never sprang.

The "Goldilocks Economy"

The U.S. economy had struggled through several recessions in the 1970s and early 1980s, but it improved markedly after the first two years of the Reagan administration. Between 1983 and 1988, unemployment and inflation declined steadily from very high levels. By the time George H. W. Bush succeeded Reagan in 1989, the jobless rate had fallen to just over 5 percent. Inflation was picking up, though, and growth was slowing. One cause was higher prices for imports due to the declining value of the dollar, a trend that began in 1985. A sharp stock market correction in 1987 had led the Federal Reserve to pump money into the economy and cut interest rates, which added fuel to an already hot real estate market. When this crisis passed and the economy continued to expand, the Fed, fearing inflation, tightened up, and interest rates rose over the next two years. In 1989 and 1990, oil prices rose as a result of Iraq's invasion of Kuwait, and markets entered a long period of uncertainty as the country geared up for the Persian Gulf War. The uncertainty and monetary tightening contributed to the end of a speculative boom in housing and commercial real estate, and eventually to the collapse of many savings and loans and some banks.

A mild, six-month-long recession hit the country in 1990, extending into 1991. At the end of 1991, economic output began to rise again, but the improvement did not show up in the job market. Most Americans measure the health of the economy by their ability to find jobs, and in 1991–92, joblessness kept rising even as output began to recover from the recession. When unemployment rose above 7 percent again in December 1991, and then hit 7.7 percent in June 1992, President Bush knew he was in deep political trouble.

How unhappy were Americans with the economy in 1992 as the election approached? The Gallup Organization's polls regularly ask, "How would you rate economic conditions in this country today—excellent, good, fair, or poor?" When this question was asked in September and October of 1992, just before the election, only 11 percent of Americans rated conditions as good or excellent.[13]

Bill Clinton recognized that voters were disgruntled about the economy, so he pounded on the theme during the 1992 presidential campaign, and it carried him to victory. James Carville, Clinton's campaign manager, posted a sign above his desk declaring, "It's the economy, stupid!" and this became a mantra for the campaign.

Signaling their discontent with both candidates, almost 20 percent of voters in 1992 supported Ross Perot, who had campaigned hard on the issue of budget deficits. In the end, Clinton defeated Bush with only 43 percent of the vote and came into office on shaky footing.

The economy continued to recover in 1993 and 1994 during Clinton's first two years in office, but it did not feel good to most voters. Partly as a result, Clinton and the Democrats did poorly in the midterm election in 1994, and Republicans took control of the House of Representatives for the first time in four decades. They seemed to have Clinton on the ropes, but the economy was about to give him a huge lift. Just at the time of the fall 1994 elections—although too late to affect their outcome—the economy began to improve in ways that people could see. Unemployment fell below 6 percent in September 1994 and continued to decline—slowly, but perceptibly.

About a year later, Clinton's pollster, Stan Greenberg, conducted a revealing study, focusing on less-educated men and union families, an important political constituency that had been moving away from the Democratic Party since the 1960s. Greenberg found that working people were finding jobs more easily and were less afraid of being laid off; this made them more hopeful about their prospects, and better disposed toward Clinton.[14]

The mood of the country seemed to be transformed. Unemployment fell below 5.5 percent in June 1996, and below 5 percent in May 1997, a level not seen since the 1960s. Equally important—and much more surprising— there were no signs of a revival of inflation that the economists so feared. The gross domestic product (GDP), another measure of the country's economic success, expanded by more than 3.5 percent each year between 1993 and 1999. Investment in durable equipment, a key to future prosperity, increased at a rate of 10.9 percent a year for eight years from 1993 through 2000.[15] Indeed, average investment growth over the eight years was 75 percent faster than the best six years of the Reagan expansion, when investment was also growing and joblessness coming down.[16] Almost miraculously, the budget deficits that Stockman, Perot, and others saw as a sign of political failure shrank toward zero and then transformed themselves into a string of surpluses.

The strong economy benefited almost all Americans. Poverty rates declined from 15 percent of the population in 1993 to just over 11 percent in 2000. The prosperity and expanding job market increased the effectiveness of the controversial new federal welfare reform program, and the number of people on welfare in 2000 fell to half what it had been in 1992.

Crime rates also went down. So did teen pregnancy. In Washington, D.C., contractors were recruiting ex-convicts to lay cable networks and to work in the booming construction industry.

Newspapers in the late 1990s were full of stories of people finding jobs and becoming self-sufficient. The *Washington Post* in September 2000 trumpeted the improvement in a headline that read, "Poverty Declines to 20-Year Low; Central Cities Account for Most of the Drop; Incomes Hit Record." In the article, Timothy Smeeding, a professor at Syracuse University who had been following poverty data for twenty years, said, "This is the best news I've ever seen," proof that obstacles to the employment of many poor people could be overcome "if demand for workers is strong enough."[17] A sense of possibility was palpable because the economy was thriving. And because inflation was nowhere to be seen, there was no reason to throttle back. In sharp contrast to the 1970s and early 1980s, when unemployment often was above 7 percent, the 1990s gave millions of people opportunities for employment.

When the good times came, Americans began to feel better about their elected representatives. When Clinton left office, 63 percent of the people Gallup polled (in December 2000) rated economic conditions as good or excellent—almost six times as many as in 1992. Although 67 percent of those interviewed said they did not approve of Clinton personally, 75 percent said they approved of his policies.[18] The U.S. economy had turned around, and people who had been angry and pessimistic in 1992 were content and optimistic by the end of the decade.

Contrasting Two Economies

Why was the economy able to perform so much better than economists thought it could? Why was it able to surge past the danger point where, in the past, low unemployment had meant high inflation? What about all the pessimistic political analysis? What should the economic performance of the 1990s mean for the future?

The answer to these crucial questions, as we will see, lies in changes that had gone unnoticed in large sectors of the economy between two eras, the 1960s and '70s, and the 1990s. These changes drastically altered the way business is done in America, and they dictate the structure and story of this book.

The Goldilocks economy of the 1990s, as it was called, was not too warm, not too cold, but just right. It had taken a long time to develop and had many fathers, and it is important to go back and recognize its origins in earlier decades. Indeed, the prosperity cannot be understood without going back. President Clinton took real political risks to support policies consistent with the ones that laid the foundations for this economy, but credit for the 1990s is due to many changes and many tough decisions taken by political leaders from both parties over a much longer period of time.

Postwar Economy: The New Industrial State. The American economy that emerged when World War II ended in 1945 and lasted until the end of the 1960s was a wonder, and Americans loved it with good reason. When the war ended, people were apprehensive. Those who had lived through the Great Depression (when unemployment reached 25 percent) thought the bad times might resume. But eleven million returning military personnel almost miraculously found jobs as they were mustered out of military service, and the public heaved a great sigh of relief.

For the next twenty-five years—until about 1970—the American economy powered the free world while generating unprecedented prosperity at home. Like the economy of the 1990s, it exceeded all expectations. In a brilliant bipartisan geopolitical move, the United States provided billions of dollars through the Marshall Plan to rebuild the economies of her wartime friends in Europe as well as her former enemies—Germany and Japan. The result was these countries became economically strong and politically reliable allies who helped contain the Soviet Union.

The burgeoning American economy also paid for investments in defense and provided the private capital that flowed into Western Europe and Japan, augmenting the governmental aid—and it did so effortlessly. The burdens of maintaining a powerful defense establishment and rebuilding Europe and Japan did not prevent the United States from becoming increasingly prosperous at home.

Incomes rose rapidly, the middle class expanded, modern highways spread across the land, and a whole new residential pattern of suburbs came into being. More and more American families were able to purchase cars, homes, appliances, and a myriad of consumer goods.

Manufacturing industries dominated the post–World War II economy. A modern economy meant an industrial economy, and the United States was the model for the world. Other countries, damaged by war, were far behind. In America, however, competition was limited within the manufacturing sector and in other parts of the economy, as economists and politicians realized.

Key manufacturing industries in the immediate postwar American economy were dominated by oligopolies—that is, a few companies that were able to synchronize prices and limit competition. While no single company controlled the market, a small number of companies shared it and cooperated to a significant degree. These oligopolies ruled the auto, steel, aluminum, and tire industries (among others), and their leaders were a tightknit fraternity, sharing a common view of the world.

Unionized workers in these industries were also a special fraternity because they could—within some limits—demand wage increases and get them, knowing that the companies could cover the cost increases by raising prices without fear of being undercut by competitors. A similar dynamic held sway in the so-called regulated industries such as transportation, utilities, and communications. Compared to the rest of the world, the United States always was a bastion of competition, since in countries such as France, Germany, and the United Kingdom (and of course in the Soviet Union and Eastern Europe) many industries were owned directly by governments; but competition even in the United States was not nearly as fierce as it would be in the 1990s.

John Kenneth Galbraith, an influential liberal economist during the 1950s and '60s, coined a term for this postwar American economy. He called it "the new industrial state," and he developed a rationale for its weak competition while touting its impressive accomplishments. Galbraith believed that the large firms in the new industrial state were part of a "planning system" that required them to have control over prices in order for the system to work. This was a time of billion-dollar paper mills, giant oil refineries and chemical complexes, mile-long auto plants, and multibillion-dollar power plants. Galbraith believed that investments of this size would be made only if risk could be minimized. Since he saw steady investment as essential to maintaining employment levels, the ability to control prices was important, and key to his theory.[19]

Galbraith wrote that "antitrust laws in seeking to preserve the market are an anachronism in the larger world of industrial planning."[20] Those who wanted to use the antitrust laws to break up monopolies and oligopolies were naïve, he thought. In any case, politicians were most unlikely to take on the giant companies and make them compete.

Galbraith's view that competition was weak in the new industrial state was widely shared, and not only by those on the Left. When it came to prescriptions, however, many Americans did not agree with Galbraith that weak competition was economically useful, desirable, or inevitable. In the 1950s and '60s, members of Congress like senators Philip Hart and Estes Kefauver were troubled by the power of the oligopolies. They held many hearings on the subject, principally in the Antitrust and Monopoly Subcommittee of the Senate Judiciary Committee (see chapter 2), looking at such things as "monopoly in the power industry," "administered prices" in automobiles, and the problems of weak competition in steel and other areas.

Postwar presidents also sensed that weak competition was dangerous in both economic and political terms. Every one of the early postwar presidents, Democrat and Republican, from Truman through Eisenhower, Kennedy, and Johnson, clashed with U.S. Steel and the other major steel companies, who were the most prominent example of corporate power over prices, the Enrons of their age. They tried to keep pressure on the oligopolists in other industries as well to prevent them from raising prices and causing inflation.

Dwight D. Eisenhower, the first Republican president of the postwar era, was elected in 1952. A five-star general who had led the Allied armies to victory in Europe, he had a reputation as a political moderate. He also was close to business leaders, many of whom had supported him for the Republican presidential nomination against more conservative elements in his party.

Eisenhower, however, like Truman (a Democrat) before him, was troubled by the power of big business. His Justice Department continued the battle with Big Steel by blocking Bethlehem Steel's attempted merger with Youngstown; this case went to the Supreme Court, which ruled that the merger violated the Clayton Antitrust Act.

Eisenhower's Justice Department also pursued a number of other important antitrust cases, including ones against manufacturing giants such as General Motors, DuPont, General Electric, and Westinghouse. In 1959, Eisenhower's appointee to head the Antitrust Division, Robert

Bicks, went so far as to make General Motors divest itself of a manufacturer of earthmovers it had bought, even though GM was not a producer
of earthmovers when it acquired the smaller firm; the case turned on the
argument that GM was a potential competitor in this field. And in the
Westinghouse-GE case, high-ranking corporate price-fixers went to jail,
even though they were executives of two of the most important companies in America at the time.

Eisenhower also warned the nation about the political influence of
large defense contractors as he was leaving office. "In the councils of government," he said in one of his last and best-known speeches, "we must
guard against the acquisition of unwarranted influence, whether sought or
unsought, by the military-industrial complex."[21] Despite the arguments
from some on the Left and Right that justified and rationalized monopolistic pricing, there was clearly a great deal of concern about the power of
businesses to set prices during Eisenhower's two terms in the 1950s, and
little disposition to let competition get even weaker.

Presidents John F. Kennedy and Lyndon Johnson shared Eisenhower's
concerns about the power of private interests to set prices and wages.
Kennedy clashed with Roger Blough of U.S. Steel, which tried to raise
steel prices by 12 percent in 1962, and Lyndon Johnson wrestled with the
steel companies and the union to avoid a strike for higher wages in 1965.
These three presidents all recognized that steel and other major industries
had the power to set prices and wages, and they looked for ways to limit
them without taking over the industries.

Inflation did not become a significant problem during the Eisenhower
years, but it was in the Kennedy-Johnson era. Prices in the United States had
surged for three years after price controls were lifted at the end of World
War II and jumped again during the Korean War from 1950 until 1953, but
then they stabilized and settled down. The hot political issue during the
1950s was unemployment, not inflation, because of the experience of the
1930s. Americans after World War II expected the government to make sure
there were jobs, and they were ready to vote presidents out of office if
employment fell short.

In the presidential campaign of 1960, John F. Kennedy hit opponent
Richard Nixon hard on the jobless rate. Unemployment stood at 5.5 percent during the election year—well below the peak of 6.8 percent that

it reached in 1958—but 4 percent was considered "full employment" at the time, and there is always a lag before perceptions catch up to reality where the economy is concerned. Kennedy promised to "get the economy moving again," and narrowly defeated Nixon in part because of that promise.

Kennedy's advisers wanted to increase government spending to stimulate the economy and get employment back up quickly. The new president accepted their advice and tried to increase spending for defense, urban renewal, education, regional economic development in places like Appalachia, and medical care for the elderly—essentially the program that Lyndon Johnson pushed through later and called the Great Society. Congress, however, would not go along with these large increases in spending, so Kennedy proposed tax cuts as an alternative way to stimulate the economy. Top tax rates were then 91 percent for individuals and 52 percent for corporations (as compared to a top rate on individuals in 2004 of 35 percent), so he had plenty of room to cut. He proposed reducing the top individual rate to 65 percent.[22] These tax cuts have long been credited with sparking strong economic growth in the 1960s—but were they really the cause?

Herb Stein, a highly regarded Republican economist, noted in 1996 that the long economic recovery that marked the 1960s began in 1961, well before tax cuts were even discussed.[23] In fact, as Stein pointed out, the recovery was moving ahead rapidly by 1962, and there was a major debate in 1963 about whether tax cuts were needed at all when Kennedy proposed them. In any case, the tax cuts became law in February 1964, and the economy continued to gain ground rapidly.[24]

The connection between employment, inflation, and competition finally became clear as the expansion of the 1960s gathered momentum. Inflation gradually became a front-burner issue—almost coequal with unemployment—because as employment rose in the 1960s, inflationary pressures increased sharply. In its first report in 1962, Kennedy's Council of Economic Advisers—Walter W. Heller, Kermit Gordon, and James Tobin—blamed a significant part of the inflationary pressures on the market power of business and labor, sharpening the concerns that President Eisenhower and the members of the Antitrust Subcommittee had voiced in the 1950s.

Kennedy, in the preamble to his 1962 *Economic Report of the President*, said that he did not expect "a level of demand for goods and services which will strain the economy's capacity to produce" and cause inflation. He warned, however, that "in those sectors where both companies and unions possess substantial market power, the interplay of price and wage decisions could set off a movement toward a higher price level."[25] He believed that business and labor leaders had the power in the new industrial state to raise prices and wages, and he pleaded with them to "hold the line."

Kennedy's analysis of the causes of inflation is important because it was very different from what most economists thought in the 1970s—or the 1990s, for that matter. Kennedy and his economic advisers believed inflation was being caused by the monopoly power of key industries and unions, and they were especially concerned about price increases in steel and autos. In 1993, it was different. President Clinton's advisers looked for the causes of inflation in an essentially mathematical relationship with the level of employment. Their approach glossed over the questions that worried Kennedy and his economists—the power of big companies and unions—and paid little attention to how that power had diminished over the years.

Kennedy's advisers estimated that "more than three fourths of the rise in the index of wholesale industrial prices during the 1955–58 period was directly attributable to price increases in [key monopolistic] industries" that then "*initiated impulses which spread to other parts of the economy*" (emphasis added).[26] The Kennedy report, therefore, explicitly recommended measures designed to increase competition—tougher antitrust enforcement, more open trade, and greater availability of investment capital to smaller businesses.[27]

Kennedy understood, however, that he had little chance of significantly increasing competition quickly in the many industries where it was weak, so he tried to influence powerful companies and unions across the board by establishing wage and price "guideposts." These guideposts were mentioned in the 1962 report, but not spelled out with precision until they were set at a 3.2 percent increase per year in 1964, just after Kennedy's assassination. The guideposts were meant to match the annual rate of productivity growth so that wage increases in this range would be consistent with stable prices.

Lyndon Baines Johnson was, if anything more concerned about inflation than Kennedy had been, and he, too, thought much of it was the
result of monopoly power of large companies. He was afraid that a rise in
inflation would threaten his cherished Great Society program, which he
was pursuing along with a major buildup of forces in Vietnam. He did not
want to cut federal spending or see the Federal Reserve raise interest rates
to slow the economy. So, like Kennedy, Johnson pressured big business
and unions to keep prices and wages down.

Johnson's approach (called "jawboning" at the time) was to try to talk
business and labor leaders into following Kennedy's price and wage
guideposts. Joe Califano, a Johnson assistant, has written an extraordinary description of these efforts, in which Johnson used all of his fabled
persuasive powers, honed during seven years as Democratic majority
leader.[28] Califano's account shows Johnson working frantically during the
summer of 1965 to head off a steel strike and avoid price increases in that
industry, which supplied a key component to so many other industries.

The president was constantly on the phone with business and labor
leaders, urging them to keep price and wage increases down. He assigned
members of his Council of Economic Advisers and cabinet secretaries,
such as Secretary of Commerce John Connor and Secretary of Labor
Willard Wirtz, to work directly with management and labor to avert the
steel strike, and he personally focused on one trouble spot after another.
In 1967 alone, the president's people met with businesses representing
over fifty different product lines.

The Johnson administration, according to Califano, labored to hold
the line on auto as well as steel prices, railroad freight rates, airfares, aluminum, copper, household appliances, paper cartons, medical supplies,
newsprint, glass containers, cellulose, chlorine, caustic soda, wood products,
and even eggs and lamb. Most of these goods and services were produced by
oligopolistic industries composed of only a few firms, whose control over
prices Johnson thought was clear.

The labor unions emerged as Johnson's biggest political problem. Like
Truman and all the other Democratic presidents, Johnson found it easier
to press business to limit price increases than to twist the arms of labor
leaders on wages. Many of these leaders were longstanding allies of Roosevelt's New Deal and the Democratic Party. Johnson, moreover, had been

a friend of the unions all his life and counted its leaders among his strongest supporters. The union chiefs, though, had their own internal political issues to deal with. Johnson knew that those who landed wage increases for their members were popular, and those who did not risked being seen as weak. He also understood that the union leaders who simply accepted the wage guidelines risked being repudiated by their militant members. Some, like I. W. Abel of the United Steel Workers (USW) and Walter Reuther of the United Auto Workers (UAW), consulted with him and tried to be helpful. Others did not.

Roy Siemiller, president of the International Association of Machinists and Aerospace Workers (AIM), was not one of the helpful ones, and the story of Johnson's dealings with him underscores the differences between the U.S. economy in the 1960s and the economy in the 1990s and today. Siemiller's machinists operated in the airline and railroad industries. Prices and competition in these industries were more controlled than in the relatively loose oligopolies that dominated manufacturing. In airlines and railroads, coordinated pricing was officially sanctioned, and anything that smacked of competition had to be approved by the Civil Aeronautics Board (CAB) or the Interstate Commerce Commission. In 1966, Siemiller, negotiating for his members in the airline industry, set his sights on a 5 percent wage increase for each of the next two years, with a 4.5 percent increase in the third year. This was more than 50 percent above the 3.2 annual percent increase suggested by the Kennedy-Johnson wage guideposts.

This was a very different world from the one in which airlines and railroads operate today. Siemiller was not worried in 1966 that some new, low-cost airline would take advantage of any wage increase he got from the established companies; the CAB had allowed no new competitors into the industry since the agency was established in 1938. Siemiller also knew that, as a practical matter, if he won higher wages for the machinists, the airline companies would ask for and receive fare increases from the CAB. It was a done deal.

The airline labor negotiations in 1966 deadlocked because Siemiller was asking for so much, and the managers at the airlines did not want to look like wimps. In April 1966, Johnson invoked the Railway Labor Act (which applied to airlines as well) to avoid, or at least delay, a strike. Then he set up a special emergency commission headed by Senator Wayne Morse, an Oregon Republican, to recommend a settlement. Morse's commission recommended modest wage increases that—with a little dissimulation—could be made to appear to fit within the guidelines.

Siemiller told Johnson he would go along with Morse's recommendation, but he did not encourage his members to vote for the deal. They voted the package down, and Johnson had to try again. He called Siemiller and the airlines' chief negotiator, William Curtin, to the White House to hammer out a deal. They quickly agreed to give the union nearly everything it wanted.

Johnson had caved but, recalls Califano, Siemiller added insult to injury, bragging that "the airline settlement 'destroyed all existing wage and price guidelines now in existence'"[29] In effect, Siemiller invited—even challenged—other labor leaders to test the guidelines. There was little that a furious President Johnson could do. Although he had prevented an increase in steel prices the previous year, he had lost the airline battle.

The next year, Siemiller again crossed swords with Johnson—and once again beat him soundly. Members of Siemiller's union also worked on the railroads, which operated within a government-sanctioned price-fixing arrangement, supervised by the hoary old Interstate Commerce Commission established in 1887. The railroads, however, were in much worse shape than the airlines. They really could not afford to give wage increases because they were steadily losing freight business to trucks and had already lost much of their passenger business to automobiles and the airlines.

Siemiller gambled that the government would push the railroads to give him what he wanted anyway, rather than allow a strike that would jeopardize the war effort in Vietnam and shut down much of the country's industry dependent on rail shipments. He was right. When the railroads resisted, his members struck, and other unions joined them for two days. Congress stepped in to require mediation—essentially, arbitration. Neither Johnson nor Siemiller wanted mediation, but it was Siemiller who came out ahead. The mediators ignored the danger of competition from trucks and awarded the railroad workers a 15 percent wage increase, nearly five times the 3.2 percent called for by the guideposts. If the airline settlement did not make the guideposts irrelevant, the rail settlement certainly did.

The 1990s and Today: How Things Have Changed. What is important about this history is the contrast between the power of business and labor leaders to set prices and wages in the 1960s and their obvious lack of such power in the 1990s and today. Bill Clinton was not concerned about the ability of auto or steel or airline companies to raise prices when he was president; neither is George W. Bush. Neither Clinton nor Bush was in any danger of having a Siemiller on his hands. Neither had to worry about the power of the airlines, rail, trucking, steel, or auto companies to raise prices arbitrarily. All of that is gone—seemingly ancient history, though it was only three decades ago.

What is clear is that Galbraith's "new industrial state" no longer exists. The near-monopolies in manufacturing, and the regulated monopolies and oligopolies in airlines, communications, and other large sectors of the post–World War II economy, were almost all gone by the beginning of the 1990s. In almost every line of business, there are new, low-priced competitors that did not exist when Johnson was president, and which—most importantly—have taken business away from the older firms. Today, most of the powerful unions that operated in these once-oligopolistic industries are much diminished, principally because competition makes it harder for companies to pass on the costs of wage increases to consumers.

The changes in these large sectors of the U.S. economy are the next part of our story.

Manufacturing. In the manufacturing sector, the 1990s were very different from the 1960s. It was not the world that had faced Eisenhower, Kennedy, and Johnson. Article after article in the 1990s reported that companies were not raising prices because they could not. "If you talk to business executives," *Business Week* said in 1997, "they'll tell you they can't raise prices. . . . When executive after executive in industry after industry tells you the same thing in convincing detail, attention must be paid."[30] This was not the economic world of the 1960s and '70s.

The auto industry is one striking example of what has changed in the last four decades. Today, there are more than a dozen major, competing auto companies, both foreign and domestic; in the 1960s, the market was dominated by the Big Three (GM, Ford, and Chrysler)—with Volkswagen providing the one real foreign, small-car alternative. Now, Toyota, Honda,

Nissan, Mazda, Isuzu, Subaru, Mitsubishi, BMW, Volkswagen, Hyundai, and more than a dozen smaller brands provide vigorous competition, with many of these "foreign" cars being made in American factories.

GM had 50 percent of the auto market in 1970, and there were years when it had more. It still had 25 to 30 percent of U.S. car sales in 2000, but it has been fighting for decades to stop the erosion of its share and, if possible, rebuild it, without success so far.

Still, competition hasn't come close to killing the domestic car industry. The United States is still a major producer of automobiles. It produced 14.9 million cars and trucks in 2000, many more than in the 1970s, but Japanese companies were building over 2.5 million of them in their U.S. plants, about 17 percent of the total. Moreover, the foreign makers continue to expand production faster than the old Big Three in the United States, Canada, and Mexico, building most of their plants in states like Kentucky, Tennessee, South Carolina, Alabama, and Mississippi where no auto industry existed in the 1960s. The quality of cars has improved markedly, in large measure as a result of tougher competition. They last longer, have many more safety features, and have amenities that no one imagined in the 1970s.

Big Steel, dominant in the United States in the 1960s, faces new domestic challengers as well as competition from imports now. As we have seen, sharp increases in steel prices led to public clashes between the steel companies and presidents from the 1940s into the 1960s, yet prices rose steadily, pushing up the costs of American products that used steel, such as industrial machinery, construction girders, and appliances.[31] In the 1960s, U.S. Steel and its chairman, Roger Blough, dominated the industry, as it had since the company was formed in 1901. A half-dozen other "integrated" companies that turned raw iron ore into steel in huge plants usually followed U.S. Steel's lead. The United Steel Workers union was powerful, too, and its leaders were important political players.

Steelmaking is not dead in America any more than car making is. U.S. production came back from 85 million tons in 1990 to 106 million tons in 1999. U.S. Steel and other integrated steel mills (several of which have recently been acquired by foreign companies), however, have lost market share to new competing domestic mills and to imports and have struggled in the new world just as GM, Ford, and Chrysler have.

The growth in steel production, as in automobile production, is taking place in new plants. Called "minimills," these plants are owned by new companies that now produce almost half of the country's steel. They use steel scrap instead of iron ore, and electricity instead of coal. Most of them are located in the South and West, and some of them (as well as some of the old mills) are now owned by foreign companies. Like the new transplant car factories, these steel mills did not exist in the 1960s.

The new steel industry, like the new auto industry, is more innovative. Both the new companies and the old ones have been forced by competition to produce better steel.

Steel today is far better because its chemistry is more consistent, making it more resistant to cracking when bent and shaped. Its dimensions are more consistent as well, so it does not get stuck in the machines that cut and shape it, and rusted-out fenders and door panels are much less common than they used to be.

Labor arrangements in the steel industry have changed, too. The old industry employed 550,000 workers in 1968, almost all unionized. By the end of the 1990s, the workforce was less than one-fifth that size, and many of the workers were well-paid, nonunion employees in the new mills. In the steel industry, important companies like Bethlehem, National Steel, LTV, and Weirton Steel have been forced to pass their huge pension obligations to the Pension Benefit Guarantee Corporation and to consolidate.

The USW and its retirees, despite the changes, have remained a potent political force in traditional steel states like West Virginia, Pennsylvania, Illinois, and Ohio. That is probably why President George W. Bush made protecting the steel industry from imports a campaign promise in 2000 and followed through when he came into office. Most of this new protection was withdrawn in 2003, however, because world and U.S. prices had risen sharply and steel customers were complaining.

The Regulated Industries. Competition also came to the airlines, railroads, trucking, and other formerly regulated industries between the 1970s and the 1990s. Roy Siemiller, the union leader who nearly drove Lyndon Johnson to distraction, did not have to worry about competition putting a lid on airfares or even about the effect of rising railroad rates when he sought big wage increases for his members. Because of airline and rail deregulation beginning in 1978, however, pilots, mechanics, and flight personnel at the oldest, most established airlines (such as United, USAir, American, and Northwest) and workers on the railroads have had to take competition and the threat of company bankruptcy into account. The advent of competition has been painful, forcing the employees of old companies to accept more flexible work rules, lower wages, longer working hours, and, in many cases, job losses, although employment in the airline industry as a whole has increased greatly.

New, lower-cost carriers, such as Southwest, AirTran, and JetBlue, play the role that the Japanese car companies and new steel companies played in manufacturing. They increasingly set the standards for airfares, service, work rules, and working conditions, gradually forcing the older companies to match them. The newcomers in airlines compete by offering passengers similar service for less money, and the Civil Aeronautics Board that used to coordinate and enforce prices so that they would be essentially uniform was abolished in 1985. Several older airlines in 2004 are likely to follow the steel companies and pass billions of dollars worth of pension obligations to the Pension Benefit Guarantee Corporation because in the competition with new airlines they can no longer charge fares high enough to cover them.

Far-reaching changes have also come to telecommunications. AT&T and the local Bell Telephone companies dominated telecommunications in the post–World War II economy. John Kenneth Galbraith could not have imagined Ma Bell and her offspring being displaced by new competitors— but that is what happened. Beginning in the 1970s, MCI, Sprint, and other new players began to nibble away at what had been AT&T's long-distance monopoly.

By the late 1970s and early '80s, real competition had come to long-distance, data, and other telephone services. By 1982, when AT&T agreed to separate from the Bells and other pieces of its empire, long-distance rates were already coming down, especially for business users. Further steps toward competition came in 1996 with the passage of additional telecom legislation. By 2004, twenty or more companies were competing for AT&T's clients, and hundreds of others had little pieces of the action. The changes were very much like those in autos and steel, with more competitors in the industry. AT&T, the company that had been dominant in the 1960s, is now a shadow of its former self, and innovation is the order of the day.

There remain plenty of warts on the telecommunications industry. The large regional Bell companies continue to have significant advantages over competitors in local markets because they still have a tight grip on the last mile of wire into most homes. Residential customers complain about poor service and confusing rate offers, and there continue to be confusion and disarray, some of it the result of speculation, overbuilding, and fraud at companies like WorldCom and Global Crossing.

But even these serious problems cannot mask what has been accomplished. The costs of long-distance or international calls, or moving data across telephone wires, are just a fraction of what they were in the 1970s. Internet access costs far less in the United States than in most countries, an important competitive advantage. Indeed, America's low prices in this and other industries have forced other countries to break up nationalized systems to keep up. Consumers have more choice and are paying less for most types of service than anyone imagined possible in 1970.

By the 1990s, competition in trucking, rail, and airfreight transportation had substantially reduced the costs of doing business in the United States. Logistics costs—basically the costs of shipping products and warehousing inventories—fell from 16 percent of the GDP in 1981 to 9.9 percent at the beginning of 2000, with the sharpest decline coming almost immediately after trucking and railroads were deregulated toward the end of the Carter administration in 1980.[32]

Since the deregulation of the 1980s, fast-growing delivery services such as FedEx and UPS have been competing more vigorously with each other and with the U.S. Postal Service. Trucking companies can no longer fix prices or set terms of service. The quality of transportation services also has improved markedly while their cost has come down. Companies needing parts and retailers restocking shelves are able to demand "just-in-time delivery," cutting the costs of storage and inventories.

Companies like UPS require corporate customers to computerize to lower their own costs of service and to make improved service possible. Today, customers expect to have next-day service or guaranteed delivery by a specific date, and to be able to track packages—all improvements introduced by the shipping companies in large part because of competition.

Changes like these have helped make even quite small businesses in the United States more efficient. Maryland Industrial Inc., a supplier of safety shoes in the Baltimore area with less than ten employees, is a good example.[33] The company has a contract to supply shoes to the old Bethlehem Steel plant at Sparrows Point, near Baltimore. In the early 1990s, Maryland Industrial still received shipments of shoes at its warehouse several miles from Sparrows Point. Shoes had to be sorted at the warehouse, logged in and out, and trucked to Sparrows Point as they were needed.

By 2000, UPS was offering a much better service for essentially the same price. UPS delivers shipments directly to Maryland Industrial's customers. This saves the company the expense of bringing shoes into its warehouse, reducing the need for warehouse space. Record-keeping is also easier, using new software from UPS that automatically produces labels and generates a shipping log at the end of the day. Packages can be tracked and are less frequently lost. Pickup and delivery are faster, and labor costs are significantly lower. And because UPS competes with other shipping companies for Maryland Industrial's business, its prices are lower and its service is better.

New competition has also produced innovations that have cut the cost of shipping by rail. Beginning in the mid-1980s, more goods were moved in containers, so fewer shipments had to be loaded and unloaded from boxcars. Now containers are loaded in the factory and moved to delivery points; it is simply easier and cheaper to load containers onto flatcars with cranes than to shift boxcars around in the big old rail assembly yards that used to exist in many large towns. The U.S. logistics system has become the model for the world.

The Financial Sector. The American financial system changed radically between the 1960s and the 1990s. Dependence on old financial institutions is a thing of the past. In the 1960s, there was relatively little competition among financial institutions for the business of smaller and medium-sized companies, and the key financial institutions were located largely in the Northeast. By the 1990s, there was much more competition, and smaller, newer firms in every line of business had financing options that had not existed thirty years earlier.

The so-called "junk-bond" market, an important market for the bonds of higher-risk firms, only came into existence in the 1970s. One of the principal roles of this kind of financing has been to provide fixed-rate capital to less-established, generally smaller firms. The NASDAQ (National Association of

Securities Dealers Automated Quotes) market for stocks of smaller and newer firms, like the junk-bond market, also was created in the early 1970s. There had long been a less formal market that handled the stocks of some smaller companies, and regional stock markets performed some of these functions; but the creation of NASDAQ was a major advance. The New York Stock Exchange had faced only nominal competition before the NASDAQ; the advent of real competition has forced it to become more efficient, lower the cost of trading, and offer better services to induce firms to list on its exchange.

Important regional banks also have grown up since the 1970s in Charlotte and Winston-Salem, North Carolina, in Atlanta, and in other cities around the country. They now challenge the great old banks of the Northeast. Many banks have either purchased or established connections to brokerage companies to be able to offer a wider range of financial services. This has made it easier to finance new businesses in areas of the country where this used to be difficult. Kennedy's economic advisers in the early 1960s had wanted to make more financing available to small businesses as a means of increasing competition. By the 1990s, that is what had happened.

There have been other changes as well in the financial area, all pointing in the same direction. In the old days, a homebuyer had to obtain a mortgage from a local bank. By the 1990s, local banks had to face competition from outside institutions, and a national market had emerged. Institutions grew up to package mortgages and other receivables as securities, increasing competition among lenders and helping lower the cost of borrowing.

The U.S. financial sector had its problems and weaknesses in the 1990s, some of which became evident only after the turn of this century. However, the system is far more open and democratic than it used to be, and new businesses and ordinary borrowers have more access to money in the United States than they do in Europe and Japan, whose systems are still more favorable to established companies and borrowers, and where, interestingly, there seem to be just as many financial scandals. That is why Europe and Japan spent much of the 1990s trying to copy changes that had occurred in the United States.[34]

Retailing. Competition in retailing, which generates as much as 20 percent of America's GDP, became much more intense between the 1970s and the 1990s. In the 1950s and '60s, department stores and small-town variety stores dominated a retailing scene that, while certainly dynamic and changing, was primarily local or regional. Discount chains selling various types of products had emerged in most regions, but competition and pressures to cut costs were not as strong as they are today. Most retail stores applied customary, relatively high, markup rates to the wholesale prices they paid for goods, and these markups usually could be maintained.

The new national retail chains changed retailing drastically, lowering costs and driving prices down. Wal-Mart grew from $40 million in sales in 1970 to more than $230 billion in 2002 largely because it found ways to cut costs and, as a result, prices. While some people object to the "Wal-Mart-ization of America," demand higher pay and more generous health benefits for its employees, and mourn the decline of independent stores, the reality is that Wal-Mart and other large discount retailers have been enormously successful because consumers like what they offer. Lower- and middle-income consumers, especially in the growing outer suburbs, were charged relatively high prices by retailers in the 1960s and '70s; today, they have more choices and better prices.

Almost every part of the retail sector has changed because of increased competition from national chains like Wal-Mart—clothing, groceries, pharmacies, office supplies, hardware, and toys, as well as general merchandise. Many boutiques still cater to consumers who are willing to spend more for service and convenience—indeed, chains of such stores have emerged. But retailing has changed in the same way that almost everything else has changed in America since the 1970s: Competition is more intense, newcomers have gained market share, the center of commercial gravity has shifted away from the Northeast, prices have stopped rising, and lower- and middle-class consumers are better served.

This is a tale of two very different economies. The changes between the two eras in these four major sectors—manufacturing, the regulated industries, finance, and retailing—are the background against which to examine the policies that made the 1990s prosperous. Competition has changed the economy. Sectors where competition had been limited in the 1960s and '70s have been opened up. The oligopolies that limited price competition and set the pattern for the whole economy in the new industrial state have lost control. Key sectors have changed, and the relationship between unemployment and inflation has changed as a result.

A Strikingly Different Economy

At the beginning of the Clinton administration, economists assumed that the country's economic performance would continue to follow the patterns of the 1960s and '70s. Why they were so wrong is a complex question that will be discussed in more detail in chapter 7. One important explanation for the error is that the central focus of economics since the Great Depression had been shifting away from Adam Smith's original focus on competition. Smith's great insight was that competition liberated the energies of ordinary people and made nations wealthy, but the Depression had made competition suspect.

Economics after the Depression of the 1930s was more focused on making sure that demand kept up with supply. It was increasingly dependent on a variety of mathematical tools that were supposed to project the future balance between supply and demand under changing circumstances. If government spending increased for guns or butter, the models assumed that demand would grow for these things and change for other things; if interest rates, taxes, or money supply rose or fell, investment, consumption, and prices were expected to behave in some predictable manner. These models looked very scientific, but they were unavoidably based on historical data and tended to assume that the past would be a reliable guide to the present and future.

The economic models in the early 1990s were based on data from the 1970s that showed inflation rising when unemployment fell. They assumed that these forces would behave similarly in the 1990s. For instance, they implicitly assumed that automobile prices in the highly competitive market of the 1990s would behave much as they did in the oligopolistic 1960s. They assumed that prices in the newly competitive telecommunications, financial, retail, air, rail, and trucking sectors would behave the way they had in the noncompetitive 1970s. They assumed, in other words, that the cumulative effect of competition-enhancing changes in all these sectors would be small.

Small wonder that Clinton's economists suspected the departing Bush team of laying a trap when they claimed that unemployment could fall to only 5.3 percent while inflation stayed at 3 percent. When unemployment had fallen to lower levels in the 1960s, '70s, and '80s, inflation had surged. Looking at dry numbers, not at what was happening in important industries, there was little reason to expect these relationships to change.

Political analysts, who viewed economists as data wizards, built a theory of American decline around the somber economic projections. They believed that America could not solve its economic problems because interest groups were too strong. Like the economists, they overlooked what was happening to some of the most important economic interest groups in the real world. Neither the economists nor the pundits paid much attention to experts who focused on competition in specific industries the way Adam Smith had.[35]

Even the industry experts themselves had too limited a sense of the importance of their work. They had been arguing since the late 1960s and early '70s that competition should be restored in American industries and had made considerable progress in convincing political leaders of that. But they did not argue with the other economists that this would change the larger workings of the economy. The industry specialists usually were expert about only one or two industries. No one saw that changes in industries such as autos, steel, airlines, trucking, telecommunications, energy, finance, and retailing had had a cumulative effect so large that they had changed the relationship between unemployment and inflation.

The British biologist T. H. Huxley once remarked that the "great tragedy of Science [is] the slaying of a beautiful hypothesis by an ugly fact." The Goldilocks economy of the 1990s turned this aphorism upside down: It was the slaying of an ugly economic theory by the beautiful fact of widespread prosperity. The theory was demolished by the fact that unemployment in the 1990s fell to record lows, and no inflation appeared. The pattern of earlier decades was broken.

How did competition increase so much, and who deserves the credit for these accomplishments? How can competition help us solve the problems of the current decade? The answers to these questions will come out of the more detailed stories of change that follow, beginning with the dramatic changes in American manufacturing.

2

The Passing of "Generous Motors"

This monopoly (which our manufacturers have obtained against us) has so much increased the number of some particular tribes (of their inflamed workmen) . . . that like an overgrown standing army, they have become formidable to the government, and upon many occasions intimidate the legislature.

—Adam Smith[1]

Auto Industry Hearings: 1958

The prospect of attending hearings on the automobile industry was exciting enough to bring me to Washington, D.C., for the first time in my life in January 1958. I had always loved cars, and the auto industry stood right up there with the American flag in my mind as a symbol of the country's strength. I had read that Walter Reuther, the head of the United Auto Workers union, wanted the Big Three auto companies to build small cars to compete with the Volkswagens that had become so popular in the 1950s. Reuther was a hero of mine, and I wanted to see him face off with the leaders of the auto industry.

The hearings were held to consider what might be done to stimulate auto sales and get autoworkers back on the job, as a sharp recession the previous year had pushed unemployment well above 6 percent. Reuther and the industry leaders were testifying before the Antitrust and Monopoly Subcommittee of the Senate Judiciary Committee, chaired by Senator Estes Kefauver. Kefauver was a populist Democrat from Tennessee who had sought the Democratic nomination for president in both 1952 and 1956.

The transcript of the testimony from forty-six years ago is revealing. It makes clear that concerns about weak competition in the auto sector go way back, and it suggests why American political leaders in later years supported policies that encouraged foreign competition and forced the industry to change.[2]

The starting point for the hearings was a proposal developed by a panel of economists from the Massachusetts Institute of Technology. They thought that the auto companies should lower prices to stimulate demand, and supported this position with extensive analysis. The MIT experts recommended a $100 per vehicle price cut—something like the rebates that are so common today—and estimated that the companies would still make a per-vehicle profit, and would sell about one million more vehicles, if they accepted such reductions.

Cars in 1958 sold for an average of about $2,000, so a $100 rebate would have been the equivalent of a $1,000 rebate on today's $20,000 vehicles. Both the UAW and the automobile dealers supported the MIT proposal because union members and dealers were being hurt by slow sales. Reuther said that if the companies accepted the plan, he would take it into consideration in future wage negotiations—implicitly promising a smaller wage increase in the next round of bargaining.

The CEOs of the Big Three dismissed the ideas of the MIT professors out of hand. They would not entertain any notions about cutting prices to increase sales. They said that the price-reduction idea could only have come from outsiders who knew nothing about how the industry worked. People didn't buy cars "on price alone," they said.

The auto executives also told the subcommittee that the union was dead wrong to urge them to build small cars. They noted that when Chrysler had tried a smaller model with the 1953–54 Plymouth, it had been a near disaster. The square-ish car sold very poorly, and the company had cut the model-run short and moved quickly to produce a longer, lower car like those coming from GM and Ford.

The auto executives declared in no uncertain terms that decisions concerning pricing and model size were the prerogative of management. Rising union labor costs, they said, were the reason for yearly price increases. They rejected the autoworkers' offer to take price cuts into consideration in future wage negotiations in return for building smaller cars. The spirit of the sometimes violent labor-management clashes of 1936 and 1937 was very much present in the hearing room. The tension was palpable.

The question of the impact of oligopolies on inflation also was very much in the room. The senators asked the auto executives specifically about the effect of steel price increases on their own costs and prices, giving them a chance to criticize the steel companies. Instead, the auto executives defended them. Steel companies, they explained, were facing rising labor costs just as they were and had to raise prices to cover these costs. As we will see in the next chapter, it took another twenty-four years—until March 1982—for GM, Ford, and Chrysler to push Big Steel to cut costs and prices.

George Romney, CEO of the American Motors Corporation (AMC), was the only dissident voice among the auto executives at the January 1958 hearings. Romney would later be a popular Republican governor of Michigan and a presidential candidate in 1968, and he served as President Nixon's secretary of housing and urban development. In 1958, however, he was CEO of a struggling smaller auto company trying to make it in a world dominated by three giants.

Romney did not sound like the Big Three automakers at all. He testified that there was "inadequate and deficient product competition in the automobile business." His principal complaint was that the large companies were hurting AMC by saying that his plan to produce 150,000 to 300,000 compact cars a year could not be successful. The dire prognostications of the Big Three were making it harder for Romney to raise money to develop new models.

Romney did more than complain that the Big Three were trying to prevent him from developing a market for smaller cars, however. He made a recommendation that almost certainly angered the other CEOs at the time, but might have saved the Big Three and the autoworkers a lot of pain if they had taken him seriously: He suggested that any company in a "basic industry" like automobiles should control no more than 35 percent of the industry, or 25 percent if it were in more than one. In effect, he recommended the breakup of General Motors.

Senator Everett Dirksen, the Republican senate minority leader from Illinois, was one of several senators who defended the Big Three at the Kefauver hearings. "Look where these men are," he told the subcommittee.

"They have risen to the top of the most powerful industry in America. They must know what they are doing." Dirksen belittled the industry's critics as uninformed meddlers in a complicated business that they knew little about.

The majority report from the hearing, which was issued in November 1958, stated that "the hard core of the monopoly problem in the automobile industry is the concentration of production and power held by General Motors." GM's position, the report said, gave it strong incentives to "maintain high automobile prices." The majority recommended that the Justice Department look into court action to break up General Motors, and possibly take antitrust action against Ford and Chrysler as well. The majority in the subcommittee essentially agreed with Romney, even though they certainly knew that a breakup of GM was far-fetched.

What is perhaps most interesting about the testimony at the 1958 hearings is that neither the auto industry's best friends nor its severest critics recognized how vulnerable it was becoming. Volkswagen got some attention because the UAW wanted to build smaller cars and take back the jobs its members were losing to the increasingly popular Beetle. No one seemed to doubt, however, that if the U.S. companies set their minds to it, they could push VW out of the market.

Another startling omission spoke to the mindset of those times. No one at the hearing even suggested that the Big Three could be facing a challenge from Japan in the future. That would have seemed absurd; the Japanese were not even on the radar screen. The Big Three's large profits obscured the warning signs of managerial arrogance, an increasingly obsolete business culture, and outmoded designs and technology. They also masked the costs of too-cozy, dysfunctional relationships with suppliers like the steel companies that also would become evident a decade or so later when the business climate changed.

An Entrepreneurial Industry Goes Wrong

Americans, at least those of us over fifty, have seen with our own eyes how competition from imports changed the auto industry for the better. If you ask people why American-built cars are so much better now than they were thirty years ago, many will tell you that competition from Japanese cars led to the improvements. Everyone understands that the Big Three had lost their edge until Japanese cars came along. Many of the American-made cars in the 1970s were poorly made gas-guzzlers. Most of us relish the fact that the big car companies got their comeuppance when competition forced them to shape up.

Most Americans also sense that the country is better off for what happened, although we understand that the transition to a better auto industry was painful; hardworking people in places like Detroit and Flint, Michigan paid the price for the executives' shortsightedness. Very few car owners, however, would go back to the time when weak competition allowed U.S. companies to get away with selling second-rate automobiles. How did the American auto industry become so vulnerable to the Japanese competitors, and what were the forces that brought competition back and turned the situation around?

The changes in America's automobile industry are emblematic of the larger changes in the U.S. economy over the last few decades. Automobiles are the heart of the modern economy, and there is much to be learned from this industry—and not only about what happened in manufacturing. To understand how the U.S. economy as a whole was changed by competition after the 1960s, it is useful to examine in detail the evolution of competition in this flagship industry.

In the early twentieth century, entrepreneurial genius Henry Ford became the first automobile manufacturer to apply assembly-line techniques to the industry. With the start of mass production of the famous Model T in 1908 and the installation of the first moving assembly line in the Ford Motor Company plant in 1913, Ford shaped the American industry in its opening decades. Like entrepreneurs in a host of new industries at the end of the twentieth century, Ford made money not by raising prices, but by driving down costs and broadening his market. In the prosperous 1920s, the family car became a fixture in the middle-class American household in large measure because of Ford.

By 1923, Ford was producing 52 percent of the 3.7 million cars turned out in America that year, and about two-thirds of the cars targeted to the fast-growing lower end of the car market. The Model T was introduced at $850 and by the 1920s sold for less than $300. Indeed, Ford played the role in America that America has played in the world for more than a century: showing that the prices of "luxury goods" can be brought within reach of ordinary people.

In 1920, only 9 million cars were in use in the United States. That number tripled by 1930. Nevertheless, there were around forty American automakers, and fierce price wars raged. Not surprisingly, this was the period of the industry's most rapid development. While Ford, GM, and Chrysler collectively had 80 percent of new car sales by 1929, dozens of other manufacturers produced cars for different segments of the market, and innovation prevailed. In many ways, the market for cars in the 1920s was like the market for computers, telephone service, and other goods and services today. It was unpredictable. Companies waxed and waned, emerged and collapsed—even large and important ones.

Ford itself was an example of this. It was the giant at the beginning of the 1920s, but it made a serious mistake by sticking with the Model T for too long. Henry Ford believed that automobiles were just a means of transportation, and that people wanted transportation at the lowest possible price. GM took a different tack. It gained ground in the mid-1920s by marketing aggressively to customers who wanted more than a plain-vanilla automobile. Chevys were more expensive than Fords, but they incorporated more innovations and were sold for style and prestige. By 1927, stubborn old Henry Ford was forced to replace the fading Model T with the spiffier Model A. Nevertheless, by the late 1920s GM had supplanted Ford as the country's leading producer, and it has remained in first place ever since.

Automobile manufacturing was the key growth industry in America in the 1920s, but a similar pattern of competition, rapid change, and product improvement with falling prices prevailed for other products as well, such as textiles, household furnishings, appliances, metal products, and chemicals. Despite rapid growth in all these industries throughout the 1920s, inflation was not a problem.[3] Living standards improved for ordinary Americans, in part because wages rose, but also because the prices of many manufactured goods and services fell. A third factor was the growth of consumer credit. By the end of the decade, two-thirds of new cars were bought on the installment plan.

Memories of the 1920s soured after the stock market crash of 1929, but the decade, like the 1990s, was a period of remarkable, raucous economic growth that was widely shared. A burgeoning auto industry marked by sharp competition, innovation, leaders with strong personalities, and a variety of business plans was a big part of that.

The Great Depression changed the pattern in the automobile and other industries. It led to the consolidation of auto manufacturing into a few giant companies that had the deep pockets required to ride out terrible times. Such companies developed dominating positions during the 1930s that were hardly challenged for the next forty years.[4]

The auto industry after World War II was very different from that of the 1920s. There was only one dominant business model—GM. Large-scale production was assumed to be the key to success, styling changes were central to keeping buyers coming back, and niche carmakers quickly faded. The kind of price competition that Henry Ford had encouraged in the 1920s was a thing of the past.

In the 1950s and '60s, the auto industry was—as it had been in the 1920s—the model for the rest of the manufacturing sector. It was also the archetype of oligopoly in John Kenneth Galbraith's "new industrial state." The question of what to do about limited competition in the car business simmered for at least two decades after the end of World War II.

General Motors, the most powerful industrial firm in the country, was riding high, but it was not universally popular. In 1952, GM president Charles E. Wilson told a Senate subcommittee, "What is good for the country is good for General Motors, and what is good for General Motors is good for the country." His words were a simple statement of fact for some and a symbol of arrogance for others.

It is always hard to argue with success, however. Wilson, despite his tactless remark, became President Eisenhower's secretary of defense. A few years later, Ford CEO Robert McNamara took the same high-level position with President Kennedy. That two auto executives became defense secretaries at the height of the Cold War suggests the importance of the industry.

As one of the largest postwar conglomerates, GM had influence that went far beyond the auto business. A giant defense contractor, it also made railroad locomotives, electrical equipment, and appliances.[5] The company had deep pockets from other connections as well. DuPont, the chemical giant, had bought over 20 percent of the carmaker's stock around 1917, and held it until the Supreme Court forced it to sell the stock in 1957.[6]

United States v. DuPont (General Motors) was an important court case. When it was brought in 1949, Harry Truman, a Democrat, was president; but when it was decided eight years later, the majority opinion was written by Justice William Brennan, who had been appointed by the Republican Dwight Eisenhower. The decision showed that the Supreme Court was concerned about the power of such big companies, and that it was not just a few mavericks in the Senate who wanted to prevent them from growing too strong.

The Big Three's grip on the American car market immediately after the war was made tighter by their power in Europe, where they had car plants and were major players. The Big Three played the international game like a cartel—a group of companies who agree not to compete and instead divide up markets among themselves, generally on a geographical basis. Each member of a cartel agrees to accept a given share of a market in exchange for an understanding that it will not cut prices or seek a larger share.

In the 1950s and '60s, GM and Ford each had 10–20 percent of the market in Germany and the United Kingdom—the most important markets in Europe—and their European operations were very profitable. They produced smaller, European-style cars in their European plants that were vastly different from the cars they made in America. The GM and Ford plants in Europe were more efficient than those of the European companies because they were owned by cash-rich American firms at a time when investment capital in Europe was scarce.

In the 1950s and '60s, the big American companies could not imagine a serious challenge at home. Early attempts by European carmakers to enter the U.S. market had petered out. After the war, British Austins, French Renaults, and Italian Fiats were brought across the water but fared poorly with American buyers. American manufacturers also experimented in the 1950s with selling their own European models—British Fords and German Opels—in the United States; these experiments also failed. This was in part because European countries (except for Germany) had not yet developed high-speed roads, so the imported cars tended to be underpowered for American highway driving. But the biggest problems were that it was costly to set up dealer networks in the United States, the European small cars were not very durable and required a lot of repairs, and the imports could only hope to carve out niche markets at best.

Very few American-made cars were exported to Europe in the 1950s and '60s, despite the dominance of the American industry at the time. American-made cars used too much gas and were too expensive for the European mass market. Protectionist policies in Europe further reinforced the separation of the two markets. The European countries that produced cars had higher import tariffs on them than the United States did. In Germany, cars were taxed based on cylinder displacement, which penalized American cars with their larger engines. France and Italy, for their part, imposed quotas and other import restrictions that made American cars curiosities, and kept Japanese cars out almost completely until well into the 1980s.

For all these reasons, the Big Three did not push hard to open the European market. GM, Ford, and Chrysler were doing fine in America and in the rest of the world in the 1950s and '60s, so they acted as though the U.S. and other markets would always stay separate. The idea of competition from Japan seemed even more far-fetched than competition from Europe. The same confidence and smugness that marked the auto hearings in 1958 colored the industry's view of the world.

Volkswagen mounted the first serious challenge to the U.S. automakers in the 1950s, turning GM's strategy from the 1920s onto its head. VW offered buyers low-cost, durable transportation—just what Henry Ford had thought they should want—and found a growing niche market. VW's tough, economical little Beetle was underpowered like the other European cars, and at first was almost rudimentary compared to American cars. The VWs imported in the late 1940s and early '50s lacked even a gas gauge; drivers had simply to remember when they last filled up and keep track of the miles. Those who liked to take chances waited for the first sputter signaling that the gas tank was nearing empty, and then released a few gallons of fuel from an emergency reserve that would get them to the next gas station. VW also did not offer an automatic transmission in the early years. Practically the only option on the early models was a radio, followed years later by a cloth sunroof.

Despite these drawbacks, the Beetle sold well. It was cheaper and more fuel efficient than even the lowest-priced American car. Once it got up to speed, it could go sixty miles per hour all day long. And it was anything but frail; VWs lasted for one hundred to two hundred thousand miles—numbers the company put in its advertising. In the 1950s and '60s, American cars with a hundred thousand miles often had to have their engines rebuilt, or were ready for the junk heap.[7]

On the strength of the Beetle, Volkswagen took a small percentage of the U.S. auto market in the 1950s and '60s, but the Big Three were not seriously concerned. They were willing to give up a small piece of the low end of the market in order to avoid cutting prices on their own models. In essence, they allowed Volkswagen into their cartel. Lowering prices to compete with VW would have been more costly than giving up 4–5 percent of the market, so the Big Three let Volkswagen have its niche.

Japanese Imports Shake Up the American Giants

Skyrocketing gasoline prices in the 1970s finally exposed the weaknesses of the Big Three that had been festering under a canopy of weak competition. Fuel-efficient, inexpensive, and, eventually, high-quality cars from Japan poured into the United States. The companies could not ignore Japanese imports the way they had Volkswagen. It became clear that they would have to make fundamental adjustments in the way they did business.

Japanese cars had not been a significant factor in the Big Three's post–World War II calculations. General Motors and Ford had been big players in Japan in the years after World War I, but they were pushed out in 1938 as Japan moved to build up Toyota and Nissan to prepare for the second world war. After the war, Japanese law prohibited American car companies from reentering Japan. Neither the American Occupation Authority nor the U.S. companies were much concerned, though, because the Japanese market for cars in the 1950s was tiny.[8]

In the 1960s, Japan's domestic market for automobiles grew—although not fast enough to accommodate the eight or ten domestic carmakers. Toyota and Nissan, the favored prewar duumvirate, had been joined by Honda, Mazda, Isuzu, Mitsubishi, Daihatsu, Suzuki, and other companies that moved from making motorcycles and small delivery vans into the auto business, despite Japanese government efforts to hold them back. The only way all of these companies could grow and prosper was to export their cars, and the only large overseas market that was open to them was the United States.

In the late 1960s, the U.S. economy was booming, and the Big Three were selling all the cars they could produce. The boom began to pull in imports, but sales by the Big Three were so strong during the Kennedy-Johnson years that they hardly noticed. Moreover, the new imports from Japan at first were of indifferent quality and often didn't sell well, and the dealers who sold them often had large inventories on hand.

But Japanese automakers learned quickly, improving their products and building a customer base by selling inexpensive cars. In 1968, Volkswagen Beetle sales in the American market peaked at 423,000 and began to drift down. By 1971, Japanese companies sold almost 700,000 cars and trucks in the United States, gaining 6.5 percent of the market and taking sales away from VW as well as the Big Three—and this was still two years before gasoline prices shot up, heightening consumer demand for fuel-efficient vehicles.

The new reality finally hit home in late 1973, when oil prices quadrupled and gasoline prices took off because of an oil embargo organized by the Organization of Petroleum Exporting Countries (OPEC). Gasoline prices shot up again during the second oil shock in 1979–80. This hit American auto companies hard, and deep recessions in 1974–75, 1979–80, and 1981–82 added to the industry's miseries.

All the problems that weak competition had encouraged and allowed to fester beneath the surface since the 1950s were suddenly revealed. American companies did not have the fuel-efficient models the public demanded. They could not develop new cars quickly. Innovations like front-wheel-drive vehicles and improved small engines were coming from overseas, not from the United States. The American industry's approach to management, labor relations, and its suppliers was out of date. The industry and its workforce suddenly were in serious trouble. Sales of Japanese imports more than doubled from 1971 to the end of the decade, reaching about 1.8 million vehicles.

The Government Rescues Chrysler

The Chrysler bailout in 1979–80 was the first unambiguous sign of the industry's reversal of fortunes and the first major challenge for government policymakers. Caught by high gasoline prices and a deepening recession, Chrysler, the number-three automaker, lost large amounts of money in 1978, and when in 1979 it lost $1.1 billion,[9] its bankers threatened to refuse further credits. Chrysler turned to the Carter administration and Congress to help it get through the crisis.

Free-market advocates in Congress and the administration did not want to put government money into Chrysler, which they believed had been badly managed. On the other side, politicians from the midwestern carmaking states argued that letting Chrysler go under would put hundreds of thousands of autoworkers on the street at a time when unemployment was already at or near record levels for the postwar period.

After much discussion, the two sides struck a deal. The UAW and congressional delegations from the most threatened states worked out a package to aid the company while implementing significant cost-cutting measures. In early 1980, with an election looming, President Carter accepted the arrangement.

The government agreed to provide loan guarantees of $1.5 billion, but the bargain required that UAW members at Chrysler plants give up some already-negotiated wage increases worth several billion dollars, and it forced changes in Chrysler management. Chrysler's creditors agreed to provide an additional $2.1 billion in new loans. The union and the company, heretofore enemies, teamed up and asked for easier terms, but the Carter administration was adamant.

Many observers, however, on both sides of the political spectrum viewed the prospect of one of the largest corporations in the country being rescued by the taxpayers as ironic at best. Folksinger Tom Paxton wrote:

I am changing my name to "Chrysler."
I am going down to Washington, D.C.
I will tell some power broker,
"What you did for Iacocca,
Would be perfectly acceptable to me."

I am changing my name to "Chrysler."
I am leaving for that great receiving line,
And when they hand a million grand out,
I'll be standing with my hand out.
Yes sir, I'll get mine.[10]

The Chrysler bailout was an easy target for critics like Paxton, but they overlooked the onerous conditions attached to the government aid, which required Chrysler to reform its poor management and labor practices. Moreover, after the initial bailout, when Chrysler's recovery was delayed by the deep recession of 1980–82, the Reagan administration added conditions that were even more demanding when it extended the guarantees. Eventually, Chrysler's more fuel-efficient models, such as the so-called K-Cars, the Plymouth Reliant, and the Dodge Aries, introduced in 1981, began to do well.

Looking for Protection

The Chrysler bailout was just the beginning of efforts by the now-struggling auto industry to get government help in a suddenly competitive world. In June 1980, the UAW made its first serious effort to shelter its members from import competition by petitioning the U.S. International Trade Commission (ITC) for protection from the Japanese.[11] The union had been moving away from its traditional support for liberal trade since Walter Reuther died in a plane crash in 1970, but this was a clear break. Rank-and-file members of the union, angry about rising unemployment, blamed the problem on imports. The UAW leadership had to get in step.

Two-thirds of the Big Three backed the UAW's efforts. Ford supported the union immediately, and Chrysler joined the petition later, after it had cut its deal with the government for the bailout. GM never signed on, although it did not openly oppose the other companies. Its management was less afraid of imports because they believed that Toyota was Japan's only serious long-term competitor, and that GM could quickly catch up.[12]

The UAW's petition to the ITC commissioners in 1980 was straightforward: Autoworkers had been hurt in 1979 by a flood of imports, and the union wanted the commission to recommend that the Carter administration grant temporary protection from import competition. The UAW did not claim that Japan was "dumping" cars—selling them at below-cost prices. Rather, they asked for relief under the so-called "escape clause" provisions of trade law, which allow an industry to obtain temporary protection from imports if they are the most important cause of "serious injury."[13]

The ITC did not make its decision until December 1980, after the election. Then, to the surprise of many observers, it voted three to two against the UAW petition. The three Carter appointees on the commission ruled that increased imports from Japan in 1979 were not the principal cause of the U.S. auto industry's problems. Two other factors were hurting the industry at least as much: the recession that had been driving down demand for all automobiles in early 1979, and the shift in the market toward small cars.[14]

The ruling, like the Chrysler bailout, subtly placed most of the blame on the American companies. It said, in effect, that American consumers were buying imports because the domestic industry was producing the wrong products. The commissioners thought the industry had to move quickly to give the consumers what they wanted, and keeping imports out was not likely to speed that process. Their decision was one of several by independent government commissions at about this time (to be discussed in chapter 5) that essentially said the government should not be in the business of protecting industries from competitors that were taking advantage of their own bad decisions.

Ronald Reagan, who defeated Carter in November 1980, had considerable leeway in deciding how to handle the ITC's recommendation. The new president could have simply taken the recommendation of the majority. He always had been an outspoken advocate of competition and liberal trade, but he came into office at a time of exceptionally high unemployment. UAW members around Detroit had been the core of the "Reagan Democrats" in Michigan in the 1980 election, and had defied their union leaders to support him. There is no doubt that they expected some consideration from Reagan in return for their support.

Reagan's top political advisers—Attorney General Edwin Meese; Drew Lewis, the influential and politically astute transportation secretary; and others—pushed the new president to get the Japanese to "voluntarily" restrain car exports to the United States. Reagan's budget director, David Stockman, and Bill Niskanen, of his Council of Economic Advisers, objected, but to no avail. Disregarding the ITC's recommendations, Reagan sent his U.S. trade representative and former campaign manager, Bill Brock, to Japan for negotiations.[15] Four months after Carter left office, the UAW got part of what it wanted: The Japanese accepted "Voluntary Export Restraints" (VERs) and agreed to roll back exports to the United States to less than 1.7 million cars per year for the next three years.

This disappointed Stockman and other free-trade advocates, but the voluntary restraint approach, like the Chrysler bailout, was not as bad as it seemed. Japanese car sales would have fallen by 8–10 percent in any case due to the deep back-to-back recessions in 1979–80 and 1981–82. The 25 percent reduction in Japanese exports that the industry wanted and failed to get, on the other hand, would have been real protection, and prices would have risen dramatically. The voluntary approach produced much more modest restrictions. While a few of the most popular Japanese cars became scarce, there were plenty of others for sale.[16]

In the mid-1980s, when car sales rebounded, the Reagan administration quickly eased quota limits to prevent shortages from developing. Quotas continued for the next decade, but they were never tight enough to reduce the competition that was shaking the U.S. domestic auto industry to its roots.

Splits in the Business Community Keep Auto Markets Open. Trade policy—America's continued openness to imports despite the VERs—broke open the auto oligopoly. There is a lesson here that applies not only to manufacturing but to all the other industries that were opened to competition during the decades leading up to the 1990s: It was splits in the business community that made it possible for political leaders to resist pressure from manufacturers and unions to close the doors on the Japanese. Both Carter and Reagan believed in keeping American auto markets open, but they might well have yielded to the protectionists' demands if it were not for countervailing pressures from car dealers who did not want to see imports slashed. The dealers were close to consumers and had support in many localities. These crosscurrents within the larger industry limited the influence of the carmakers and the unions, and they did much the same in other sectors of the economy.

When we talk about these countervailing forces, we should start with the dealers. By the early 1970s, Japanese auto companies had built a network of more than four thousand U.S. dealers. These small-businesspeople fiercely opposed strict import restrictions because the availability of imports made them less dependent on the Big Three. Dealers and the Big Three had longstanding conflicts; the manufacturers had often tried to establish tight "vertical" control over the local dealers, but the dealers always resisted.

A little history is again important. In 1956, dealers succeeded in pushing the "Dealer's Day in Court Act" through Congress. Individual dealers wanted the right to be able to sell Volkswagens and other foreign makes as well as American cars. The law forbade manufacturers to take away franchises from dealers that sold imports. It also outlawed other punitive measures, such as establishing competing franchises close to existing ones or denying dealers access to their most popular cars. Dealers also succeeded in persuading many state legislatures to enact similar laws.

For the dealers, the 1980s were essentially a continuation of the earlier fights. They saw the threat of tight import restrictions as another way for the Big Three to limit their independence. Restricting their supplies of popular imports would have been as painful as cutting them off from the best-selling American cars. And while the automakers and the UAW were strong in the traditional car-manufacturing states such as Michigan, Ohio, Indiana, and Illinois, car dealers had influence in every single state. Both the Carter and Reagan administrations had to take their interests into account.

This splitting apart of related business interest groups—the car dealers and the auto companies—in the 1960s and '70s was characteristic of how the American political system works. Car dealers, like many other small businesses, had to be reckoned with. They often had the ear of their congressional representatives, and their trade associations in Washington had real clout. Since they were spread throughout the country, they had important advantages over big auto companies. For the same reason, heating oil dealers have often seemed to have as much influence on energy policy as big oil companies.

In Europe and Japan, by contrast, auto companies have had far more control over the dealers. Henry Misisco, a Commerce Department expert on the Japanese auto industry, said in 2001 that "no Japanese dealer in his right mind would think of representing an American or European make without getting permission from his Japanese supplier."[17]

In 2002, the European Union moved to increase competition in its auto market by letting dealers handle different makes of cars and sell them to customers from other countries—rights comparable to those Congress guaranteed to American dealers in the 1950s. Where American car dealers have had real political power based on their importance in local politics, in Europe the idea of giving dealers the right to sell multiple makes came principally from the European Commission in Brussels—that is, from the top down, not bottom up.

Japanese "Transplants" Make It in America. Imports of Japanese cars in the 1970s and '80s set off a chain reaction. One important feature of it was the reinvestment in the United States of a significant portion of the profits Japanese companies were earning from their U.S. car sales. Some of this investment was defensive. As Japanese companies increased their American exports, they became increasingly vulnerable to the potential loss of these markets if the U.S. government were to set serious limits on imports. For this and other reasons, Japanese companies began to invest in new plants (termed "transplants") in the United States. This created formidable new domestic competitors for the Big Three in the 1980s, intensifying the competition they were already feeling from imports.

Throughout the post–World War II era, American policymakers had urged other countries to bring in foreign investment and, consistent with that policy, had encouraged foreign companies to invest in the United States. The UAW had likewise long been a champion of foreign investment in the United States, to provide more jobs and act as a spur to American auto management to keep up with worldwide developments. Many states actively sought out foreign investors who were seen as a source of high-paying jobs. Even the U.S. automakers encouraged the Japanese to invest, reasoning that foreign companies operating in the United States would face the same difficulties with unions that the Big Three thought were the root of their problems.

Honda was the first Japanese carmaker to open a plant in the United States.[18] It started producing motorcycles in 1979 but quickly broke ground for a car factory in 1982 near its Marysville, Ohio, motorcycle plant. It was not far ahead of the bigger Japanese firms. Tennessee, Kentucky, Illinois, and other states courted Japanese car companies and parts suppliers, creating new competition—and new checks and balances—for the Big Three. By the mid-1980s, with encouragement from the federal government and the states, almost all Japanese carmakers were building vehicles in the United States.

Toyota built its first U.S. car plant in Georgetown, Kentucky, in 1986;[19] over time, it grew and attracted a network of suppliers and related investments. Nissan started in Tennessee and grew in a similar pattern, while Isuzus were made in Indiana. In 2002, Nissan built a billion-dollar facility in Canton, Mississippi, attracting both U.S. and foreign parts makers—and lowering costs by providing modules instead of parts to the assembly facility. In 2004, hundreds, perhaps thousands, of Japanese parts makers have plants in the United States that compete with U.S. parts makers.

By the mid-1980s, the Big Three recognized they had a great deal to learn from the Japanese, so they teamed up with them on specific projects. In 1984 GM agreed to a joint venture called NUMMI, to be managed by Toyota at one of GM's older plants in Fremont, California. Mazda worked with Ford at its plant in Flat Rock, Michigan. Mitsubishi, linked to Chrysler, built its plant in southern Illinois.

GM's joint venture with Toyota in California was interesting. GM management believed that much of the Japanese advantage came from not having to deal with the UAW, so part of the agreement concerning the Fremont plant required Toyota to hire UAW members. George Eads, GM's chief economist in the mid-1980s, says that GM also suspected Toyota was benefiting from some kind of "secret automation." GM was investing billions in new robots and similar technology and believed that Japanese companies must be doing the same.[20]

GM learned a lot from the joint venture. One surprise was that the Japanese-managed plant in California did fine with its unionized workforce. GM also learned that "secret automation" was not Toyota's secret. The real difference was that Toyota managers saw workers as part of a team that worked with management to squeeze out costs and make continuous improvements. It was this mindset, not different workers or machines, that gave Toyota its advantage. The Big Three's corporate cultures had been shaped by the worker-management conflicts of the 1930s and by the ethos and arrogance of oligopoly. These bad habits were hard to shake, even when it was clear that they were holding the American companies back.

The Fremont joint venture offered GM a third painful lesson. The plant made small Toyotas, but it also produced identical cars that GM sold under its own Chevrolet nameplates, like Nova and Prism. To GM's embarrassment, the Toyotas still sold better than the Novas or Prisms, even though the identical "American" versions cost several hundred dollars less in the showrooms.

The reason for this was obvious. A friend of mine bought a Chevrolet Citation in the early 1980s and had such trouble with it that ten years later he still said he would never buy another GM car. Another friend who had bought Cadillacs for decades had the same experience in the late 1980s, and made the same vow. American consumers had learned to expect quality from the Japanese competitors, while memories of poorly made American cars persisted. Cars from Japanese firms, both imported and produced in the United States, had 30 percent of the market in 2000.

Studies of the auto industry in the 1980s and '90s summarize the problems that afflicted an industry where competition had become, at best, limited and stylized. In a 1980 article entitled "Managing Our Way to Economic Decline," Bill Abernathy and Bob Hayes attributed the auto industry's decline to a failure in "product design, process technology and manufacturing technique."[21] Paul Ingrassia and Joseph White, who won a Pulitzer Prize for their book, *Comeback: The Fall & Rise of the American Automobile Industry,* called GM "a backward looking culture."[22] Weak competition created an industry that was rotting from the inside during the very years when the oligopoly had seemed most imposing. While ignoring its critics, it had dug a very deep hole for itself. The leading edge of change in manufacturing had shifted to Japan and other countries.

Competition, however, forced the auto industry to modernize and improve its products after three decades. In 2004, it is still behind the

Japanese, but it has improved enormously. If American policymakers had yielded to the union and the companies and closed the market more tightly, they would have saddled the United States with a second-class manufacturing sector that, in the end, would have required an even more painful process of reform.

3

Steel

Steel Industry quarters are . . . asking how many mills will remain suppliers to GM and what kind of price discounts they will have to concede in order to stay in.

—*Metal Bulletin*, 1982[1]

The Construction Industry, Minimills, and Imports

The steel experience in the postwar years was similar to the auto industry's. Like the auto giants, American steel companies emerged from World War II in strong shape, but attitudes and practices developed during this period of weak competition cost them dearly.

U.S. Steel had dominated the industry since its creation in 1901, when J. P. Morgan merged his steel interests with those of Andrew Carnegie. Bethlehem Steel was created a few years later as the result of another merger and, for much of the century, was the second-largest U.S. steelmaker. Other companies, like National, Inland Steel, and Armco also were important.

Rapid growth after World War II and the fact that the steel industries in Europe and Japan had been destroyed made the U.S. steel industry as overconfident as the auto industry. That changed in the 1960s. The European and Japanese industries were back on their feet, and, when demand soared during the Kennedy and Johnson administrations, imported steel poured into the country for the first time. Most of it came in to meet the needs of the construction industry, which was desperate to find adequate supplies, especially of relatively crude products like reinforcing rods for concrete and steel construction beams.

The most important part of the story of increasing competition in the steel industry since the 1960s begins with a man named Ken Iverson. Iverson was a naval officer in World War II who had engineering degrees from Cornell and Purdue. He had started his business career as a customer of Big Steel, and he understood the construction industry. In 1962 he joined the Vulcraft Division of the Nuclear Corporation of America, which bought steel from the large American steelmakers and made it into joists and similar products for buildings, bridges, and other construction projects. Iverson quickly made Vulcraft profitable, and the board soon chose him to head the whole company.

Iverson and others who supplied the construction industry needed steady supplies of steel at fair prices. Like auto dealers, they did not enjoy being dependent on the big U.S. companies, who they felt treated them shabbily. Iverson heard about new steelmaking furnaces being introduced in Europe that used electric arc technology to melt scrap metal, and he thought this technology might solve his supply problem. He decided to build new steel plants in the United States using it. In 1965, he moved the company from Arizona to North Carolina, sold off its other divisions, and changed its name to Nucor Steel. In 1969, he opened his first new steel mill in, of all places, Darlington, South Carolina, far from Pittsburgh and other smaller American centers of steelmaking.

Over the next thirty years, Iverson made his new company the biggest and best-known of a new breed of steelmakers. By the 1990s, Nucor and other "minimills" were producing about fifty million tons of steel a year in the United States, about half of U.S. domestic production. Imports, by contrast, accounted for just twenty-five to thirty million tons. Iverson's company made money steadily, while the big companies flirted with bankruptcy. He was a modern manager, with none of the habits common in the older Big Steel companies. He was famous for answering his own phone and running his headquarters with a staff of fewer than fifty people. There were no executive dining rooms, special elevators, executive parking spaces, or company cars. Iverson's pricing philosophy was very different from that of the Big Three auto companies and the older steel mills as well. By cutting prices to keep its mills running at full capacity instead of laying people off and closing facilities, he kept Nucor's order books full.

Iverson and Nucor saw the weaknesses of Big Steel, and they rede-
fined American steelmaking by doing things differently. The old mills,
which depended on coal and iron shipped by water, had been built along
the Great Lakes or on the coasts. The new mills used electricity to melt
scrap metal, which was in abundant supply across the country; the mills
could be set up wherever their customers were. Many were located in the
South and West, where roads and buildings were being built faster than
elsewhere in the country, and where Big Steel had few plants and less
influence.

Some Nucor and other minimills were also located near ports such as
Houston and Savannah and on the West Coast, where most of the imports
were coming in. This gave the minimills a transportation cost advantage
over the old steel firms in competing with imports. It also meant that
Iverson and the minimills, like the transplanted Japanese auto companies,
could count on political support from southern and western governors
who wanted to attract new business to their states and were not beholden
to Big Steel or the union.

Nucor, like the Japanese carmakers, also found existing distributors
who would handle its products so it did not have to finance a completely
new distribution system. It sold roughly 75 percent of its steel through
independent service centers, which also became important political allies.
Like U.S. car dealers, these wholesalers wanted multiple sources of supply to provide leverage with the big companies, so they flocked to buy
from Nucor. Their counterparts in Europe and Japan, in contrast, almost
always were controlled by the large steelmakers, and often would not
handle imports or even local steel from independent mills.

Nucor and the minimills had even more advantages. Hostility between
labor and management was a fact of life in the old unionized steel industry, as it was in the auto industry. Bitter strikes before and after World
War I and in the 1960s and '70s were part of the history of Big Steel.
Nucor and Iverson had a different approach and could start fresh.

Nucor's large steel complex on the Mississippi River at Blytheville,
Arkansas, built with Yamato Steel in the late 1980s, provides an example
of these better relationships. The Blytheville plant is nonunion, as is most
though not all of the minimill industry. When I visited in November 2000,
Blytheville employees were working three twelve-hour shifts a week instead

of five eight-hour days. Employees said they liked this schedule because it gave them more time with their families and allowed them to take advantage of educational benefits the company provided.

Work rules at Blytheville were far more flexible than at the traditional steel mills. Workers changed tasks every few hours, helping to break up the monotony of long shifts. During a single workday, team members would man computers that checked the characteristics of the steel being melted, manage the computer console of machines that made beams out of hot metal billets, fix machinery, mark beams for shipment, and run cranes that moved the molten steel and finished products.

Computer screens at many locations let the teams know how they were doing in terms of the productivity goals that determined a large percentage of their take-home pay. Incentives and procedures were designed to encourage team members to do what needed to be done, rather than waiting for a supervisor to give instructions when something went wrong. Workers said they liked the responsibility, and they knew they had a stake in keeping the plant productive and competitive; they viewed management more as a partner than as an antagonist.

Big Steel: Caught between Two Fires

Iverson and Nucor began to build their new steel mills in the United States in the late 1960s. The U.S. economy was booming, a vast coast-to-coast interstate highway construction program was in full swing, and the Vietnam War was adding to demand. Steel imports had risen from 5 percent of the U.S. market in 1960 to 17 percent in 1968, just as the new minimills were starting to get into production. Iverson, who was always opposed to protection against imports, regularly undersold the foreign producers; indeed, he drove them out of several of the product lines he produced.

The established mills, however, wanted protection. Big Steel and the union always believed that their problem was imports, and they worked politically for three decades to cut them back. They had many apparent successes, starting in 1969, when President Nixon negotiated so-called Voluntary Export Restraints on steel imports.[2] Such negotiations with foreign countries to limit exports to the United States through a variety of mechanisms continued through every succeeding administration, right through the 1990s.

In addition, the old steel interests won a welter of cases at the International Trade Commission, which on several occasions agreed with the steel companies and the union that specific foreign countries and companies were "dumping" steel in the U.S. market. Indeed, the definition of "dumping" in the U.S. trade law, and eventually in the laws of other countries, was heavily influenced by the lawyers hired by Big Steel and the United Steel Workers to help them in Washington.

Old steel seemed to get much of what it wanted, but, as with the Voluntary Restraint Agreements for the auto industry in the 1980s, the political process made sure that the protection came with loopholes. The "voluntary" steel quotas, "trigger-price" mechanisms (which came later), and similar arrangements limited the growth of imports, but they never really halted them. The big domestic mills could raise prices and handicap their own steel-using customers in their efforts to compete, but the restraints on imports were never enough to arrest Big Steel's steady decline. Steel buyers shifted their business to the minimills or found overseas producers in countries that were not covered by the restrictions. Producers overseas could shift their exports from lower- to higher-value products that were not covered by the restrictions, the way the Japanese did with higher-value automobiles.[3]

So Big Steel was caught between two forces: Political leaders slowed, but would not stop, the steady stream of imports; and Nucor and other new steel companies grew rapidly, taking ever-bigger pieces of Big Steel's market.

The Auto Industry Delivers a Crucial Blow

The real turning point for the steel oligopoly—the sign that its power over prices was gone—came in the spring of 1982. For the third year in a row, imports of Japanese cars and trucks exceeded two million, despite the voluntary export restraints that had been put in place in 1981. By then even GM, the most powerful of the auto companies, knew that it had to change the way it was doing business to meet the Japanese challenge.

The old oligopoly was vulnerable because it was increasingly depend-ent on sales to the auto companies. The construction industry was buying imports and steel from the minimills, which had taken almost all of the lower end of the market. The new mills were producing 30 percent of the nation's steel, and that share was growing by about 2 percent each year as new plants came on line. So it was a crushing blow in 1982 when the auto companies broke ranks, too.

In March 1982, General Motors announced what the *Metal Bulletin* called a "radical change in its steel purchasing policy." It shocked the major steel mills by saying that it would no longer allow individual GM plants to buy their own steel supplies. Instead, GM would tally up the steel requirements of all of its plants and accept bids from its suppliers. The companies that gave GM the best deals would get more business.[4] GM's declaration "was not the only wakeup call for the industry, but it was the one it understood best," recalls Kempton Jenkins, then corporate vice president for international affairs at Armco Steel.[5]

For many years, General Motors had been nicknamed "Generous Motors" for the way it treated its suppliers and employees. It had had strong profits, so it could allow suppliers regular price increases. The 1982 announcement was the end of all that, for one basic reason: It had become clear to auto industry executives that their companies would have to help themselves. U.S. politicians were not going to protect Detroit in a serious way from import competition, so the automakers would have to cut costs to become more competitive even if it meant changing the way they treated old friends.

The high-quality, "flat-rolled" steel that Big Steel sold to the auto com-panies was the core of its business, since it was a product the minimills could not make. Having lost most of the lower end of the steel market to imports and the minimills, Big Steel now saw its most important and prof-itable market put at risk by GM's shift.

The announcement, as Jenkins recalls, hit steel industry executives "like a collective heart attack," but it was also a signal to the whole man-ufacturing sector.[6] The decision signaled that business was going to have to be done differently in the whole economy. The new industrial state was dead. Between the lines of the announcement was an important political message: Not even GM or Big Steel had the power to avoid competing if government would not help them. Without a protectionist government, they had to find ways to improve efficiency, cut costs, and compete with more innovative companies.

It took time, in some cases a decade, but competition gradually changed business practices in all the industries, large and small, that were linked to steel and autos. The oligopoly culture came unglued.

The Parts Makers and Competition

Jerry Jacobson was executive vice president of the Bendix Corporation, a major auto parts supplier in the 1980s. Curious about how Bendix negotiated price increases for its parts with the auto companies, he asked a friend at the company to describe the process. It was simple, he was told: Bendix added up its costs, tacked on a few percent for profit, and told the car companies what it wanted to be paid. The carmakers would agree, and the "negotiation" would be over in a few minutes. This cozy process with parts makers—much like the steel arrangement—was another artifact of weak competition, and it was about to change, as the effect of competition from the Japanese spread slowly through the whole sector.

The beginning of this shift in the parts area is difficult to date precisely, but GM played a big role in it, too. An important participant was Jose Ignacio Lopez. Lopez had been a star manager at GM's assembly plant in his native Basque region of Spain, where he had been successful in applying Japanese parts-purchasing practices.[7] Lopez was willing to break eggs and make enemies to cut costs. Promoted and given the task of cutting the cost of parts at GM's European operations, he did so—by as much as 30 percent—by forcing suppliers into round after round of competitive cuts, tearing up contracts, and driving ruthless bargains.

In the late 1980s, when GM needed someone to do the same unpleasant work in the United States, Lopez once again angered suppliers and generated controversy, but he delivered comparable savings. While his approach culled out many smaller suppliers, the larger ones who survived provided GM with better parts at lower costs.

The new demands auto companies placed on parts suppliers had repercussions on other businesses. The parts makers had to find ways to meet these demands, and they began looking more carefully at what they paid for steel and for the machine tools they used in their operations.

The Parts Makers Turn on Big Steel. The independent parts makers, like the construction companies, had never loved Big Steel, and as pressures to cut costs intensified, they struck another blow at the steel companies. In 1988, the Precision Metalforming Association (PMA), which represented many parts makers, decided to oppose steel quotas, which President George H. W. Bush had promised in his campaign to extend for five more years. It joined the Coalition of American Steel-Using Manufacturers (CASUM), a coalition of parts and appliance makers and other steel users that was at the center of the fight against steel import quotas.

CASUM was largely the brainchild of Caterpillar, a major producer of construction machines and a large steel user itself. Caterpillar had long been something of a maverick in the U.S. manufacturing sector, having continued to export its products after the steel, auto, and appliance makers had retreated to the domestic market or given up product lines in the face of European and Asian challenges. In the 1960s, when U.S. domestic sales were strong, Caterpillar had nevertheless decided that giving up exports to focus on domestic sales would undermine its ability to compete with imports in the future.

Caterpillar invested boldly in its beliefs. In 1963, in order to deny Japan's biggest equipment maker, Komatsu, an uncontested market at home, Caterpillar formed a joint venture with Mitsubishi in Japan, Shin-Caterpillar, which is still the second-largest maker of construction and mining equipment in Japan. As CAT had hoped, this joint venture proved strong enough to compete with Komatsu in Japan at the same time the Peoria, Illinois–based company sold thousands of American-made machines in that country. To compete with Komatsu head-to-head, CAT had to keep up with its rival technologically and could not slack off and fall behind the way American automobile and steel manufacturers did.

Caterpillar in the late 1980s was not afraid to get in a public political fight with the steel companies. It recruited PMA and its small-business members into the antiquota coalition, knowing that PMA's regionally dispersed membership would give the group an important boost. Several

American makers of home appliances, also large users of steel, took similar leadership roles.

Ken Iverson of Nucor, who believed he could compete with anybody, supported the effort as well. CASUM's leadership tried but failed to get GM and the American auto companies to join. It was an interesting difference in leadership styles—GM was pushing the steel companies quietly behind the scenes and certainly opposed the steel quotas, but was trying to avoid an open political fight; CASUM, led by Caterpillar and Nucor, had no such hesitation.

PMA, representing parts makers, was an important ally for Caterpillar and the appliance makers. It had over a thousand members spread across many states who, like car dealers and the steel service-center owners, were often on a first-name basis with members of Congress. The steel users understood that President Bush would not completely drop his support for steel quotas, but they hoped for half a loaf. This hope was fulfilled when the administration developed a compromise, extending steel import quotas for two and a half more years, rather than the five years it had promised. As with early concessions by the government to the big companies and unions, it was once again weaker protection than they had wanted, and it gave Big Steel no protection at all against the new domestic mills that were adding millions of tons of new capacity each year.

Competition Comes to Machine Tool Builders. Parts makers, under pressure from the car companies to cut costs, also resented the fact that the American machine tool builders seemed to pay little attention to smaller customers. They produced mostly big machines for the Big Three automakers, and the parts makers felt exploited and ignored. So in the 1980s, the parts makers began to look overseas for alternative sources of machine tools, as well as steel. They discovered that Japan, Taiwan, Korea, Switzerland, and Germany made tools that were often more affordable, more readily available, more suitable for small businesses, of better quality, and more advanced, incorporating improved computerized controls.

The U.S. machine tool industry reacted by complaining to the Reagan administration that it was the victim of unfair foreign practices, pointing out that the Japanese government had subsidized its machine tool makers, and it sought protection from imports. Even though Japan was only one of the foreign sources of excellent machines, the Reagan administration set quotas for machine tool imports from several countries in 1986 that were renewed in 1991.

The protection was again "leaky," however. The flow of imported tools continued, and eventually the American makers had to respond to the increased competition. Like the auto, steel, and parts making industries, machine tools had fallen behind during the immediate postwar period when competition was weak. By the late 1980s and early '90s, American companies came out with new lines of smaller, more flexible machines, designed to meet the needs of smaller users and of good enough quality to compete with tools from overseas.

In the Rearview Mirror

Business plans changed in almost every area of U.S. manufacturing in the 1980s because the cozy relationships of the postwar era were no longer tenable. Companies facing import competition could not afford to carry suppliers who were less than world-class. As imports increased, manufacturing companies were forced to look for new ways to cut costs and improve quality. Eventually, in 1988, in an effort to lower their electric bills, even the big steel companies and their umbrella organization, the American Iron and Steel Institute (AISI), found themselves supporting regulatory changes that would force their electricity suppliers to compete.[8] It was a stunning change in direction for the steel industry, and one that confirmed the end of oligopoly dominance and the emergence of a new, competition-centered business model in the manufacturing sector.

Economic change spread from one American industry to another, and a succession of administrations let it happen, even though they almost always made some concessions to the struggling domestic industries. European companies faced the same problems American companies faced, but governments there responded differently. They poured public money into established companies—like the Chrysler bailout in spades. They established more rigid quota arrangements, took over debts and pension costs from the laggards, and did more than American politicians were willing to do to shield managers and employees from the pain of adjustment.

Japan behaved in a similar manner. Entrepreneurs there tried to do what Ken Iverson had done in the steel business, but the Japanese government was more single-mindedly committed to helping the existing steel mills. High prices drew domestic competitors into the business, just as they did in the United States. But the Japanese government supported a tight cartel that limited imports more severely than America did and used its power to prevent independent producers from undercutting the prices of the established mills.[9]

Japanese steelmakers who might have been tempted to follow Nucor's strategy and cut prices to gain market share feared retribution from the government, which allocated quotas to export to the United States and could deny obstreperous firms a share of exports to the U.S. market. It threatened construction firms who might have been customers of upstart mills with the loss of government-financed work if they bought lower-priced steel—an act that would have been politically unthinkable in the United States. Yamato Steel, an independent Japanese minimill that feared its expansion would be blocked by the government's control of sales to both export and domestic markets, ended up joining with Nucor to build a large facility in Blytheville, Arkansas.

The old American steelmakers and the union no doubt would have liked the kind of government support that their counterparts in Europe and Japan received, but they could not get it. The politics of protectionism were different, the structures of government were different, and the cultures were different. In the United States there was more of a balance between producer and consumer interests. The construction firms, service centers, parts manufacturers, appliance makers, and other steel buyers opposed the steel companies just as car dealers had opposed the auto manufacturers; these competing interests knew they could find support and that American political leaders would not ignore them. That does not mean that standing up to established interests was easy or that our elected officials have always done it. But it does mean that established interests in the United States have been challenged more often and more successfully than in other parts of the world.

There is a lot to learn from the changes in manufacturing that were ushered in by import competition in automobiles. The import challenge led to the breakup of old business relationships and forced businesses to find ways to keep costs down. This encouraged the kinds of investment, innovation, and creativity that are held back in countries not willing to expose their establishments to the fierce winds of change and competition.

The decisions to give special trade protection and help to the manufacturing industries by various presidents—although they seemed to be major at the time—turned out to have only modest effects. The concessions, problematic as they were, were part of a larger complex of policies that generally supported more open trade.

Another important lesson is that the economy can change rapidly. The post–World War II auto industry, dominated by a single company and characterized by weak price competition, grew in only a decade or two out of an industry that had previously been fiercely competitive. By the 1950s and '60s, a manufacturing sector and, indeed, a whole economy with limited competition seemed to John Kenneth Galbraith and others to be the natural order of things, one that would last for a very long time. But then the '70s and '80s brought fierce competition to the industry once again.

Battles to keep U.S. markets open to imports are ongoing. The auto workers, as well as textile, garment, and other unions and employers, continue to try to limit imports from countries like Mexico that are part of the North American Free Trade Agreement (NAFTA), and from elsewhere in the world. The new auto firms and minimills that (together with imports) brought competition to the manufacturing sector could quickly become like the entrenched interests that they once overthrew.

GM's decision in 1982 to change the way it did business with its suppliers is another important model that is relevant today. Competition that keeps pressure on American companies to continue to cut costs could, for example, lead to real competition and downward pressure on the cost of health care, which is discussed in the final chapter.

Adam Smith said more than two hundred years ago that the fight to make monopolists compete required political action and would be harder than demobilizing "an overgrown standing army."[10] These words are as true today as they were when Smith wrote them. The fights to restore competition at the end of the twentieth century made him look like a prophet.

Politically difficult, sometimes muddled decisions to allow auto imports and competition from foreign auto plants began ripples of reform in manufacturing. The next chapter will show how competition came in much the same way to other industries that were, in effect, government-sanctioned monopolies—ones whose pricing arrangements and terms of entry had been directly regulated by the federal government since the Great Depression and where imports played little if any role.

4

The Demise of the Government-Supported Oligopolies

*I don't want to impose a system on this country that will set aside
the anti-trust laws on any permanent basis.*
—President Franklin Delano Roosevelt[1]

Jack the Giant-Killer

In the early 1960s, about the time that Ken Iverson started Nucor Steel,
Jack Goeken was selling two-way radios in Joliet, Illinois. His principal
customers were truckers, many of whom drove between Chicago and St.
Louis and used two-way radios to keep in touch with their head offices.
Goeken thought he could provide a service by building microwave
repeater towers to give the radios he was selling more range. Barges along
the Illinois River and businesses in the towns along the way were also
potential customers.[2]

Goeken had been toying with ideas like this for several years, and he
knew he would have to apply to the Federal Communications Commission (FCC) to build the towers. So he got an FCC application, filled it out,
and mailed it to the regulatory agency. A few weeks later, trucks began
pulling up to his door to drop off packages. In them were copies of briefs
addressed to the FCC that had been filed by various regional Bell Telephone operating companies. These companies were owned by AT&T, and
they all opposed his application.

In a regulated industry like communications, potential new entrants
had to show the federal regulatory agency that additional service was

needed to do business. In all the briefs, the various local Bell companies emphatically told the FCC that Goeken's microwave service for two-way truck radios was not needed.

The packages got Goeken's attention, and he did what savvy challengers did in every industry; he started looking for a lawyer. He had read about Michael Bader, a telecommunications specialist, and he flew to Washington, D.C., to visit him. Why, Goeken asked Bader, was he getting legal documents from all over the country attacking his proposal to build a couple of towers in downstate Illinois? Bader replied that AT&T always tried to stop potential competitors before they got off the ground. In 1957, for instance, it had fought an entrepreneur who was selling a plastic device called a "Hush-A-Phone" that merely slipped over the mouthpiece of phones owned by AT&T so that conversations could be more private.[3] The Federal Communications Commission had decided against AT&T, so it was clear that the company was not invulnerable. But Ma Bell had a near-monopoly on long-distance communications and controlled most local service; it was not about to let Goeken build his towers. AT&T's stable of lawyers was always geared up to fight anyone who dared to challenge its monopoly, and they could spend whatever it took to wear their would-be rivals out.

But Goeken was not intimidated. AT&T's opposition suggested that his microwave towers could turn into something much bigger. If the monopoly was spending this much money to block a couple of towers, there had to be a lot of money to be made in beating it. Goeken decided to fight for his licenses. This was the beginning of Microwave Communications, Inc., the company that would become MCI. It was also the beginning of a fight to bring competition to telephone service that is still going on forty years later.

Goeken relished the idea of taking on AT&T, and the media loved the ebullient entrepreneur. To those who covered communications issues, Goeken was "Jack the Giant-Killer," David against Goliath. He became an American hero, one of those happy warriors the public has long celebrated. The joke in Washington was that "MCI was actually a law firm with an antenna on its roof," but it survived in the late 1960s and early '70s largely by winning law cases.[4] The Giant-Killer was extraordinary, but he and Bill McGowan, who later headed MCI, were not one of a kind. Similar challengers rose up against the regulated monopolies in other areas, and there were people in the government and at regulatory agencies like the FCC, the Civil Aeronautics Board, and the Interstate Commerce Commission who believed in the benefits of competition. Like Goeken, they were willing to take on some of the most powerful interests in America—the special interests that supposedly dominate the country's politics with their money.

The Way It Was in the Regulated Industries

The oligopolies and monopolies and the powerful unions that dominated U.S. telecommunications, airlines, trucking, railroads, pipelines, electricity, and the other so-called "regulated industries" from World War II into the 1970s were even more sheltered from competition than the Big Three car companies and the oligopoly steel industry in manufacturing. The limits on competition that protected these companies, unlike those in manufacturing, were actually enshrined in law and regulation. Moreover, these industries provided the kinds of services that could not be challenged by imports and foreign companies. By the 1990s, however, these companies were also shadows of their former selves, their power over prices and ability to block new competitors broken. How did this happen, and what can we learn from it?

In the post–World War II period, each of the regulated industries had its own regulatory agency with its own idiosyncrasies. Each had been set up by a different piece of congressional legislation. Each was supervised by a different set of congressional committees, and each had its own history in administrative law. All, however, had one key thing in common: Firms in the industry were protected, by law and regulation, from competition from newcomers.

The incumbent firms in the federally regulated sectors counted on the agencies that supervised them to agree to price increases that guaranteed a good return on their investments. These firms also could be sure that potential new competitors would have to prove to the federal regulators that the additional services they proposed to provide were needed, or—in the term of art that was used—served "the public convenience and necessity." If a new company wanted to provide trucking services between

New York City and Boston, it had to show that they were needed. If an airline wanted to serve Chicago from Los Angeles, there was a similar costly and contentious process.

In 1970, long-established companies dominated the growing airline industry, such as American, Braniff, Delta, Eastern, Northwest, PanAm, TransWorld, and United, as well as a few smaller operations. They provided airline service over approved routes and on regular schedules. They had to get permission from the Civil Aeronautics Board to add a new route, abandon a route, or change fares. When an airline proposed to do something that might increase competition in the industry, there would be hearings with lawyers and economists testifying in droves for both sides. The applicant would try to convince the CAB that new service would be good for the public; the incumbent invariably argued that it was unnecessary.

There were similar hearings for other industries at the Federal Power Commission, the Interstate Commerce Commission (ICC), the FCC, and other regulatory agencies. Setting rates and adjusting services was a very big industry in Washington that supported a host of lobbyists and lawyers. I attended a hearing on electric rates that filled the large auditorium and an overflow room at the Federal Power Commission with lawyers and their assistants, taking notes for client memos. State regulatory agencies with overlapping responsibilities created a similar dynamic in state capitals. Sometimes the states did less to limit competition than the federal regulators, but in other cases state regulation was more intrusive and restrictive, and less subject to criticism and pressures for reform.

Unions were strong in the regulated industries. The unions for airline mechanics, pilots, baggage-handlers, and other airline workers wielded considerable political power. As discussed in chapter 1, Roy Siemiller of the airline mechanics' union overcame President Johnson's efforts to limit wage and price increases in 1966.

The American Trucking Association and the Teamsters union dominated the trucking industry, regulated by the ICC. Outwardly, trucking was very different from the airlines. There were thousands of trucking companies, not just a few, but they were allowed by law to get together in regional "rate bureaus" under the aegis of the ICC and set rates for different services. These arrangements also kept newcomers out, and parallel regulation in most states reinforced the system.

Long-distance telephone service was an AT&T monopoly. The FCC regulated the rates Ma Bell charged for interstate telephone service, and intrastate rates were set by parallel state regulatory authorities. The Bell operating companies owned by AT&T controlled local service in most heavily populated areas. The prices they charged were regulated, of course, by the states. "Independent" local phone companies often served rural areas, but they were dependent on AT&T for long-distance connections.

The Communications Workers of America, AT&T's dominant union, was correspondingly dominant. Wages made up a relatively small share of the costs of providing many of the regulated services such as telephone, natural gas, and electricity. In these capital-intensive industries, it was even easier for the regulators to allow companies to pass on wage costs to consumers than it was in the airline area, where labor accounted for a larger proportion of total costs.

The overlap of federal and state agencies that regulated prices and the entry of new competitors often created tensions. Important differences between the states and the federal regulators, and among the states themselves in some cases, created loopholes that the lawyers for new competitors were able to use to enter the business. Airlines and truckers operating within just one state (in *intrastate* commerce) were not subject to federal regulation; they operated under the regulations of that state, and in some states were not regulated at all.

The differences between regulated interstate and unregulated intrastate airfares in similar markets were cited in dozens of academic studies because prices in the regulated markets were usually higher. Other studies contrasted the costs of trucking for businesses like Sears or General Motors, which ran their own trucking operations, with the costs of shippers who had to use regulated "common carriers." The fact that many companies chose to operate their own transportation subsidiaries rather than rely on regulated trucks in itself made clear that regulation was making the cost of "common carriage" trucking more expensive than it had to be. Another indication was the significantly lower rates charged by truckers hauling agricultural goods and a few other products that were exempt from regulation.

In the telephone business, similar comparisons could be made between regulated and unregulated parts of the market. Private companies were always trying to bypass AT&T and establish their own internal phone systems to save money. AT&T fought and often stopped companies that set up their own systems between facilities, but the fact that users kept trying suggested how costly regulation was in this area, too.

This is a thumbnail sketch of the way price and entry regulation operated in important industries in the 1960s and '70s. Similar rules operated in other industries, affecting natural gas, oil pipelines, barge transportation, cable TV, and coastal shipping. Most of these rules have been relaxed if not eliminated as part of the general movement to increase competition in transportation and communications. Only coastal shipping remains largely as it was, a tribute of sorts to the truly exceptional power of the maritime lobby.

Limits on Competition: Another Legacy of the Great Depression

How did these limits on competition in the major regulated industries develop? What led to the elaborate structures that replaced competition with price and entry regulations?

Again, it was the unprecedented economic crisis of the 1930s that led to most of the limits on competition. The regulation of railroad rates by the Interstate Commerce Commission dated further back to a period of economic stress during the 1880s, and it served as a model for the newer regulatory agencies.

In hard times, falling prices and intensified competition in a shrinking market force companies and individuals that lack deep pockets to sell out to richer firms or fall into bankruptcy. Companies and individuals that depend on credit are particularly vulnerable. Those who are at risk often seek help from governments to cancel or lighten the burden of their debts and to protect them from competition that would drive them under. During these periods business leaders want to keep prices from falling, and working people want to avoid layoffs. Price-fixing and limits on new competition are seen as measures to save jobs and make it possible to provide subsidized service for especially hard-pressed consumers.

The horrific economic collapse of the Great Depression sank prices and wages, sharply cut employment, and brought enormous pain to workers and businesses that had prospered during the 1920s. In 1933, the unemployment rate reached 25 percent, and almost 13 million Americans were out of work. Corporate profits before taxes were 98 percent lower than they had been in 1929, and commercial and industrial failures were almost 40 percent higher.[5] Small wonder that beleaguered businesses pleaded with the government to let them act in unison to reduce and limit capacity, avoid "cutthroat competition," and prevent more price reductions. Small wonder also that labor and much of the public wanted the government to prop up failing businesses, shore up employment, and arrest the decline in wages. As a result, the economic collapse created broad support for regulated prices and limits to competition.

New Deal Economic Measures. Franklin Delano Roosevelt was elected in 1932, promising to take action. He had no consistent plan—perhaps no one did—but FDR promised a "New Deal" that included considerable price-fixing and limits on competition. The National Industrial Recovery Act of 1933 (NIRA), introduced by Roosevelt in May 1933 and passed a month later in June, was his most sweeping and comprehensive effort to restore the economy. It sanctioned price- and wage-fixing in broad sectors of the economy and, in Roosevelt's words, "relax[ed] some of the safeguards of the antitrust laws" in order to stabilize production and employment. Roosevelt said that "the antitrust laws [would still] stand firm against monopolies that restrain trade and price fixing which allows inordinate profits or unfairly high prices"[6] but he was clearly sending a mixed message to those who had to implement the NIRA on the one hand and his administration's antitrust policies on the other.

The National Recovery Administration (NRA) established under NIRA was headed by the colorful and outspoken Hugh S. Johnson, who was named *Time*'s Man of the Year for 1933. Johnson's task at the NRA was to halt falling prices and wages by working with businesses to establish limits on output and prices. The act, in effect, made it legal for businesses to act in concert and divide among themselves the Depression-limited markets for goods and services.

NIRA also required businesses to agree to better labor conditions, eventually including a forty-hour workweek and minimum wages—reforms that have endured.[7] Business and labor groups never shared with each other the same objectives for NIRA, although they both supported it. Businesses cared about reducing capacity and agreeing on prices, and they wanted the government to sanction such actions. Labor wanted to use limits on competition to maintain job and wage levels, improve working conditions, and strengthen the hand of unions. But for the time being, they worked together to limit competition.

The first NIRA price and production codes, established in 1933, covered only a few key industries and were developed by the industries themselves with significant input from the government. The regime of codes spread quickly, however, to cover about five hundred other industries. After a while there were so many of them that codes were being developed almost entirely by the interests concerned, and merely ratified or blessed by the public authorities.

The Supreme Court in the spring of 1935 refused to accept this broad delegation of congressional authority and government power to private code-setting bodies. The codes by then had come to regulate even slaughterhouses for chickens. In what was called the Schechter "sick chicken" case, the Court declared large sections of the National Industrial Recovery Act unconstitutional.[8] The decision, however, did not say that regulating prices or limiting competition was unconstitutional; rather, it held that the delegation of congressional authority to the code-setting industries to do such things went too far. Moreover, the Court was clearly put off by the "huge number of codes."[9]

President Roosevelt and the Congress responded angrily to the torpedoing of the NIRA. They denounced the Court but eventually settled for separate pieces of legislation that regulated specific industries individually, which the Court accepted.[10] Labor got much of what it wanted despite the demise of the NIRA because the Supreme Court accepted provisions that limited the workweek to forty hours and provided for a minimum wage. In addition, the Wagner Labor Relations Act, which passed in the summer of 1935, had even stronger reforms in these areas than those that had been incorporated in the NIRA.

FDR, upon reflection, may have felt relieved about the Schechter decision. The president was himself ambivalent about the sweeping limits on competition implied by the NIRA, which substituted code-setting bodies for the antitrust laws. "I don't want to impose a system on this country that will set aside the anti-trust laws on any permanent basis," Roosevelt said, according to Frances Perkins, his secretary of labor.[11] Consistent with this stance, Roosevelt opposed antitrust immunity for telecommunications carriers when some in Congress pushed to include it in the Communications Act of 1934, before the NIRA was declared unconstitutional. He also opposed an antitrust exemption for truckers under the Motor Carrier Act of 1935, but Congress granted it.

Roosevelt also recognized from the beginning in 1933 that "many good men voted [for the NIRA's price-fixing arrangements] with misgivings,"[12] recalled Hugh Johnson. But the president and many others got behind it because the Depression had created a clear emergency. It is, nevertheless, awful to contemplate what the United States would have been like after World War II had there been over five hundred industries with legal price-fixing, regulatory bodies, and no real competition, instead of only a dozen or so.

The Supreme Court, in effect, resisted and limited the passion for price-fixing that had swept Congress and the executive branch as a result of the economic crisis. The Court forced the elected officials to reflect further on what they were doing and gave them a way to resist the popular ideas of the day. Eventually the emergency and the sense of fear dissipated, and conditions turned around after World War II. The fact that the Court had limited the scope of price and entry regulation then made it easier to restore competition in those limited areas where it had been legally abridged.

Concern Grows about Weak Competition after the War. The onset of World War II ended the Great Depression, and after the war people began to complain that limits on competition involved a lot of red tape and some obvious waste. By the 1960s the idea began to take root in academia, at a few think tanks, and among businesses and consumer groups that cheaper and better service might be available if regulation could be streamlined and, perhaps in some areas, replaced by competition.

In 1960, president-elect John F. Kennedy commissioned a study of the regulatory agencies by James Landis, who had succeeded the president's father as head of the Securities and Exchange Commission in the 1930s. Landis's criticisms of the agencies in his December 1960 report were repeated over and over again during the next several decades.[13] He detailed the time-consuming, legalistic rules and the lengthy administrative and judicial procedures that had developed at every regulatory agency. Most important, he and others complained that the costly hearings and procedures of the regulatory agencies made it almost impossible for small companies or new entrants to challenge incumbents. The Landis report was especially critical of the ICC, which had regulated railroads since 1887 and had gained new powers over trucking, pipeline, and barge traffic in the 1930s.

Liberals and conservatives viewed the issues raised in the Landis report differently from the start, but there was something in the report for both groups. Liberals tended to believe that the problems at the regulatory agencies arose because they had become captives of the businesses they were supposed to regulate. More competition, therefore, would break the grip of business over these agencies and help consumers. Conservatives saw price regulation as government interference with free enterprise. They thought the commissions usually were antibusiness and wanted more competition for this reason.

President Kennedy agreed with Landis and wanted to reduce the bureaucratic red tape, but neither he nor his successor Lyndon Johnson did much in this area. Both seem to have hoped that they could work with the oligopolies and unions and enlist their cooperation without having to confront them. The issue was beginning to boil beneath the surface, though. President Johnson's final *Economic Report of the President*, released in January 1969, had a lengthy and very strong section on competition and antitrust policy. The report, drafted by a young economist, Roger Noll, laid out the problems of regulation in communications, electricity, transportation, electric utilities, natural gas, and other areas. When Johnson left the White House, Thomas Gale Moore, a conservative economist on the staff of President Nixon's Council of Economic Advisers, picked up the deregulation portfolio.[14]

Competition's Comeback: Regulation Slowly Unwinds

President Nixon was sympathetic to deregulation but, like Kennedy and Johnson, he hung back. Although he talked about deregulating trucking and telecommunications and appointed people to key posts at the ICC and CAB who shared his views, he did not make a political commitment. When he encountered strong opposition from both the truckers and the Teamsters union, he let the trucking issue drop.

Gerald Ford was the Republican minority leader in 1971 when Nixon was considering taking action on trucking. Ford told the Nixon White House that trucking deregulation was a political hot potato, and that the president should maintain the status quo. According to Sam Peltzman, who was working in the Nixon White House at the time, Ford said he had 435 congressmen who had trucking companies in their districts, and none of them wanted to change regulations.[15]

But when Ford became president in August 1974, he reversed his position and fought for more competition in trucking and in other areas. Presidents have a very different perspective on many issues than do members of Congress. Commentator Louis M. Kohlmeier said in 1975 that Ford as president went "further out on the deregulation limb than Kennedy, Johnson, and Nixon ever allowed themselves to get."[16]

Ford set up a group within the White House Economic Policy Board to develop a deregulatory strategy for trucking and other industries. The group was headed by William Seidman, a businessman and friend of Ford's from his hometown of Grand Rapids, Michigan; its assignment was to advance some of the very measures to restore competition in regulated industries that Ford had earlier opposed. Roderick Hills, Ford's White House counsel, and Paul MacAvoy, a member of Ford's Council of Economic Advisers, were also leaders of the group.

Ford told the group to move boldly while making sure the process was bipartisan. He specifically directed Seidman to speak to Howard Cannon of Nevada, the Democratic chairman of the Senate Commerce Committee, and to Massachusetts Senator Ted Kennedy, who both would later play important roles in airline and trucking deregulation. Following Ford's instructions, the White House also put together a bipartisan group of two dozen congressional leaders who agreed to work with the president on reform of the regulatory agencies.

When Ford began the effort, the idea was to streamline and improve regulation more or less as Landis had proposed in 1960, because ending it seemed like too big a step. There was a two-part game plan. First there would be a push for "in-house reform" at the agencies to reduce red tape and the costs of regulation and encourage competition within the existing framework. Ford hoped such changes might get him halfway to where he wanted to be, and that legislation could eventually be pushed through to achieve the rest.[17]

Still, restoring true competition in the federally regulated industries seemed a distant goal. In 1975, Edwin Zimmerman of the prestigious Washington law firm of Covington and Burling wrote that the old companies and unions had a stranglehold on the system that deregulation advocates would find difficult to break. "Pessimism about the prospects of increased competition in the regulated area is well founded," he wrote.[18]

Paul MacAvoy said much the same thing three years later, just after Ford had left office. "[D]eregulation initiatives have been put forward in railroads, trucking, airlines, natural gas, oil, and cable television," he wrote, yet there had not yet been "a single case of reduced controls."[19] He attributed the failure to the way Congress worked and to stiff industry opposition. MacAvoy said that business leaders called deregulation proposals "the worst rantings of ideologues who have not worked in the industry." Every industry claims to be special, and MacAvoy and others heard this contention over and over again. Business also caviled that although regulation might have some "ill effects . . . deregulation would be worse." MacAvoy complained that Congress paid too much attention to industry fears and to the short-term problems of transition from price controls to competition.

The Pessimists Are Proved Wrong

Even in the late 1970s, advocates of competition like MacAvoy remained pessimistic. They had written hundreds of papers arguing that competition would lower costs. Presidents Kennedy, Johnson, and Nixon had backed them in spirit. President Ford had made a real public effort, and courts had encouraged regulatory agencies to apply antitrust policies in their decisions. Yet those closest to these issues still feared that nothing was going to happen. The status quo interests all had strong support in Congress and seemed to be unshakable.

But significant changes either were afoot or were just going unnoticed. The telephone monopoly had already been much weakened by regulatory changes, airfreight had been deregulated in 1977, and the dam of fixed airfares was about to break. By 1980, the big prize, trucking, was deregulated, and railroads followed. Pessimism about the American political system and its willingness to confront special interests soon turned out to be unfounded.

Competition Comes to AT&T. In 1968 Jack Goeken, having just barely gotten MCI off the ground, teamed up with Bill McGowan, a business and organizational genius, whose name would later be more closely associated with the company than that of Goeken himself. McGowan knew how to raise the bigger money, through financiers like Michael Milken, to fight the monopoly in court and at the same time expand MCI's customer base.[20]

MCI needed political support in Washington in the 1960s to survive, and the company found it. The earliest came from the FCC's Common Carrier Bureau, headed by Bernard Strassburg. There were civil servants like Strassburg at most of the regulatory agencies, people who remembered that the legislation that had created their agencies had been intended to help consumers, not the regulated companies. Strassburg backed MCI on the microwave license and was usually in the new company's corner.

In August 1969, MCI won its first battle. The FCC narrowly approved Goeken's application to build the towers, despite opposition from Ma Bell and the Bell operating companies. By then Strassburg and MCI had begun to focus on the emerging market for data transmission services for business. The ponderous monopoly had only slowly moved to meet the growing needs of American businesses in this area. MCI saw this as an opportunity and promised to move faster.

Following the recommendation of the Common Carrier Bureau, the FCC asked potential customers if AT&T was providing the data services they wanted. Important companies such as DuPont, American Express, Mobil, and the American Petroleum Institute (representing much of the oil industry), said no; in 1970, the FCC allowed MCI and others to begin signing up customers for data services, which was a growing area.[21] As with the splits between the Big Three and their dealers, and the rifts between Big Steel, the construction industry, and the parts makers, customers wanted competition, and they remembered how they had been treated by the monopolists. AT&T, with its highhanded tactics, had made enemies in the business world, at the FCC, and among political leaders, and now it was about to pay for these mistakes.

MCI's effort to get approval for its microwave towers and then for the right to compete with AT&T in providing data services to businesses was not front-page news. Industry experts, lawyers who specialized in FCC cases, and policy analysts at a few journals knew about the fight, but the public was not much involved. An antitrust case filed by President Nixon's Justice Department in 1974 against the AT&T monopoly, however, finally brought the issue before a larger public. The MCI legal team prepared the ground by funneling information to the Antitrust Division of the Justice Department, describing in detail AT&T's efforts to prevent MCI from competing. When the Justice Department brought the suit, the struggle was out in the open. It was no longer Jack, scraping together money for his legal fees, against the Giant and the army of lawyers it could deploy. It became *United States v. AT&T.*

The political tide already had turned against the telecommunications monopoly, however, well before the Justice Department filed, and certainly before the antitrust case was resolved in 1982. In 1977, five years before the final telecommunications antitrust settlement was made, Richard Cohen of the *National Journal* wrote that "competition had come to the telephone industry, and the federal government [was] largely responsible."[22] Nixon, Ford, and Carter appointees to the FCC and the Justice Department had been backing competition for years. FCC decisions allowing newcomers like MCI to challenge AT&T had been supported by the judiciary all the way up to the Supreme Court. Indeed, said Cohen, all three branches of the government had "reaffirmed . . . their commitment to competition."

Cohen reminded his readers that AT&T had the largest number of employees and shareholders of any company in the United States, and it mobilized all its forces to stop competition. The Communications Workers of America was a big union, and it backed AT&T all the way. Yet, in late 1976, when AT&T supporters introduced a bill in Congress to halt the expansion of competition, the legislation "was never seriously considered by the House and Senate communications subcommittees," which was a "dramatic illustration of the national mood against bigness and for competition." Despite its size and wealth, the AT&T Goliath lost out to little David, because David had more political support.

In January 1982, *United States v. AT&T* was settled. The agreement split the mother company from its Western Electric subsidiary that made equipment, and from the regional Bell operating companies that controlled local service. The judge in the case, Harold Greene, did not have to rule and later said that he did not know how he would have ruled had he been forced to do so. Judge Greene's brisk, evenhanded management of the trial, however, prevented AT&T from dragging it out, and no doubt pushed the monopoly in the direction of a settlement. But the die had been cast earlier. Three administrations had backed Goeken, McGowan, and the customers who wanted more competition against Ma Bell and its union—another case of well-heeled interests losing out to the more powerful American preference for competition. AT&T eventually had to face competition because regulators and political leaders gradually were persuaded that it was the right idea.

The End of Airline Price-Fixing Begins a Legislative Parade. The deregulation of the airlines represented a breakthrough because it was the first legislative step in the dismantling of the price and entry regulation put into place during the Depression. In 1975, Gerald Ford appointed John Robson, an Illinois Republican who had served as the "price czar" in the Johnson White House, to head the Civil Aeronautics Board, which regulated competition among the airlines. Robson's instructions were to see how far he could go toward competition in the industry without any new legislative authority.

Robson, the Ford administration, and broader bipartisan deregulation efforts were strongly influenced by the work of Michael Levine of Yale, who had written about airline regulation in the 1960s. Levine's argument that consumers would gain significantly from competition made an impression upon other young lawyers coming to Washington, one of whom was Stephen Breyer, a Harvard law professor and early advocate of increased competition, and a staff aide to Senator Ted Kennedy in the 1970s.[23]

Breyer, whom President Clinton later appointed to the Supreme Court, persuaded Senator Kennedy to hold several days of hearings on the subject of airline price and entry regulation in 1975, which showcased the economic arguments for competition. At about the same time, Robson used his authority at the CAB to make some significant procompetitive changes. He loosened the rules limiting charter carriers and allowed airlines to flexibly offer discounted "supersaver" fares for various long-distance trips, including, prominently, vacation trips to Florida.

By 1977, pressures for more competition were building in the airline industry. The first step was taken when Fred Smith of Federal Express and other airfreight companies persuaded Congress to get the CAB out of the business of regulating airfreight shipments. Smith, who came from Memphis, Tennessee, had developed an idea when still a student at Yale: Why not use a hub-and-spoke system to move packages around the country overnight? Packages would be brought to Memphis, quickly sorted, and promptly sent out to their destinations. Smith hoped to charge low prices and expand his business rapidly.

It was difficult to do this when the company had to work through a set of CAB legal proceedings whenever it wanted to add, reduce, or change service. Smith, like others who wanted to compete, found ways to exploit loopholes in the regulatory system while pushing for greater freedom to compete. For instance, Federal Express often sent packages in small planes because they were not regulated by the CAB. On some nights, FedEx flew a dozen small planes wing-tip to wing-tip from Memphis to California, even though all the packages could have been carried on one big plane, saving fuel, and at less cost to consumers.

One reason airfreight was deregulated first was that it seemed like a small matter at the time. No one anticipated that FedEx could become the biggest air transport company in the United States. As Fred Smith pointed out in 2002, these are the kinds of changes that are "never envisioned" and that can happen only if competition is allowed to work.[24]

Carter Picks Up Where Ford Left Off. Jimmy Carter became president in January 1977. Although Carter was from a different political party than Ford, like Ford he continued to push the regulatory agencies to permit more competition.

Like Ford, Carter chose people who were strongly in favor of competition for senior staff positions at the White House and regulatory agencies. Stuart Eizenstat, Carter's chief assistant for domestic policy, was a noted strategist in this area. He later became undersecretary of state for economic affairs and then deputy secretary of the Treasury in the Clinton administration. Eizenstat's deputy was Simon Lazarus, who had contributed to Mike Levine's airline deregulation writings at Yale in the 1960s; he also attended some of the early meetings on deregulation held at the Brookings Institution in 1971.[25]

Carter's staff knew that the president placed a high priority on restoring competition, and that he would back up their actions. Lazarus tells a story that illustrates this confidence. In 1977, Mary Schuman, a young lawyer who worked for Lazarus and Eizenstat, was arguing in favor of airline deregulation with Frank Borman, the former astronaut who was then chief executive officer of Eastern Airlines.

Borman took umbrage at Schuman's vehemence and said if she didn't ease off he would write a letter to Carter. According to Lazarus, the young Schuman stood her ground and shot back: "Go ahead. When he gets it he'll send it to me, and I'll answer it."[26] Whether Borman wrote Carter or not is unclear, but he certainly did not dissuade the president from supporting increased competition.[27]

Alfred Kahn replaced John Robson at the CAB. Carter's White House staff wanted Kahn in the position so much that when the president asked them for three candidates for the job, Lazarus says they suggested "Alfred E. Kahn, Fred Kahn, and Alfred Kahn."[28] Kahn was a well-known professor of economics from Cornell who would become a media favorite in Washington. He had headed the New York State Public Service Commission, which regulated electricity, natural gas, and telephones, among other industries, and had written textbooks on the subject.

Carter expected Kahn to push for more competition within existing CAB rules the way Robson had, and he did. Kahn expanded discount fares to cover new destinations. He gave airlines the right to cut fares by as much as 50 percent without getting CAB approval, causing much muttering in Congress. The CAB began to award domestic routes to any eligible carrier that wanted to operate them, without allowing other airlines to argue against the merits of additional service. Some in Congress grumbled again, but Carter backed Kahn, and the opposition never coalesced.

Roderick Hills, who had worked on these issues in the Ford White House, says that he and others who had served President Ford marveled at Kahn's nerve. The Ford administration, which had taken plenty of chances, had hesitated to test the CAB's authority to increase competition to the extent that Kahn did. He seemed to be way out on a limb, but Carter supported him, and Congress did not try to stop them. And when the airlines themselves brought suit to stop the initiatives, the courts let Kahn proceed.

Kahn's initiatives were opposed by all but United and PanAm among the major airlines and by all the unions representing the pilots, mechanics, baggage-handlers, and other airline workers.[29] One popular industry tactic was to tell members of Congress that their states and localities might lose airline service if deregulation came. Legislators from sparsely populated states had long crowded onto the House and Senate commerce committees that supervised the CAB in order to ensure good airline service for their constituents.[30] For example, Norris Cotton, a New Hampshire Republican, sat on the Senate Commerce Committee, the authorizing committee for the CAB's appropriations. While regulation lasted, large, almost empty jets provided frequent service to little Keene, New Hampshire, near his home. The airlines knew which side their bread was buttered on, and they made sure members of the committee got what they wanted, even if the services they provided cost them a river of money.[31]

Senator Barry Goldwater, an Arizona Republican who called himself a "free enterprise fellow all the way," at first hesitated over and then opposed airline deregulation, concerned that Arizona's air service might suffer.[32] Senator Warren Magnuson of Washington, a Democrat and the chair of the Senate Commerce Committee, also hesitated to support airline competition, fearing that the wide-open spaces of eastern Washington State might be neglected in a competitive system. "Competition is a nice word," he said, but he wasn't so sure in this case that it was the right one.[33]

Arguments for deregulation piled up as the process of deliberation went on. Some of the studies cited most often came from think tanks like AEI and Brookings, but the CAB produced its own study in 1975, and the subject became a hot one in academic circles. Deregulation advocates pointed to Southwest Airlines, which operated entirely within Texas and thus was not regulated by the CAB. Southwest founder Herb Kelliher had initiated cut-rate fares in 1962 and found that, even in depressed times, they increased passenger traffic and profits significantly. Southwest's per-mile fares were much lower than those of the CAB-regulated airlines. In California, by the same token, intrastate service was 40 percent less expensive than service over comparable distances in the regulated inter-state market.

These studies and examples had an effect. In the end, competition came to the airline industry because key legislators came to believe it would lead to better service and lower prices.[34] They became convinced that smaller communities could be served by feeder airlines—but they set aside a pot of money to subsidize service in less-populated areas, just in case. It was a classic political compromise, similar to the agreements that made modest concessions to the auto industry while competition from imports continued. The Airline Deregulation Act passed in October 1978. By 1983, most price controls on airfares had been phased out.

Ford and Carter Take On the Truckers and Teamsters. Airline deregulation in 1978 was not expected to establish a precedent for the bigger and more powerful trucking industry. The Teamsters, the biggest union in the country with almost two million members, and the American Trucking Association, with members in every congressional district, opposed deregulation. Teamsters president Frank Fitzsimmons had helped talk Richard Nixon out of an effort to bring competition to trucking in 1971.[35] There were good reasons to think that he would be able to do the same with Gerald Ford.

One story from Paul MacAvoy, who served on Ford's Council of Economic Advisers, captures the flavor of the Teamsters' opposition.[36] In 1975, MacAvoy and John Snow, then deputy undersecretary of the Department of Transportation, were assigned the unpleasant task of visiting the huge white marble union headquarters and informing the Teamsters that Ford was going to support legislation to deregulate the industry. MacAvoy and Snow were ushered into a small conference room and seated among a half-dozen burly union vice presidents, who yelled at the two for half an hour.

Finally, employing a sort of good-cop, bad-cop approach, Fitzsimmons spoke up. He suggested softly that the trucking industry "isn't broken. Why do you want to fix it?"

The federal officials responded that more competition would lead to more growth in the industry, and lower costs.

Fitzsimmons was not impressed. He replied that traffic was growing anyway, and ending price and entry regulation "would be a terrific blow to the Teamsters." There would be hardships, even bankruptcies. Why, he asked pointedly, would the administration want to attack the Teamsters, the only large union that had supported Republicans?

The meeting ended. Of course, both the economists and Fitzsimmons were right. Most Americans would gain from competition, and the cost of doing business in the United States would be lower; but the Teamsters and the established trucking companies were right too; they would lose. It is impossible to end a monopoly without causing some pain to the monopolists and their employees.

A month or so after the session with the Teamsters, Ford was discussing the trucking issue with his transportation secretary, William Coleman. According to MacAvoy, he asked Coleman, "How are we doing on trucking?" Coleman responded that the industry and the Teamsters continued to complain that more competition "would destroy the industry and the union, and end civilization as we know it." Ford laughed. "By God that's good," he said. "You have so many weak deregulation bills out there. Now you have a bill with some cut in it."[37] MacAvoy recalls that Ford made a joke out of the dire predictions from the Teamsters, the airlines, and others about the consequences of competition. The president said that if he succeeded in reducing regulation he probably would have to drive to his hometown of Grand Rapids, Michigan, to rescue his old aunt because he had been told that all the services to the city would collapse, and there would be no other way to get her out.[38] A trucking lobbyist had said that if competition came the trucking companies would no longer be able to charge high enough prices in richer markets to allow them to subsidize service to Grand Rapids. It would not be profitable, the lobbyist said, to serve smaller cities, so there would be no milk, fuel oil, or propane deliveries trucked in.

The airline lobbyists had told Ford the same thing, so there would be no air service to Grand Rapids. The railroad lobbyists told him that rail service would end. Some predicted that even bus service would stop. AT&T lobbyists warned that telephone service would leap in price and might be disrupted.

Ford and his procompetition advisers did not buy this line of thinking. They knew that private companies not protected by price guarantees or sheltered from competition served small cities all over the world. They believed that transportation and other regulated services would turn out to be no different.

As the politics of deregulation heated up in 1975, Roderick Hills and the White House staff checked back with Ford on several occasions to see if he was having second thoughts about trucking. But the president held firm. If everyone was against it, Ford told his staff, "It must be the right thing to do."[39] But he was not able to make much progress with Congress before he left office.

Jimmy Carter's staff knew about Ford's difficulties. They also cautioned Carter about the risks of taking on the truckers. But, as with the airlines, Carter took up the challenge where his predecessor left off, and told the staff to let him worry about the politics. Like Ford, he first pushed for reform in trucking regulation within the limits of ICC regulation while considering his legislative options.[40] He made A. Daniel O'Neal chairman of the ICC, even though Nixon had first appointed O'Neal to the commission. O'Neal pushed for changes, but he never was the media favorite that Kahn became.

O'Neal, however, was more aggressive than many realized. He eased entry requirements for new trucking competitors and relaxed the requirement that new entrants show a need for their services before they could offer them. To lower costs, he also adjusted rules to reduce empty backhauls—that is, the number of trucks returning empty after making a delivery rather than carrying a second load on the way back.[41]

Once airline deregulation was signed into law in October 1978, Carter had to decide if he should take the next big step and seek legislation to deregulate trucking. He decided after a significant debate in the White House to submit a full-blown legislative proposal. Stu Eizenstat, his White House domestic policy chief, drew the short straw and, like MacAvoy and Snow a few years before, was sent to tell the Teamsters of the president's intentions.

At the Teamsters' offices, Eizenstat was treated to a slightly different version of the performance experienced by the earlier envoys from President Ford. He recalls being ushered into a room outfitted with one of the largest conference tables he had ever seen.[42] On the table were heavy marble and metal plaques representing each of the Teamster union locals.

At the place where he was to sit, he saw his name hand-lettered on a paper sign.

The room was full of the same oversized vice presidents who had surrounded the two Republican White House staffers a few years before. Eizenstat, of course, was aware that foul play had been suspected in the 1974 disappearance of Jimmy Hoffa, three years after the former union head's release from jail. It crossed his mind, he said, that he might end up as part of a pier in a Jimmy Hoffa memorial bridge somewhere. Nonetheless, he told the Teamsters that President Carter intended to go ahead with trucking deregulation.

The Teamsters, like other powerful interests, overplayed what might otherwise have been a strong hand. In an effort to block legislation to restore competition, they apparently tried too hard to influence Senator Howard Cannon of Nevada, who was chairman of the Committee on Commerce, Science, and Transportation that was considering the legislation.

Cannon decided not to support the Teamsters and let the process take its course. The deregulation train gathered speed, and congressmen and senators jumped on board as they had with airlines. The Motor Carrier Act of 1980 ended federal regulation of interstate trucking and bus services. Rates, routes, and other terms of service were now set by competition. The ICC, like the CAB, eventually disappeared. It took a long time, but the powerful interests that are supposed to get what they want from politicians lost again.

Trucking regulation at the state level, however, continued long after federal regulation had largely disappeared, and this is very important. Forty states, including large ones such as California, Texas, Ohio, and Michigan, continued to regulate trucking rates and service conditions within their borders well into the 1990s. Nevertheless, the end of federal regulation created a big, new loophole that could be used to evade state regulation: Trucks from other states could bring in products and charge low rates as long as the goods were not unloaded at some intermediate point within the state.

Warehouse centers sprang up in Shreveport, Louisiana, and Ardmore, Oklahoma, to distribute goods in Texas, where there continued to be onerous state regulation. A similar warehouse and distribution center grew up in Sparks, Nevada, to serve the vast California market, which also remained regulated. Why? Because it had become less costly to distribute goods in Texas or California from warehouse complexes across the state line in Oklahoma, Louisiana, and Nevada than to do so from depots in Dallas or Los Angeles that would be subject to the complexities and costs of state regulation.

There was no consistency. It was the airline situation turned upside down. Unregulated airline competition in Texas and California had been models for what deregulation could do at the national level. In trucking, the two states were avid regulators. In the end, however, the demise of entry limits and price-fixing at the national level forced states to end similar restrictions.

Congress is usually reluctant to interfere with state regulation, but it happened in the case of trucking. Gradually, pressure built up to end state limits on trucking competition, and a second piece of federal legislation, which President Clinton signed in January 1995, finished the job.[43]

The Dam Has Burst. With the passage of the Motor Carrier Act, the principal form of transportation where competition remained legally circumscribed was rail. Experts were surprised that trucking competition had come before railroad freight deregulation, because the truckers and Teamsters were so imposing. Then, when the Motor Carrier Act became law, most assumed that nothing would happen with railroads. But in October 1980, one month before the presidential election, Congress again surprised observers and passed the Staggers Rail Act, which opened that industry to competition, too.

The legislative process works in mysterious ways, but trucks had been taking business from the railroads for years, so legislators probably realized that the passage of the Motor Carrier Act would kill the railroads if they did not have the flexibility to compete. The deregulatory dam burst. Trucking had been the toughest nut, second only perhaps to natural gas (which is not discussed here, but which Carter also began to deregulate, albeit with a seven-year phase-in period, in 1978).

By the 1990s, the costs of once-regulated services were much lower than they had been before political support for competition had opened up the regulated industries. The breakup of AT&T drove down long-distance rates, led to new services, and lowered the cost of doing business in the United States. Low telephone rates gave Americans a major advantage when the Internet came along, and nationalized European and Asian telephone companies rushed to catch up, following the indispensable road map traced by the Americans. In the transportation sector, airfares were half what they might have been, so more Americans could afford to travel. Freight transportation costs were lower, which meant that businesses could ship their products within the United States for much less, and with much better service, than they could before. The same pattern prevailed in other industries where economic regulation had suppressed competition, so that by the 1990s they became hotbeds of investment, innovation, technological change, and growth.

The Bottom Line: The Economic Impacts of Deregulation

How big an impact did deregulation have on prices and the costs of doing business in the United States? It is hard, perhaps impossible, to estimate the impact of the changes on all the affected industries, but clearly it has been considerable.

Consider, for example, the reductions in the costs of doing business over the past two decades at Guardsmark, a privately held security firm whose president, Ira Lipman, is a family friend of the author's. Lipman is an innovator and hands-on manager in the fiercely competitive business that provides guards to businesses and communities around the country. In 2000, long before 9/11 gave the security business another huge push, Guardsmark's revenues were about $350 million, or about 8.5 times what they were in 1980. The company had grown at an average compound rate of 12 percent a year, adding thousands of employees and more than a hundred new offices across the country. By the end of 2000, it provided security services at several thousand locations and had become the fourth- or fifth-largest such firm in the country.

Guardsmark's story tells a great deal about the impact of more intense competition on the American economy: Despite being more than eight times as large in 2000 as it was in 1980, Guardsmark was paying half what it had spent for telephone service when AT&T still was a powerhouse. Adjusted for the increase in revenue, that is one-sixteenth of what the company was paying before. Moreover, this understates the company's savings because it does not reflect the fact that Guardsmark now uses telecommunications far more than it used to, with the advent of faxes, e-mail, and electronic data transfer. This more intense use of communications has made employees more productive. Taking everything into account, phone-related services after the advent of competition cost the company only 3 to 5 percent of what they did when Ma Bell had a near-monopoly.

And telephone costs are only one part of the story. Guardsmark's managers travel frequently, often on short notice, as do agents and representatives of many other businesses. The company estimates that at the end of the 1990s, airfares in the now-competitive travel market were only about half what they were in the 1980s.

And it does not stop there. Guardsmark's cost of working capital is 25 percent lower than it used to be, because the company can borrow at a rate based on a competitive market index instead of at prime, a rate set by the banks and the Federal Reserve. More competition in almost every area benefited Guardsmark and thousands of other American companies by lowering their costs of doing business and helping them to grow.[44]

The changes in the regulated industries mirrored changes in the manufacturing sector, with some important differences. The most important was that imports—the result of open-trade policies—were not a significant factor in the regulated sector. It was, rather, political decisions by a succession of presidents, first to promote competition within the context of continuing regulation and then to attack economic regulation more directly through legislation, that forced these industries to change. And antitrust also played a role.

It is important to note that in neither manufacturing nor the regulated industries did tax or monetary policies have much to do with the changes that took place in the way business had to be done. The key was a political system that supported people who were willing to face down the airline executives, withstand the efforts of the Teamsters to maintain the status quo, and stand up to AT&T and its supporters. Those who ran the political interference for the new entrants and took the political risks were political leaders—presidents, members of Congress, and the leadership and staff of regulatory agencies—who took the side of the new competitors. As in manufacturing, even the most powerful regulated monopolies lacked the muscle to shut out competitors once the political pendulum began to swing away from the mindset of the 1930s and the immediate postwar years.

Counterattacks

The battle to maintain and expand competition and flexibility in the economy is not over. Jack the Giant-Killer won his battle against Ma Bell, and Gerald Ford and Jimmy Carter faced down the airlines and the Teamsters, but it is an ongoing fight. The interests that are always hurt by competition will continue to try to persuade political leaders and the public to protect them. The troubles of the airlines and California's electricity crisis in 2000 are two cases in point.

The Airline Crisis. Improving economic conditions at the end of the 1980s and all through the 1990s made it possible for some of the established airlines to delay and soften the painful adjustments needed to meet new competition, such as cutting layers of management, reducing payrolls and pension obligations, and increasing flexibility in the use of both airplanes and staff. The older companies, although burdened with higher costs, still had important advantages over newcomers. They had near-monopolies of landing slots at major airports like New York's LaGuardia, Atlanta, Chicago's O'Hare, Dallas-Fort Worth, and Washington, D.C.'s Reagan National. As a result, fares at those locations remained above competitive levels. They also had long-term relationships with business travelers who remained willing to pay high prices for the convenience of using specific airports.

Newer carriers such as Southwest, JetBlue, Vanguard, Frontier, and AirTran were able to fight their way into some airports. Others, like People Express and New York Air, came and went. Where newcomers succeeded, fares were lower than at airports where only a few older carriers predominated. For the most part, however, the newer carriers broke in at expanding airports like BWI and Dulles near Washington, Providence (near Boston), and Long Beach, Ontario, and other airports in the Los

Angeles basin that were more eager for new business than, for instance, LAX. But it took years—even decades—for this process to work.

Several older airlines such as TWA, PanAm, Eastern, and Braniff disappeared quickly for various reasons. The strongest of the older ones, however, made sufficient adjustments and had enough shelter from competition to stay in business as long as traffic was growing. In the year 2000, the airline industry was carrying three times as many passengers as in 1978, at prices that averaged 35–40 percent less when adjusted for inflation.[45] But older airlines, like the old automakers, still had higher costs than the new competitors. They had cut costs, but not enough to match those of the newer competitors.

A slow economy after 9/11 made matters worse. In April 2003, the *Washington Post* reported that 115,000 airline workers had lost their jobs in the previous two years.[46]

The vulnerability of the older airlines is still apparent in 2004. USAir, which was already struggling before 9/11, had to file for bankruptcy in August 2002, and may have to do so again. United followed USAir into bankruptcy in 2003 and is struggling in mid-2004 to deal with its large pension obligations. American is also in precarious shape. Indeed, among the major airlines, only Southwest, which had never developed the high costs and bad habits that are a product of weak competition, was consistently profitable.

The problem is similar to the one in manufacturing industries like steel. Costs that could be carried under business plans that were developed when competition was weak cannot be carried in a competitive world where newcomers do not share such costs. The question is, who will pay for the adjustments that must be made to level the playing field? Will it be stock- and bondholders, current workers, and retirees, or will it be taxpayers and the flying public through subsidies or handicaps imposed on the new competitors? Economists call these "transition" costs, but that description is bloodless and misleading. These changes involve real economic pain and tough political choices.

More change is clearly coming. Low-cost airlines built a client base by covering underserved routes and appealing to leisure travelers. Now they are attracting business travelers, who pay the highest fares, increasing pressure on the older carriers to complete the modernization that started with deregulation in 1978. The political battle about who will pay and how much to cushion the changeover from weak to strong competition will continue in the airlines, and will be fought in many other industries as well.

The California Energy Crisis. The California energy crisis during the winter of 2000–2001 is another example of the painful transition from limited competition to freer markets.

In the immediate postwar period, electric utilities were essentially local monopolies. Each had its own generating facilities and distribution lines, and the connections between the systems existed largely to permit the sale or exchange of power during peaks in demand or when a utility had some of its plants down for repairs. There were regional "power pools" to coordinate exchanges of power, which kept costs down to some extent, but utilities ran their own generating facilities as much as they could. Prices differed significantly from one state or region to another because there was no national market for electricity. And, indeed, prices differed enormously within states because there was no real competition.

Federal legislation during the Carter administration in 1978 began to increase competition in electric generation by allowing a small number of special facilities to sell power on the open market. Legislation in 1992 encouraged electric utilities and others to develop independent generating units so they could sell electricity in a developing wholesale market.

The beginnings of competition at the federal level did not automatically mean there would be competition within any given state. The prices that state utilities could pay or charge for electricity continued to be set by state regulators. States, however, especially in the East, began to expand competition within their borders. California decided to follow. In 1997, it passed legislation to move away from price-fixing and eventually "deregulate" the state electricity market, but only after certain conditions were met.

The most difficult problem faced by California and other states was how to treat electric utilities that had what were called "sunk" or "stranded" costs. These were for the most part the costs of investments in nuclear plants, which had been so expensive that they could not be sold without wiping out utilities' investors. If the state regulators insisted on moving quickly toward competition and did not allow the utilities to charge high prices until they could recover the cost of these unsaleable investments, the utilities would be bankrupt.

Before going to "deregulation" and a competitive market, therefore, California's utilities wanted to recover these stranded costs by charging higher rates to consumers, and the state let them do so. The state's legislation provided that residential electricity rates should stay regulated—and high—until the utilities recovered the money they had invested in the nuclear plants. This provision was meant to let the utilities avoid the painful declines in values that had taken place in autos, steel, trucking, airlines, and other industries whose sunk costs—bad investments and large pension liabilities—for the most part had to be absorbed by stock- and bondholders. As one news story succinctly explained, "Under the legislation, the price of electricity was temporarily fixed at 6.5 cents per kilowatt hour which was substantially higher than the market price until 2000. The utilities were allowed to use the difference to recover 'stranded' costs which were costs for the nuclear plants, which could not be sold to the new independent generators."[47]

To be fair, electric companies across the country had built the nuclear plants with the approval of state regulators, so they assumed, with some justification, that state agencies would guarantee them a good return. Voters, however, might well have opted to let the stock- and bondholders pay the price for this folly, rather than pay high electricity prices to shield them, if they had been given the choice.

California's deregulation scheme contained other questionable elements. The utilities' efficient generating plants, most of them powered by natural gas, were sold quickly to private buyers. The utilities planned to buy electricity from these and other plants operated by outside power producers and brokers, such as Enron and Duke Power, at what they expected would be low market prices. They would charge customers high prices nevertheless until the nuclear plants were paid off. Then they would make money by charging other generating companies to use their power grid and distribution systems for electricity, which for a long time would continue to be the only way to reach customers.

This was supposed to be a painless, bloodless adjustment to competition that protected investors and the companies, not a rough and tumble changeover that would unavoidably bring pain to the beneficiaries of the earlier noncompetitive system. It was a cozy arrangement that delayed real competition until all the bad investments of the regulated period had been paid off.

But the plan hinged on the assumption that natural gas prices and electricity from the Pacific Northwest would remain cheap, because most of the electricity the utilities planned to buy came from these sources. This seemed like a safe bet, because since 1985 prices for electricity and natural gas to generate power had been cheap and stable. Indeed, natural gas was cheaper in 1997 when the deregulation legislation passed than it had been in 1985, and even cheaper in 1998 and 1999.

The idea was that the California utilities would be able to buy cheap power generated from gas, sell it at a profit, and eventually pay off the high-cost nuclear plants. This scheme, however, rested on a gamble—the weather—and California lost. In 2000, a hot, dry summer was followed by a cold winter, which pushed up natural gas prices for the first time in fifteen years. Other states had protected themselves against the dangers of price increases for gas and hydropower by generating more power from coal and oil, or by signing long-term contracts to buy electricity or gas at fixed prices. California regulators, however, had not wanted to allow these kinds of precautions, because they could have raised prices. Instead, the regulators essentially required the utilities to depend on sources of electricity whose prices were set on the "spot" market, day to day. Such supplies had been cheap for many years, but in 2000 prices on the day-to-day market rose to astronomical heights.

Some of this spike may have been due to Enron, other energy brokers, and the pipelines having rigged the markets and made the situation worse, but the underlying cause was the failure to insure against a worst-case scenario and allow the utilities to line up long-term supplies of either electricity or natural gas. Like a foolish private investor, the utilities had not diversified, in large part because the state regulators would not let them spend what it would have taken to do so.

For some observers, like S. David Freeman, head of the city-owned Los Angeles Department of Water and Power, the California energy crisis was a morality play. Freeman had been a strong, outspoken proponent of electricity regulation since at least the 1970s, when he worked in the

Department of the Interior. He had also worked for the Senate Commerce Committee and the Department of Energy and headed the Tennessee Valley Authority before going to California. California, in his view, should not have trusted the "so-called free market," as he put it.[48]

In Freeman's version of events, Californians were betrayed by the market, gouged by Enron and other greedy business interests, and abandoned by the federal government. The solution was to rely again on utility monopolies like those set up in the 1930s. It was better, in Freeman's view, to have the government fix prices with guaranteed returns to investors, or to have public ownership of the plants themselves, in order to make sure that employees in the industry were well taken care of, and that somehow natural gas and electricity shortages would not occur.

In fact, the California electricity story shows something different: It demonstrates what happens when political leaders are not willing to stand up to the interests that have benefited from monopoly. Freeman addressed his remarks to a union audience, and one of the things he held out to them was that in a world of fixed prices and guarantees for investors, utilities would again be able to pay premium wages and hold onto workers they did not need. Management could be fat, investments could be gold-plated, and innovation could lag, but consumers would pay.

Competition Becomes Contagious

Like competition in the manufacturing sector, deregulation was contagious. The introduction of price competition to the airfreight sector helped to ease the deregulation of the passenger segment. Trucking deregulation made it inevitable that railroads would have to compete to maintain a share of shipping. Competition in trucking at the federal level eventually led to competition within states. The opening of long-distance telephone service to competition in the 1970s led to increased competition in many telephone-related services, and the process is still underway at the state level. Even changes in federal regulation of electric power led to important changes at the state level, although the California debacle set the process back. Competition has spread from one industry to another, and from one level of government to another, because America's federal system makes it difficult for powerful local groups to isolate themselves from pressures around them and to hold onto the political support needed to do so.

Divided power and responsibilities within and among federal agencies, Congress, and the states have given newcomers a chance. Politicians from both parties, at various levels of government, have stood up to the companies and the unions in the name of consumers and the broader public interest. Competition has become more intense, although inconsistencies continue to abound. States that were hotbeds of competition in one industry have been deeply committed to continued limits on it in others. Individual legislators who favored competition in one area have opposed it in another.

The spread of competition has never been clean, complete, or even final, as we will also see in the case of the financial sector, discussed in the following chapter. Adam Smith wrote that "changes . . . should never be introduced suddenly, but slowly, gradually, and after very long warning."[49] The father of modern economics would have been pleased at the way the deregulatory process worked in America in the last three decades of the twentieth century. A lot was accomplished, but the struggle goes on within a political framework that Smith would have understood and applauded.

5

Opening Up American Finance

Elite institutions no longer dominate the commanding heights of finance as they did earlier, and still do in countries like Germany and Japan.

—Mortimer Zuckerman[1]

A Financier Who Said Yes

In 1984, Frank Cruz, who had been an award-winning reporter at ABC and NBC affiliates in Los Angeles, went to see financier Michael Milken. Cruz wanted to talk to him about raising capital to launch a second Spanish-language TV station in the city. Cruz was happily surprised by his reception. His group of would-be borrowers thought it would be a hard sell, so they brought reams of background statistics about the size of the potential Hispanic audience and the market potential of their project. But even before Cruz could make his pitch, Milken began talking about the demographics of Spanish speakers in the Los Angeles area, which he seemed to know almost as well as they did. Milken was on board from the beginning. He was a financier ready to say yes to new ideas.

Milken moved quickly, according to Cruz, and helped the group to open KVEA-TV, Channel 52, which was an immediate success. Like other financiers, Milken knew a lot of people he could reach out to for the things it took to make an investment successful. He put Cruz in touch with a wide circle of financial groups that helped the emerging Telemundo Network acquire additional stations and cable affiliates, making it the country's second-largest Spanish-language TV network. He also introduced

Cruz to advertising executives on New York's Madison Avenue. Once Milken opened these doors, it was easy, because Cruz, like other leaders of emerging companies, knew how to sell.[2]

It had not always been this way, which is why Cruz was surprised. The postwar financial world had been dominated by large New York banks like Chase Manhattan, with its connections to the Rockefellers; Manufacturers Hanover, which later merged with Chase; City Bank of New York (later Citibank); and the New York Stock Exchange (NYSE) and the old securities houses that controlled it; and large insurance companies like The Hartford and Travellers, also located in the Northeast.

These pedigreed financial institutions largely determined which businesses and consumers could borrow and how much savers could earn in the new industrial state of the 1960s. The old financial behemoths had close ties to the oligopolies that bestrode manufacturing and to the monopolistic regulated industries, like telecommunications and electricity. Firms such as GE, GM, U.S. Steel, the major oil companies, and the large utilities, with their old connections, secure revenue streams, and sufficient collateral to guarantee their loans, found little difficulty raising money.

For newcomers and outsiders like Cruz, obtaining financing was harder. Even when America was "the new industrial state" it was easier to finance new companies and new ideas here than it was in Europe, but Cruz and his fellow entrepreneurs would have had a much harder time before people like Milken and sources of finance like his high-risk bonds came on the scene.

The sector began to open up in the 1970s and '80s, and by the 1990s it had been significantly reformed. Mort Zuckerman wrote in 1998 that "elite institutions no longer dominate the commanding heights of finance as they did earlier [in the United States], and still do in countries like Germany and Japan." There had been a vast "diversification of investment outlets." Zuckerman—editor in chief of *U.S. News & World Report,* commentator, and major real estate developer—has been in the middle of the financial world as a borrower since the late 1960s, securing tens of billions of dollars to finance the development of commercial properties. Zuckerman notes that older financial institutions have been forced to compete to manage funds and make loans, sharply lowering the cost of obtaining financing. The United States has capital markets that fuel, in Zuckerman's words, "the future not the past."[3]

The Changing Structure of American Finance

The growth of new financial institutions between the 1970s and the '90s—and the corresponding decline of the older banks—was remarkable. In 1970, traditional commercial banks and insurance companies controlled roughly 57 percent of the country's savings—the money that borrowers can tap to finance investments. Private pensions and government retirement funds controlled by so-called "nonbank" institutions had grown rapidly since the 1950s but still accounted for only 13 percent of funds available for investment. By 2000, the share of lendable funds controlled by banks and insurance companies had fallen to 32 percent, and various pension and mutual funds had grown to 37 percent of the total.[4] Nontraditional sources of funds had grown enormously, creating new opportunities for borrowers.

The savings pool in these alternative institutions grew in part because it became less costly to put private savings in the stock market. Brokerage rates dropped from thirty cents to fifteen cents per share overall from 1980 to 1995, and from about fourteen cents to about three to four cents for institutional trades.[5] More options appeared for ordinary Americans seeking mortgages or investments for retirement, as well as for businesses seeking finance capital.

Finance followed the pattern we have seen in other areas. The new variety of financial vehicles and their lower cost to users are measures of the democratization of the financial sector in the United States. This chapter describes the transformation of the U.S. financial system of the post–World War II era into the more open, flexible, decentralized and competitive one of the 1990s. It relates the story of Michael Milken and the high-yield bond instruments ("junk bonds") he created, which financed many of the rising stars of the new economy. It discusses the rise of the NASDAQ that brought competition to the old New York Stock Exchange, inspired by demands for reform from Congress and regulators. It traces how the center of gravity of American banking, like other economic activity, shifted away from the venerable institutions of the Northeast and spread into the South and West. In each of these stories there is an unexpected underlying political story, because none of the changes would have taken place without political support. Finally, the chapter compares American financial trends with those in Europe and Japan, and evaluates developments in the United States from the perspective of the economic situation of the past few years.

The financial world of the immediate postwar period—like the auto industry, trucking, communications, and other sectors—was profoundly affected by the Great Depression. It would have been much less the preserve of blue-chip borrowers after the war had it not been for the belief that one of the principal causes of the Depression was risky loans made during the 1920s.

In the 1920s, people in the financial world had tried out new approaches. Commercial banks (those that take deposits from businesses and consumers) were competing vigorously and developing new financial services to attract business. They lent money to industrial companies, bought and sold securities, and were developing financial products similar to today's mutual funds.

The Great Depression not only put a stop to these developments, but it also rolled them back. The banks owned securities, which fell in value. They faced additional large losses when many borrowers, who also had lost money in the stock market, defaulted on loans. Hard-pressed depositors pulled money out of the banks, and in order to pay them, the banks had to "call" (cancel) loans, even to solvent borrowers. Beset on all sides, thousands of banks saw their reserves of lendable funds disappear.

The last straw was the Federal Reserve's abdication of its responsibilities. It had been created (and named) precisely because it was supposed to provide "reserves"—cash—to banks so they could keep lending in times of fiscal uncertainty. Divided and ineptly led at just the wrong time, it did not do so.[6] Thousands of banks failed, smaller and newer businesses that depended on credit were wiped out, and depositors lost their money as well. The businesses that survived were principally the ones that did not depend on credit, which usually meant the oldest and best established.

The Depression demanded scapegoats, and the banks were among those singled out. Politicians and the public believed that banks had made risky loans and betrayed depositors. Few understood how the Federal Reserve was supposed to work, but everyone thought they understood the greed of bankers. The political pressure was on to reduce risks, and the idea was to prevent banks from getting involved in risky businesses in the future so they would be sure always to be in a position to pay depositors.

The mood was similar to the one that prevailed after the stock market bubble collapsed in 2001, but far more serious. There had been plenty of shady dealing and manipulation by insiders, as there often is in a boom. Some banks certainly had made foolish loans in the 1920s. But these transgressions would not have led to a collapse of credit and the whole economy if the Fed had acted wisely.

Nevertheless, banking legislation was put in place. The Banking Act of 1933, called the Glass-Steagall Act, made it illegal for the commercial banks to deal in securities or own manufacturing firms. These steps were meant to reduce risks to depositors and prevent conflicts of interest. The Banking Act also provided for federal insurance for depositors, which would prevent the kind of runs on banks that—in the absence of Fed action to supply reserves—brought many healthy ones down in the 1930s.

Glass-Steagall, however, had its downside. It allowed investment banks, which did not take deposits from ordinary citizens, to continue lending money to companies, but it made it much harder for new businesses to get financing from commercial banks, which held a large share of the country's lendable funds. The largely New York–based investment banks were, in turn, relatively averse to risk and lent principally to established businesses with adequate collateral. The insurance companies tended to follow their lead, financing the same kind of companies and investing in the bonds and stocks of fewer than a thousand blue-chip firms.

A similar desire to reduce the risk held sway in the stock market and also made it harder for new firms. The New York Stock Exchange had purged itself of what were thought to be its riskier stocks after the financial crisis of 1907, but another purge followed 1929. The NYSE wanted to avoid the kind of regulation that had been imposed on the banks, so it reduced the number of "listed" stocks that could be traded, again cutting off newcomers and companies seen as risky. The result was that the NYSE became even more exclusively a market for blue-chip stocks.

The NYSE and the banks adjusted to the rules that limited their activities and encouraged them to place limits on their lending to riskier firms. The Big Board, as the NYSE was called, charged high rates for stock trades, so the securities firms that were members did well under most circumstances.

The exchange had been organized as a cartel in 1792, when twenty-four stock traders gathered under a buttonwood tree (the common name, at that time, for a sycamore) at 68 Wall Street. The traders did what Adam Smith said business people always do when they get together: They agreed to fix prices. In this case, they agreed not to charge less than one-quarter percent commission on stock trades, and to favor one another in trading stock.

The Buttonwood Tree Agreement served its members well. They made good incomes brokering stocks and had little incentive to develop the kinds of alternative products—mutual and money-market funds, for example—that they developed in the 1970s, when commission rates tumbled.

There were markets other than the NYSE in which companies could sell stock and raise money, but they were subject to more frequent abuse and gave the sellers less access to substantial sums. Stocks pushed off the Big Board were traded in the over-the-counter market, which was large, if ill-defined and mysterious. And there were exchanges in cities like Boston, Chicago, and Philadelphia, and on the Pacific Coast. These smaller exchanges were more willing than the NYSE to handle local stocks, but they gave smaller companies only modest access to the nation's pool of savings, in part because they never could bring enough investors into the market to be real competitors to the NYSE.

The Junk-Bond Market

The financial markets that had been shaped by the Depression began to open up slowly after the war, but the pace picked up in the 1970s. Entrepreneurs like Frank Cruz and smaller companies were forced to rely heavily on banks for fixed-rate financing. Banks, however, were reluctant to lend to such firms, and when they did, the loans were usually short-term.

Worse, when money tightened, as it sometimes did, banks might cancel loans to smaller borrowers, leaving them to scurry to find new lenders, if they could. Even when companies were willing to pay higher interest rates to get long-term, fixed-rate financing, there was no place for them to turn. The junk-bond market, which made stable, long-term capital available to thousands of growing American companies in the 1980s and 1990s, was one innovation that addressed this problem.

Junk bonds were the brainchild of one man: Michael Milken, who created a whole new market for the bonds of entrepreneurial companies and made it possible for thousands of them to grow and change the American economic landscape. It may be difficult to picture Milken, who went to jail in the early 1990s and paid almost a billion dollars in fines for securities law violations, as an American hero. Milken, however, was a financial genius. Many in the Wall Street establishment that he challenged wanted him convicted and cheered when it happened. But even his critics recognize that Milken had changed the financial world. In 1989, a dozen years after he began financing new companies with junk bonds and a year before his fall, the *Wall Street Journal* called him "arguably the most important financial thinker of the century" and one of the century's ten most important business leaders.[7]

Michael Milken was a student of finance and of risk, which is a large part of what finance is about. He had graduated *summa cum laude* from the University of California at Berkeley in 1970 and gone on to get an MA at the Wharton School at the University of Pennsylvania in the early 1970s. There he picked up on the argument that the debt of many promising medium-sized companies was not significantly riskier than that of established blue-chips. Academics were debating this idea at the time, but Milken was thinking about its real-world implications.

Smaller companies had trouble selling long-term debt at fixed interest rates to the big eastern banks and insurance companies because, in the jargon of the trade, their debt was not "investment-grade." Many were willing to pay higher interest rates to get long-term loans, but there was no such market for higher-risk obligations. Milken believed that if lenders could get 8 percent from blue-chip companies, they could get 11, 13, or even 15 percent from newer, medium-sized companies, and the risk would not be much greater. It would be a good deal for both sides because, his research showed, these higher interest rates would more than make up for any increased risk to lenders.

Milken finished at the top of his class at the Wharton School and went to work with Drexel Firestone, a small but venerable Philadelphia investment bank that underwrote stocks and bonds. The firm was acquired in 1973 by an astute financier named I. W. "Tubby" Burnham, who had been running a small family brokerage business. Burnham saw the acquisition of Drexel Firestone as his way to become a major financial player, and he was right. His most important decision, however, was to persuade Milken to stay with the growing firm and not go back to Wharton to teach.

At Drexel Firestone, Milken began dealing with what were called "fallen angels"—the bonds of companies that had once been investment-grade but had become riskier and gone down in value. Milken's studies told him that it was only a short step to creating a similar market for the bonds of smaller and newer companies, and Tubby Burnham backed him.[8] Drexel began marketing new issues of high-yield securities for these kinds of companies, and the market for them quickly took off. Milken made breathtaking amounts of money—$550 million in one year—and so did Drexel Burnham.

Milken's reputation grew rapidly, and in 1976 he moved his office back to his native Los Angeles, sure that a steady stream of entrepreneurs would still beat a path to his door. Milken looked for good ideas and financed them. His successes—including Telemundo, CNN, Mirage Resorts, and MCI—were legion.

Ted Turner and CNN are a good example of a Milken success. Turner envisioned a potential market for a TV channel that would show news twenty-four hours a day, around the world, as it was happening. NBC, CBS, ABC, and other established networks showed news in specific time slots—in effect, saying that people could wait for the news until 5:30 or 11:00. Turner made his case to Milken and secured the financing that he could not get from the usual sources, and CNN began broadcasting in 1980. By the 1990s it had spawned rounds of copycat news channels and revolutionized the news business.

MCI was another new business Milken helped finance. Bill McGowan, who had become the driving force at MCI even before Jack Goeken left the company, liked doing business with Milken.[9] McGowan was eager to sell MCI's debt to a market that included many buyers, rather than depend on personal relationships at a few banks and insurance companies. Bank financing, he believed, restrained MCI's ability to grow. At one crucial point, Milken raised a billion dollars for MCI in only a day.[10] He eventually raised $3 billion to help MCI build a fiber optic network that AT&T had not wanted to build.

By the late 1980s, over a thousand companies in all the major areas of the U.S. economy were using high-yield bonds to finance expansion and modernization, and a new financial form had been created.

Critics say that investments in high-yield bonds contributed to the collapse of the savings and loan institutions in the late 1980s, and that corporate takeover artists used the bonds to break up successful companies and feast on the leavings. Economics policy scholar Glenn Yago, director of capital studies at the Milken Institute in Santa Monica, disputes these assertions.[11] Only a few S&Ls were large buyers of higher-yielding securities, so these bonds could not have been the primary cause of the collapse of so many of these institutions in the late 1980s. A dozen or so S&Ls in California and other states had made heavy purchases and were hurt when junk-bond prices fell at this time. Fundamentally, however, it was their own decisions to make highly speculative commercial real estate loans, not junk bonds, which caused the S&L crisis.

Yago argues convincingly that the role of high-yield bonds in corporate takeovers was also exaggerated. The early deals did not involve takeovers at all. Most of the money from junk bonds in the late 1970s and early '80s was used to finance expansion, purchase divested divisions of older companies, and pay for leveraged buyouts by management teams that thought they could add value to their acquisitions. Hostile takeovers were not an issue.

By the mid-1980s Drexel Burnham had created a new junk-bond industry, but there was no patent on the idea. Other financial houses also began creating high-yield bonds. It was during this period that someone—it is not clear that it was Milken or Drexel—hit on the idea of using them to finance hostile takeovers. Yago says that the use of junk bonds for takeovers was never more than 15 percent of the total bonds issued, and usually less. The established companies that were the targets of corporate raids, however, reacted angrily and blamed Milken. The older financial houses on Wall Street hated Milken and Drexel Burnham for other reasons. They were the sharp, uncouth newcomers on the block, taking away their customers.

The use of junk-bond financing in hostile takeover attempts aimed at several oil companies in the 1980s generated a great deal of controversy. Some of the oil companies had added a lot of staff during the 1970s and early '80s when oil and natural gas prices were high. Good times led to overconfidence, and when oil and natural gas prices began to erode in the mid-1980s, some companies did not adjust quickly. The stocks of several that had large oil and gas reserves and other assets, such as Unocal, Gulf Oil, and Getty Oil, fell well below what analysts considered to be the long-term value of these assets, making them attractive targets for takeovers.

T. Boone Pickens of Mesa Petroleum, a Texas independent oilman and entrepreneur, made an immense fortune by lining up financing to take over some of these companies. In the 1960s and '70s he developed Mesa as a large independent oil and gas producer that had sizable reserves of its own. By the 1980s, however, Pickens decided that acquiring other companies, some of them much larger than Mesa, could be more profitable than finding oil and gas. His favorite tactic was to buy up stock of bigger oil companies at prices that he thought were low, acquiring enough to threaten a takeover. The target companies then had a choice: yield to Pickens, sell to another company that would pay more, or buy back the stock Pickens had acquired at a higher price. It was called "greenmail," and Pickens, who was a Milken client in the 1980s, used junk-bond financing to challenge some of the most established energy companies, including Gulf Oil, Cities Service, Diamond Shamrock, and Phillips Petroleum.

Pickens had plenty of enemies already. In 1985, however, he especially outraged some in the oil industry when he tried to acquire Unocal using junk bonds. Unocal was a California company that was almost a hundred years old; its assets included oil and gas wells in the Gulf of Mexico and California. It also owned refineries and had extensive marketing operations.[12] Pickens failed to acquire Unocal, but he angered its managers and made a ton of money for himself and stockholders by bidding up its shares.

The reaction in Congress to the use of junk bonds to finance hostile takeovers was fierce. In 1985 alone, more than two dozen bills were introduced to restrict high-yield-bond financing of takeovers and to limit holdings in these bonds by pension funds, insurance companies, commercial banks, and savings institutions. Irate oil companies and the American Petroleum Institute were important players in these efforts.[13] In addition to these legislative proposals, pressure was brought to bear on the Securities and Exchange Commission, the Federal Reserve, and other regulatory agencies to restrict the use of high-risk bonds.

The Reagan administration opposed these restrictions because it was generally pro–small business and critical of the old business groups. It was not tied to the Wall Street establishment and defended junk bonds on the grounds that they were a wake-up call to lackluster corporate managers. In the end, some legislative and regulatory restrictions were put in place to limit takeovers, but they acted more like speed bumps than barriers. Borrowers wanted access to this new source of financing, and investors, including most insurance companies and pension funds that were making money by buying them, resisted the restrictions.

George H. W. Bush and his new administration in 1989 were more sympathetic to the concerns of the companies who did not want to have to deal with upstarts like Pickens. It is fair to say, however, that the S&L crisis had hit by the time Bush took office, and his administration had to respond to the perception that a decline in junk-bond prices had endangered some S&Ls. In any case, the Bush administration adopted regulatory changes to prevent S&Ls from including junk bonds in their portfolios, and the S&Ls had to dump their holdings at steep discounts.

The market for junk bonds went quiet as the economy went into a slump between 1989 and 1993. It expanded again during the 1990s but generated less attention because most of it was going to the stock market. Nevertheless, Michael Milken had changed the financial world by developing high-risk bonds to serve a large number of would-be borrowers that were being ignored by the financial establishment. Like the Japanese automakers and Ken Iverson, he created an alternative for customers that had been less than well-served. Medium-sized companies got access to long-term debt capital because Tubby Burnham and Michael Milken and the companies they financed helped to expand competition in other areas of the economy. The old financial interests and the blue-chip companies tried to use their political muscle to stop the newcomers, but for the most part they failed.

Competition Comes to the New York Stock Exchange

The Securities and Exchange Act of 1934—the New Deal legislation to protect stock investors—was more flexible and less intrusive than the laws aimed at curbing abuses in banking. The Securities and Exchange Commission (SEC), the New Deal's regulatory agency for the stock markets, sought to protect securities buyers by requiring that companies provide more public information than in the past. The SEC enforced transparency, but buyers had to assess the risks for themselves.

The availability of equity capital for new businesses and ideas was a problem, just as fixed-rate financing was. To avoid regulation, the NYSE had pushed many smaller companies off the exchange by setting strict rules for who could "list." Thousands of companies that issued stock and followed SEC rules were not listed on the NYSE. They had to sell stock in a less formal over-the-counter (OTC) market that was also less well-policed. These companies also found it more difficult to reach a large community of potential investors.

Nevertheless, American stock markets were always more open and inclusive than those overseas. Brokers operating in the OTC market bought and sold stocks in companies not listed on the NYSE or other exchanges. They did this based on "pink sheets," a service for professional stock traders that listed prices daily.[14] Selling stock in this way cost both buyers and sellers more than on a formal exchange, the market was smaller, and it was risky.[15]

The OTC in the 1950s was a lively place, however. It was then called "the electronic market," just as today's NASDAQ is called the "high-tech" exchange. It was a source of capital for parts makers selling to big electronics companies like GE, IBM, Sylvania, and RCA in the fast-growing TV industry, as well as smaller startup companies such as Harman-Kardon, established by Sidney Harman, a pioneer in high-fidelity home stereo equipment, who was still a successful entrepreneur in related areas in 2003.[16]

The expansion of opportunities for smaller firms to sell stock started with efforts to clean up problems in the OTC market. Congress in the 1960s was afraid that investors were being bilked because they were not sure of what they were buying, and the spreads between bid and asking prices (which was the margin for the brokers) tended to be wide; so it asked the SEC to look at the OTC and see what could be done to make it work better. The study began during the Kennedy administration in 1963 and was completed toward the end of the Johnson years.[17]

In 1971, the SEC imposed new regulatory requirements on the OTC—regulations that helped it grow, rather than placing restrictions on its activities. The SEC told the National Association of Securities Dealers (NASD), the industry group that managed the OTC, that it had to give buyers of stocks more information, and directed it to open up the trading process in order to protect both buyers and sellers. The SEC encouraged the NASD to move from closed, opaque trading based on telephonic communications to an open, transparent, and accessible electronic system offering computerized listings and real-time quotes—a real breakthrough. The OTC market quickly developed such an electronic trading system, expanded, and in 1971 became the NASDAQ.[18]

The over-the-counter market operated differently than the NYSE even after this transformation. There was no trading floor or auction-style bidding for stocks as there is on the Big Board. Unlike the tightly knit NYSE, the NASDAQ never limited the numbers of brokers who could trade stocks. Any dealer who passed a test for knowledge and probity could trade on the NASDAQ. Also, where the NYSE required companies listed on the exchange to meet certain performance criteria—to be of a certain size and to have significant revenues—the NASDAQ would list companies without profits or even sales, as long as they met the disclosure requirements. NASDAQ required firms to disclose a great deal of information as a condition for listing, but it let investors themselves decide if they wanted to invest in riskier firms. The NASDAQ became a place where newcomers like Microsoft, Intel, and Apple had a chance to raise money before they became large and profitable. Like Milken's junk-bond market, the NASDAQ became the stock market that served the newcomers and the country's most dynamic entrepreneurs.

The changes imposed on the old OTC traders by the SEC in 1971 began a process that, over the next three decades, made the NASDAQ into a true competitor to the NYSE. The SEC's reforms reassured investors and made them more willing to purchase the stocks of companies listed in the new system. Competition between the NASDAQ and the NYSE for new listings also encouraged other innovations. The NASDAQ's computerized processing of stock trades was more modern than the comparable back-room operations of the NYSE. NASDAQ could perform a trade more quickly, in a second or two. To keep up, the NYSE had to add computer capacity and modernize its backrooms. It is also moving away from its traditional open trading floor with live brokers toward computerized trading.

NASDAQ, for its part, also had to make adjustments to compete with the NYSE. Traders on an auction floor like the NYSE usually received a smaller profit margin than brokers on the OTC/NASDAQ. As the two markets began to compete for listings, brokers on the newer exchange had to narrow the spreads between the bid and asking prices to limit the Big Board's advantages, and the cost of trading became more comparable.

The existence of the NASDAQ drove other changes. It created a market for the securities of new companies that venture capitalists could turn to quickly once they got a company started. The NASDAQ enabled venture capitalists to sell stock in startup firms more quickly, so they could move on to other projects. It let them sell on a broad and well-run market, long before the startup firms were profitable enough to move onto the NYSE. To some extent, the NASDAQ helped formalize the venture-capital process. Venture capital became a great deal more than just a matter of rich people taking fliers on risky new enterprises.

The NASDAQ, however, is not just a minor-league stock market, a way-station for firms waiting to graduate to the older exchange. Although eighty or so of the more than four thousand firms listed on the NASDAQ may make the move to the Big Board in a given year, the NASDAQ retains many more companies than it loses, including giants such as Microsoft.[19]

The desire in Congress and the SEC to curb abuses in the OTC market was one factor that helped create competition for the NYSE and increase opportunities for investors and those who were seeking financing. The courts and the antitrust authorities also encouraged changes in the stock markets, as they did in manufacturing and the regulated industries. In the 1960s, buyers of stocks and, especially, pension funds began to complain about the NYSE's fixed commission rates, and unhappy business customers proved again to be a powerful force, as they had been in manufacturing and the regulated industries.

Pension funds were growing in the 1960s, and increasingly aggressive pension-fund managers wanted brokers to waive their high fixed commissions on high-volume stock trades, just as GM in 1982 wanted better terms from its steel suppliers. Reformers also disliked the fixed commission rates that had existed since the Buttonwood Agreement because they encouraged corruption. Money managers at the pension funds and agents, it was alleged, were funneling the most profitable high-volume orders to favorite brokers. In exchange, the pension managers and agents were wined and dined lavishly by the brokerage houses seeking the profitable business, and payoffs were said to be rampant. It was comparable to the situation in the 1990s, when stock analysts were corrupted because they got paid for steering business to the investment-banking arms of their firms. In the 1960s, pension managers also got under-the-table payments from the brokers for bringing in business.

The pension funds and others began to press for changes. In the late 1960s, the Justice Department filed an antitrust action on behalf of investors, challenging fixed commission rates. In August 1971, Congressman John Moss of California began hearings on this and related subjects in the Committee on Interstate and Foreign Commerce, and over the next four years support for an end to fixed rates developed in both parties and at the White House.

Not surprisingly, the established interests—in this case the old brokerage houses and the NYSE—fiercely defended fixed commission rates. They made all the same arguments against abandoning their monopoly rates that truckers, airlines, utilities, and oligopolistic manufacturers had made to Gerald Ford and Jimmy Carter when their fiefdoms were threatened.

Echoing the truckers, the brokers and the stock exchange claimed that if fixed rates were abandoned, smaller investors would pay more than big investors, and no one would serve the smallest investors at all.[20] Small brokers would be driven out of business, consumers would have fewer brokerage houses to choose from, and people would lose their jobs in New York's financial district. None of this proved to be the case.

Pressured by antitrust suits, money managers, and the expanding mutual funds, the SEC banned rate-fixing on larger stock transactions in 1971 and 1972.[21] In 1973, the agency banned price-fixing, effective in 1975. John Moss's legislation soon caught up. In May 1975, Congress, with the support of President Ford, ended fixed commission rates on stock trades. "Opposite and rival interests" within the business community clashed as they did in other areas. The challengers and critics got support from the SEC, the Antitrust Division of the Justice Department, the Johnson, Nixon, and Ford administrations, and Congress. Again, the established interests lost, and the winners were the newcomers and consumers who pressed for change.

Competitive brokerage rates created a cascade effect, encouraging other innovations in U.S. financial markets, in much the same way that competition from Japanese cars led to more competition in a half-dozen connected manufacturing areas. Just as the old brokerage houses had feared, the end of fixed commissions put brokerage earnings under pressure. Old established houses that had depended on high fixed rates to make money had to find other ways to remain profitable. Merrill Lynch hit on one: the idea of setting up money-market mutual funds that small savers could use as an alternative to checking accounts. Merrill and other brokerage firms began to buy and package government bonds to create such funds, earning enough to pay depositors a good rate of interest, pay for checking privileges, and make nice profits for the houses.

The advent and rapid growth of money-market accounts with checking privileges created competition for bank deposits that hit the commercial banks hard. Banks were no longer the only place where depositors could put their savings and get a checkbook. In the 1930s, a Federal Reserve rule (regulation Q) had been put in place to bar "cutthroat competition" between banks for deposits, with the twin aim of bolstering bank profitability and protecting depositors.[22] The rule prevented commercial banks from paying interest on checking accounts and put caps on the rates they could pay on larger savings accounts, time deposits, and certificates of deposit (CDs), as well. In the absence of competition, it was a great deal for banks. Competition gradually led the Federal Reserve to raise the interest-rate caps on large deposits, and competition from the new money-market funds finally gave small savers more options as traditional, zero-interest checking accounts under regulation Q became untenable.

Understanding this, when money-market funds began to take hold in the mid-1970s, Alan Greenspan, then on President Gerald Ford's Council of Economic Advisers, and Arthur F. Burns, the chairman of the Fed, repealed regulation Q so that the commercial banks could continue to attract customers by offering interest-bearing checking accounts. Banks had to fight for customers, forcing existing businesses to improve their own services as competition continued to spread throughout the financial system.

Government policies aimed at making the OTC market fairer and more transparent improved the market enormously and created a much larger marketplace for the stock of smaller, more entrepreneurial firms. So did antitrust and legislative efforts aimed at ending fixed commission rates, because these forced securities firms and banks to become more innovative and to offer better, lower-cost services to their customers.

Other changes in government policy also helped increase the availability of investment funds for small and medium-sized businesses. One of the most important was a change in the rules that governed the investment of pension funds.

The Employment Retirement Income Security Act (ERISA) of 1974 was the first national legislation setting rules for pension plans, a growing source of investment capital. The legislation was in response to the collapse in the 1960s of the Studebaker car company, whose workers lost most of their pensions. ERISA, among many other things, set rules for the investment of pension funds by pension managers. A change in the legislation in 1979 during the Carter administration really helped smaller companies: The so-called "prudent man" rule was amended to allow pension funds and insurance companies to hold a larger proportion of lesser-known companies listed on the NASDAQ and even high-yield bonds, which gave both the NASDAQ and the junk-bond market a significant boost.[23]

Regional Banks Challenge the New York Establishment

The changes relating to the stock market—the NASDAQ, the end of fixed brokerage rates, and changes in ERISA—increased borrowing opportunities and lowered borrowing costs for newer firms. The growth of important regional banks outside of the Northeast did the same thing. By the 1990s, northeastern banks were no longer so dominant within the banking community because world-class banks had developed in the Southeast—banks that had hardly counted in the 1970s. North Carolina emerged as a major banking and financial state with institutions large and sophisticated enough to compete with those in the old financial heartland around New York City.

The shift in relative power from the old banking centers to the new ones was remarkable. As late as 1983, North Carolina banks had assets worth only about 10 percent of those of New York banks. Over the next seventeen years, the value of assets held by the New York banks almost tripled, but those of the North Carolina banks grew by a factor of thirty.[24] By 1999, North Carolina banking assets were valued at 80 percent of New York's. The medium-sized city of Charlotte had become the headquarters of two large institutions: First Union (which later merged with Wachovia) and NationsBank-Bank of America. NationsBank's 1998 takeover of the California-based Bank of America made a very large contribution to this increase in assets, but it could not have occurred if North Carolina had not already become a major banking center.

One reason that banks, like other economic institutions, were merging and becoming national enterprises was that the spreads between what they were paying for money and their lending rates had been pushed down by competition with other changing financial institutions, forcing the banks to consolidate and cut costs. According to Richard Tilghman, the former CEO of Crestar Bank of Virginia (which was acquired by SunTrust in 1999), more intense competition among the large banks lowered the cost of almost every type of loan—commercial loans to businesses and construction loans, as well as mortgages and home-equity loans.[25]

The prospect of being taken over by big New York and foreign banks was another reason for banks to merge. The idea of easing limits on inter-state banking was a topic of discussion throughout the 1970s as other reforms of the larger financial system were taking place. In the early '80s, President Reagan was committed to ending most of these New Deal restrictions. Reagan's plans triggered action by leaders in New England and the Southeast, who feared that the big out-of-state banks would be allowed to gobble up their smaller local ones. States also feared losing tax revenues from local banks if they were taken over by out-of-state entities.

New York banks were big and powerful because New York City was the business and financial center of the country. New York and northeastern banks had been the most important banks in the United States since the Revolution, and fear of domination by them had been a concern of the other states for centuries.

But outside the Northeast, it was differences among the states' complex banking laws that made banks stronger and larger in some states than in others. North Carolina, Ohio, and California historically had relatively large banks because their state laws allowed them to set up branches statewide. Many other states, especially in the West and Midwest, had a populist tradition of mistrust for banks, so some of them limited banks to only one location or allowed multiple locations only in one town or county.

Virginia offered a good example of the problems presented by laws in some states as their banks tried to position themselves to face possible out-of-state challengers. As Tilghman remarked, "Banking competition in Virginia meant preventing other banks from getting in."[26] Virginia law allowed banks to have some branches in limited locations, but not across the entire state. Texas law was even more restrictive: It allowed each bank to operate at only one site. Smaller banks in most states opposed interstate banking because keeping outside banks out gave them local monopolies. Of course, that argument would have been too self-serving to make publicly, so they claimed instead that banks from outside the state or county would not make loans to local businesses and would only drain money out of them to lend in the big cities outside the regions.

In the 1970s, a little-noticed provision in the Bank Holding Company Act of 1956, the so-called Douglas Amendment, began to get attention as a way to strengthen regional banks against takeovers by outsiders. It generally gave states the authority to decide under what rules out-of-state banks could operate within their borders. In other words, banks in one state could own banks in another if the other state passed a law specifically allowing it. State officials, bankers, and lawyers used this provision creatively to help local and regional banks prepare themselves for the competition they feared was coming from the big northeastern and foreign banks.

The New England states were the first to strengthen their banks to resist takeovers. Maine, with its eye on the Douglas loophole, passed a state law in 1975 to allow banks from other New England states to own banks in Maine, as long as the other states reciprocated. The Maine statute and the reciprocal laws that followed in other parts of New England became the basis of an "interstate compact" between Maine and the five other New England states. A similar compact emerged in North Carolina, South Carolina, Virginia, West Virginia, Georgia, and Florida in the early 1980s. The compacts allowed a bank in one participating state to acquire banks in another participating state, while effectively preventing New York banks from making similar acquisitions.

Smaller banks would have liked to have remained independent, but they saw the handwriting on the wall. So did state regulators, who preferred mergers of local banks to mergers dominated by banks from outside the regions. The interstate compacts were a political middle ground that created a bigger regional market while excluding New York and foreign banks.

The big northeastern banks objected in court to the interstate compacts, arguing that they limited interstate commerce. The Reagan administration, frustrated in its effort to get comprehensive banking reform, supported the state compacts, and in 1985 the Supreme Court ruled that the compacts were legal.[27]

North Carolina's banks were the greatest beneficiaries of the compacts. Since they had long operated statewide, their managers were accustomed to competition and ready to manage larger institutions. In addition, their would-be competitors in Georgia and Virginia were held back by local factors. Virginia, although it had not allowed branching across the whole state, had several good-sized banks that might have become regional powerhouses. Unfortunately for them, they were preoccupied at the crucial moment in the late 1980s by their concerns about some apparently shaky real estate loans they had made in Washington, D.C., and its Virginia suburbs. The problematic loans weakened the Virginia banks just when they needed capital to expand, giving the North Carolina banks an advantage.

North Carolina banks grew in part by acquiring several of the Virginia banks. North Carolina banks also moved into Georgia before the banks in Atlanta, the region's largest city, could expand. North Carolina National Bank (NCNB) was an especially fast mover. Using the provisions of the Banking Holding Company Act, its enterprising management had acquired small banks in Florida and Texas, even before the regional compact was in place. Under the regional compact NCNB expanded, acquiring other banks and S&Ls that were on the market and becoming NationsBank in 1991, when it acquired C&S-Sovran Bank of Virginia.[28]

Glass-Steagall Act provisions that had prevented banks from owning securities firms and engaging in investment banking were crumbling, too. North Carolina had always allowed its banks to sell some kinds of insurance and provide a limited range of other financial services. Its expanding banks, therefore, were more comfortable with the idea of acquiring investment banks and securities firms during the late 1990s.[29] Small, regional securities firms and investment banks that had never been able to compete with the long-established Wall Street firms became available for acquisition and were bought up. The regional banks were then in a position to offer a range of financial services that could only have been found in New York in earlier years.

In 1999, President Clinton finally pushed through Congress banking legislation that did most though not all of the things Ronald Reagan had wanted to do in the early 1980s. It repealed many of the limitations on commercial banks imposed during the Great Depression out of the country's earlier antipathy toward large banks. The legislation, however, had less impact than it would have had if it had been adopted earlier, because by 1999 the regional banks were already a force, and there were so many more alternatives to commercial banks for both savers and borrowers.[30]

The evolution of banking reform thus followed a typical pattern. The executive branch pushed for increased competition and supported court cases and action in the states that moved in that direction. Loopholes were exploited by entrepreneurs and their lawyers who wanted to compete, and these entrepreneurs found political support. Powerful interests who wanted to maintain the status quo succeeded in blocking national legislation for almost twenty years, but they were softened up by legal actions and gradually moved aside. Eventually, legislation completed the process.

Copying the Americans—More or Less

In the quotation that heads this chapter, Mort Zuckerman contrasted American finance with that of Europe and Japan, and it is important to return to that point. How did the financial sectors in European countries and Japan evolve while the American sector was being transformed?

In the 1970s, there was concern that large Japanese and European banks would take over and swallow up small U.S. banks. Overseas banks had never been handicapped by the kinds of limitations that had long been characteristic of the American financial system. Foreign banks were really financial conglomerates, nationwide giants linked to insurance companies, other financial institutions, and corporations.

The Japanese financial institutions looked especially threatening. Each powerful *keiretsu* (grouping of companies) in Japan had a main bank to finance the group's activities. These banks maintained ties to the group's insurance companies and industrial firms, links that would have been illegal in America under Depression-era banking laws. The Japanese government, especially the potent Ministry of Finance, thought in the 1980s that the country's banks were ready to expand internationally.

The Japanese financial institutions were sitting on hundred of billions of dollars in lendable funds, deposits, and profits they had taken in during the Japanese stock market and land booms during the 1980s. To make use of these funds, the Japanese banks, security houses, and insurance companies opened hundreds of offices in the best locations in New York, Atlanta, and other U.S. financial centers, and in European cities like London, Brussels, and Frankfurt. They loaned a great deal of money to Japanese speculators to buy famous buildings, choice real estate, prestigious golf courses, and fine works of art at stupendous prices, and they wanted to lend money to the clients of the American financial houses as well. The Japanese Ministry of Finance encouraged these financial giants to move into the American market the way the Japanese automakers and other manufacturers had.[31]

Nicholas Brady, who had headed the investment banking house of Dillon Read and Company in New York, was George H. W. Bush's secretary of the treasury. He was concerned about the rising power of the Japanese financial institutions and believed that they threatened American financial institutions. Brady and President Bush, like Ronald Reagan in the early 1980s, wanted to liberate U.S. banks from the limits of New Deal legislation so that they could defend themselves against the foreigners. Brady repeatedly warned that if the United States kept restraining its banks from moving into related businesses as their overseas competitors were free to do, American banks would lose their independence.

Investment banker Eugene Dattel had a different view of the Japanese financial conglomerates. Dattel lived in Japan from 1987 to 1992, working first in the Tokyo office of Salomon Brothers and then for Morgan Stanley. His 1994 book, *The Sun That Never Rose,* described the fear many felt in the late 1980s and early '90s about Japanese financial power.[32]

Dattel's perception was that the Japanese financiers were overrated and were lending to firms and businesses that were paying too much for all the things they were buying. He knew from his own contacts in the country that the Japanese bankers did not understand the complicated new securities that were appearing on the markets. The conventional wisdom held that although the Japanese firms that were the banks' clients might be paying too much for some of their purchases, they would still come out ahead.

It was the classic rationale for "irrational exuberance" whenever it breaks out. The Japanese were willing to pay more, the logic ran, because they understood that everything was going up and that, over time, the value of these assets would rise enough to justify the seemingly high prices they were paying. This was the same argument people made about the American stock market ten or twelve years later, and it was just as wrong.[33]

Suddenly, in 1990, the Japanese stock market bubble collapsed. Between 1990, when it reached almost 39,000, and 1998 when it fell below 13,000, the Nikkei lost about two-thirds of its value. Land prices in Japan plunged to 80 percent below the highs reached in 1991.[34]

The Japanese banks and insurance companies had loaned huge amounts of money to borrowers, accepting these now-depreciated assets as collateral. When the value of the collateral vanished, borrowers stopped repaying hundreds of billions of dollars worth of loans. In the bloodless jargon of banking, the loans had become "nonperforming." But if the banks had foreclosed, forcing borrowers to liquidate the depreciated assets, it would have bankrupted both the borrowers and the banks. Under these circumstances, the Japanese government and the banks preferred to nurse the illusion that the loans would someday be paid back. But the banks' aura of invincibility disappeared overnight.

The collapse of the Japanese financial system made more apparent the virtues of the American one. When the U.S. stock market nosedived in 2001, American banks were hurt, but they were not as exposed as banks in Japan, and they were not nearly as big a part of the financial system. By the end of the 1990s, America had developed a broader array of financial institutions that distributed risk.

Junk bonds gave companies long-term financing that could not be terminated by a bank, and that shifted risk to bondholders from the company itself. The NASDAQ was also a broad market that allowed millions of stockholders to share both rewards and risks. And a whole new list of banks and financial institutions outside of the Northeast distributed risks and benefits and broadened opportunities for tens of thousands of entrepreneurs.

In the Rearview Mirror

Leaders in other countries understand that the United States gained enormously in the late twentieth century because it had developed financial markets that allowed people like Frank Cruz and companies like CNN and MCI to challenge the establishments in their industries. Foreign policymakers have therefore tried to copy what America has done.

In Europe and Japan, high-yield-bond financing for small and medium-sized firms appeared in the mid- to late-1990s, but the spirit was different from that in the United States. Junk-bond markets overseas emerged as top-down efforts to mimic what had been successful here, but they remained much smaller and more marginal. Standard & Poor's estimated the U.S. junk-bond market in 1999 at $500 billion, more than twenty-five times larger than its European counterpart, which stood at $18 billion.[35] Fixed-rate financing for most European businesses, therefore, continued to come principally from large banks.

European efforts to give entrepreneurs better access to stock markets were a similar story. The NASDAQ had been so successful in the United States in the 1990s that almost every government in Europe and some in Asia tried to copy it. New markets were promoted in Germany, the United Kingdom, the Netherlands, Italy, Spain, France, Japan, and probably other countries.

The instinct in Europe, however, was to work through the old financial establishments to create these new markets. European countries did
not do what the United States did and encourage brokers who had been
dealing in the OTC to organize a new market.[36] The European notion was
to ask the established stock exchanges in each country to set up a market
to handle stock issued by newer, smaller, high-tech companies. In most
cases, it was like asking the NYSE to set up a separate market to compete
with itself, and companies were slow to list on the new markets.

The question is whether new markets created by the old stock
exchanges, with all their interests in moving companies onto the established exchanges as quickly as possible, can give new companies in
Europe the benefits that competition among the exchanges has brought
in the United States.

New stock markets in Europe face other problems as well. The
NASDAQ and the junk-bond markets in the United States received a
boost when ERISA was amended in 1979 to allow private pension funds
to invest larger percentages of their assets in relatively risky securities. The
problem of funds for new enterprises in Europe is aggravated in France,
Germany, and some other countries by their government pension systems.
U.S. private pension plans are huge compared to those in Europe, and the
funds are invested heavily in stocks. In Europe, on the other hand, private
pension plans are small, and current workers pay for retired workers in
the government plans.

There is a growing understanding in Europe that pension or savings
plans that have to funnel funds into government securities deprive the private sector of access to investment funds, slow down job creation, and dis-
courage saving. It has proved difficult, however, to change these policies
because, much as these countries want to grow the way the United States
was able to in the 1990s, strong interests defend the status quo.

Abuses Are Not a Reason to Reverse Reforms

The collapse of the U.S. stock markets, starting in the spring of 2001, was mirrored in Europe, where stocks had risen more or less in parallel with those in
the United States. European markets are not protected from speculation

because they are less accessible to new entrepreneurial companies than markets on the more open side of the Atlantic.

In the United States, abuses by brokers, investment analysts, and corporate leaders that took place during the 1990s boom should be punished, and, where possible, better regulation is in order. But because the abuses are reminiscent of what went on in the boom times of the 1920s, the danger is that we will throw out the baby with the bathwater once again. Then, as in the 1990s, insiders and stock analysts hyped stocks, and investors wanted to believe them. Corporate chieftains were greedy almost beyond measure. Ordinary people took risks they could not afford to take.

Still, these abuses should not become an excuse to reduce competition in financial markets and impede the flow of investment funds to unproven enterprises and new competitors. There are fair risks and unfair risks, and it is important to distinguish between them. Entrepreneurs take risks, and the people who buy stocks and lend money to them have to expect risks, too. The idea that stocks are an easy and safe way to get rich is just wrong.

That being said, it is unfair for insiders and analysts to disguise risks from investors, to dilute stock without informing them, and to hype a company by disguising its problems. Markets must be policed to ensure transparency—to make sure that the scales work and weights and measures are honest, or, in the case of investments, that statements of profit and loss, corporate debt, and revenues and sales are not misleading. Article 1, section 8 of the Constitution makes the federal government responsible for setting the standard of weights and measures in markets; cheating in financial markets is little different from cheating with regard to weights and scales.

The collapse of high-tech stocks and the sharp decline in the broader markets of 2000 did not result from the changes of the previous thirty years that made the American financial system more competitive. The worst excesses in the late 1990s were the result of inadequate policing of corporations and stocks promoters, who employed the kind of scams that are as ancient as society itself.[36] Corporate officers and Wall Street insiders were allowed to enrich themselves by setting their own pay scales and manipulating stock prices to dupe investors. Accounting firms covered for them. The reforms that opened up the U.S. financial system after 1970 to new investors and increased competition had little or nothing to do with the speculation and collapse.

The changes in the American financial system after about 1970 had much in common with changes in other American industries—making competition more intense, turning relatively local markets into more national ones, facilitating the growth of the South and the West, and giving a boost to new entrepreneurial companies that took on established ones.

As they did in manufacturing and the regulated industries, lawsuits and the courts played a big role, but so did government policies. The Reagan administration protected the new junk-bond market against attempts by powerful interests with support in Congress to restrict it drastically. Congress and the SEC promoted the NASDAQ to reform and modernize the old OTC market and limit the ability of insiders to manipulate it. The Antitrust Division of the Justice Department supported the end of fixed rates for brokers, which encouraged the brokerage houses to develop money-market funds. States in New England and the South used interstate compacts to encourage the development of regional banks to temporarily prevent the New York banks from moving in.

When new financing institutions grew up, the reforms in the banking laws that had been the focus became less important. Legislation came slowly after regulators, lawyers, and the courts had sanctioned crucial changes. Established interests opposed the changes, but, for the most part, they lost and had to adjust.

As a result, the U.S. financial system does a better job of funneling investment capital to the economically promising rather than the politically powerful. The developments during the 1970s and '80s brought in new blood, increased competition, and made the American financial system the match of any in the world. From our perspective today, the sudden ending of the boom years sits in the foreground, obscuring our view of the successes of the slightly more distant past. Yet America is far better positioned now than it was in the 1970s to finance the new ideas that will be needed to solve today's problems.

6

The Revolution in Retailing

[Wal-Mart] did more to fight inflation than the Federal Reserve.
—Daniel Akst[1]

Out-of-Town Shopping

In the 1980s, it seemed a little strange to me that our friends who lived in New York City did all of the back-to-school shopping for their kids in western Massachusetts, where they spent summer vacations. There were no outlets or Wal-Marts then, and the stores where they bought clothes and shoes were not very special. Why waste a day or two out of a vacation when there were all those stores in New York City?

Later, I saw many more New Yorkers shopping in the new malls outside the city because it was so much less expensive. On a Sunday heading back into the city, dozens of cars filled with shopping bags could be seen on the roads. It was not just the high city taxes sending them away to shop.

One reason New York City is beginning to loosen restrictive zoning rules and allow stores like Costco, Home Depot, Target, and Ikea to open in Queens, the Bronx, and Staten Island is that tens of thousands of New Yorkers shop in these stores anyway. In America it is possible to evade local restrictions by going to a nearby community with different rules, or to another state. Bus companies advertise trips to lower-cost outlet malls and similar shopping locations.

New Yorkers are hardly the only Americans willing to struggle for lower prices. Americans have never liked government-imposed restrictions on what they could buy or whom they could buy it from. Persistent cultural factors have always encouraged an aggressive, highly competitive, technology-adaptive style of retailing in America that has made limits on competition difficult to enforce.

One reason for this is that commerce has always been more respectable in the United States than in other places. America has never had the caste and class-based systems that were common in India, China, and much of Europe right up into the twentieth century. Although some Americans may have thought commerce was beneath them, in general, our culture has celebrated entrepreneurs. European Marxists appealed to the elites of many older civilizations by endorsing their disdain for commerce. The hostility of many intellectuals to business has deep roots in earlier value systems. Even today in the United States, elite commentators talk dismissively about 22 million "dead-end jobs" in retail, and view businesspeople as somehow beneath those who choose the supposedly less commercial professions.

In any case, many of America's early leaders engaged in commerce. Colonial commercial interests were major supporters of the Revolutionary War, in part because British merchants tried to limit competition from their overseas cousins. Supreme Court Chief Justice John Marshall, as well as George Washington and other Founding Fathers, speculated in land and carried on other forms of trade.

Traveling salesmen were common in the earliest colonial days, serving customers on remote farms and reservations. American farmers were never isolated peasants with a sharply different culture from those who lived in cities, because commerce touched them every day.

By the 1830s, American farmers could order from seed catalogues; salesmen for John Deere spurred the use of the modern steel plow in the Midwest in the 1840s, well before the Civil War, preceding the advent of government-sponsored agricultural colleges and the Agricultural Extension Services. Deere also insisted on constantly improving his plow, telling associates that if he did not, others would soon be taking his customers. The mail-order catalogues of Montgomery Ward and Sears, Roebuck and Company made manufactured products available to rural Americans in the late nineteenth century, boosting the development of both manufacturing and agriculture.

And so Americans have never really lived in isolated communities, and they are used to having retailers fight for their business. No wonder New Yorkers often go outside the city to buy back-to-school clothes and do their heavy-duty grocery shopping.

Wal-Mart Remakes the Playing Field

In 1970, Wal-Mart was a dot on the retail horizon, with sales of only $44 million. Just over thirty years later, its sales exceed $200 billion, roughly 7 percent of retail sales in the United States, and it has become the largest retailer and employer in America.[2]

Sam Walton, Wal-Mart's founder, was to retailing what Ken Iverson was to steel, Jack Goeken and Bill McGowan were to telecommunications, and Michael Milken was to finance. He was out to change the status quo. Like the new competitors in other industries, Wal-Mart grew by lowering prices and providing service to people who had been served poorly. And, like the others, Walton made established firms shape their strategies to his, or go out of business.[3] As Daniel Akst quipped in the *New York Times*, when you lower costs in a sector that accounts for 20 percent of U.S. GDP, as well as 20 percent of employment, you may indeed have a bigger effect on inflation than the Fed.[4]

Sam Walton and other new retailers had to fight off established businesses large and small that wanted to freeze or slow down changes in retailing and maintain the status quo. Walton said that "small-town merchants" fought him, and that "department stores put a lot of pressure on vendors to keep them from selling to discounters like us because they hated what we were doing: offering our customers prices much lower than theirs. Our vendors [also] resented us for prying the lowest prices out of them." Middlemen, jobbers, and distributors did not like Wal-Mart, either, because it often tried to deal directly with manufacturers. Even manufacturers, who benefited from the volume business Wal-Mart could bring, were unhappy with the pressure for lower prices.[5]

But opposition never fazed Walton. He seemed to know from the beginning, when he was driving a trailer around the Southwest to find low-cost merchandise, that in America the established interests would not be able to stop him.

At the time that Walton began in the retail business after World War II, the sector was very different from what it is now. Big-city retailing was dominated by large department stores. Discounters were only beginning to come in, mostly at the local and regional levels. Shoppers in small towns were expected to sacrifice quality for cost and to forgo wider choices for the convenience of shopping locally.

Rural residents on tight budgets did their shopping at variety stores—really small-town department stores—which were sometimes independent and sometimes linked in chains. Some commentators are nostalgic for those times, but this Norman Rockwell world was really not great for rural and small-town shoppers. Variety stores in small towns often stocked lower-quality merchandise and lesser brands. They typically used "high-low" pricing—drawing in customers with low prices on a few items and making their money by sharply marking up their other goods.

Sam Walton wanted to grow his business by selling more recognizable brand-name products at what he called "everyday low prices." Walton started out managing variety stores for others. He had a vision of a low-price strategy, but found he could not get from wholesalers or the owners of the chains the good deals that would allow him to pursue it. In 1962, he started Wal-Mart.

Walton turned comparison-shopping into an art form. He wanted customers to be able to compare the prices of brand-name products and popular models at his stores against his competitors' so it would be clear what good deals Wal-Mart was offering. He also sought out managers and employees for his stores—many of them veterans of other variety-store chains—who were ambitious, knew the merchandise, and would instill confidence in customers. It turned out to be a winning strategy, because buyers came to believe they could trust Wal-Mart to deliver on its low-price promise and do the comparison-shopping for them.

To be able to sell brand-name goods at lower prices than his competitors, Walton had to be more efficient, so he adopted a "big-box" store format. He located his stores in rural areas where property was cheap and stayed away from downtown areas and malls. He also found out what other discounters were doing and tried to do it better. He borrowed ideas from Fed-Mart, which was founded by a legendary California retailer named Sol Price in 1954, and later from Price's Price Club, which became the model for Walton's Sam's Club stores. Walton copied from his competitors the things that worked, and learned from their mistakes. He fought to get lower prices from manufacturers and wholesalers that he could pass on to customers. In time, Wal-Mart's buying power would mean that it could force manufacturers, transporters, and its other vendors to become more efficient and lower their prices. Sears, Roebuck and Company had done this in the late 1800s, but Wal-Mart did it better.

Even as Walton copied others, he forced others to copy from him. Inspired by his enormous success and fearful that he would put them out of business, a whole group of retailers began offering fashions and brand-name goods at prices that department stores and independents could not match.[6] Wal-Mart became the leader of a new mass-marketing category of retailers.

Many of Walton's retail innovations were similar to those that worked in other sectors of the economy. His stores improved service to the lower end of the market just as Japanese cars, steel minimills, and the new financial institutions did. He managed his retailing empire with a small headquarters staff that was characteristic of other success stories, such as Nucor. In time, like the leaders in transportation and telecommunications, he applied advanced information technology to all aspects of retailing and distribution. But above all, like the success stories in other industries, Wal-Mart won customers by offering them a better deal.

The company's birth in northwest Arkansas and early growth in small towns in Texas, Missouri, Oklahoma, and Arkansas—far from the East Coast—were also characteristic of entrepreneurs in other sectors. The auto plants of the Japanese transplants were located away from the old centers of industrial power. Nucor started by serving the South and West. Wal-Mart grew up in the same area. It later moved to challenge older chains in the Northeast and Midwest, but it began in the underserved, fast-growing parts of the country.

A wave of change and modernization swept over the whole retail sector as new formats and competing chains burst onto the scene. Discount prices spread, as laws that had protected local retailers and allowed manufacturers to set retail prices were undermined by the courts and legislatures. Suddenly, manufacturers were cutting prices and costs to get contracts from the new retailers, suggested retail prices became meaning-less, and customers learned that they had options.

The politics behind the changes in retailing resembled in many ways the dynamic that operated in other areas of the economy. Retailing was not dominated in the 1970s by oligopolies and monopolies with national reach, as was the case with autos, steel, telecommunications, and some types of finance. Yet in cities and towns all over the country, retailers, like electric utilities, were locally powerful. The associations that represented these older retailers went to local, state, and federal governments to argue that competition from the emerging national or regional chains was unfair, a danger to established neighborhoods and employment, and a threat to the environment. And, as in other areas of the economy, the status quo interests generally lost.

The Politics of Retail Competition

The battles that Wal-Mart and other aggressive new retailers fought all through the 1980s and '90s against efforts by established retailers to limit them actually were the continuation of a long war. Smaller retailers have tried over and over again to stop successive waves of larger new competi-tors since early in the twentieth century, if not before.

One approach has been to try to get manufacturers to require that their products be sold at high fixed prices that would guarantee even small retailers a good profit. In 1911, the Supreme Court decided that the Sherman Antitrust Act prevented manufacturers from requiring retailers to sell at predetermined prices in interstate commerce. The Court also said, however, that states could allow retail price-fixing within their own boundaries if they wanted to do so, so smaller retailers pursued this possibility.

Just as the Great Depression made price-fixing in manufacturing appealing, so, too, did it make price-fixing in retailing seem like a good idea. (Recall from chapter 4 the National Industrial Recovery Act of 1933 with all its codes.) California and other states, anxious to keep small shops in business and prevent prices from falling further, passed statewide legislation allowing manufacturers to set minimum prices. The courts, however, stepped in again, deciding that even state-level legisla-tion violated antitrust principles, and throwing out the California law and similar state statutes.

Proponents of minimum prices did not give up the fight. Many sup-porters of small business in Congress sought federal legislation to allow states to pass what were called "fair-trade" laws. In 1937, while the Depression still held the country in its grip, these forces pushed through the Miller-Tydings Retail Price Maintenance Act, exempting the California retail law and similar statutes in other states from the antitrust rules. In time, more than forty states passed fair-trade laws that allowed manufac-turers to sign contracts with retailers setting minimum resale prices.

The question of minimum pricing as a way to safeguard small mer-chants from competitors became moot during World War II. States were reluctant in wartime to enforce such pricing when inflation, not cutthroat competition, had become the issue. After the war, however, pressures to limit price competition resurfaced. A key Supreme Court case in 1951 involved a liquor merchant in Louisiana who wanted to compete by slash-ing prices. He insisted that, despite Miller-Tydings and Louisiana fair-trade laws, the antitrust laws made it illegal for his suppliers to require him to enter into a price-fixing arrangement. The Court agreed with him.[7]

In response once again, Congress passed another fair-trade law in 1952, the Maguire Act, which closed the loophole that had allowed retail-ers to reject price-fixing contracts and cut their prices. States varied in their willingness and ability to enforce fair-trade laws in the 1960s and '70s, no doubt because most did not want to deny their residents the advantages of shopping at the new discount stores. Finally, Miller-Tydings and the Maguire Act were repealed in 1975 by the Consumer Goods Pricing Act.

The Miller-Tydings approach was meant to appeal to both manufac-turers and small retailers, and it assumed that the former preferred to sell at high fixed prices. Some manufacturers, however, did not want to keep their prices high, preferring instead to sell to large chains who would make volume purchases. Small retailers tried to limit the ability of manu-facturers to pursue this approach.

One way to do so was to back laws that prevented manufacturers from giving large discounts for volume purchases. In the 1920s, small grocers, druggists, and tire dealers focused on this approach to slow the growth of chain stores but, predictably, did not get far while prosperity lasted. The Great Depression increased the pressure for such measures and brought Washington into the picture. Advocates for the small retailers argued that larger retailers were using their bargaining power with manufacturers in a deliberate effort to put the "little guys" out of business. They claimed that, once the small retailers had disappeared, the chains would boost their prices.

This led to the Robinson-Patman Act of 1936, which was meant to force manufacturers to justify or even eliminate discounts to the chains. This approach, like efforts to force retailers to maintain prices, never got very far because lowering prices to get business was very much a part of the American tradition. Except in very hard times, it was always an uphill battle to persuade the public that lower prices were not a good thing.

Challenging the Department Stores and Groceries

Sears was the Wal-Mart of the nineteenth and early twentieth centuries. It became a powerful retailing force by providing good-quality, low-cost goods of all kinds to farm families. More than a hundred years ago, its 500-page catalogues reached into tens of thousands of communities. Mail-order sales provided competition for the high-priced small-town and rural stores.

Sears's distribution centers before World War I were a technological marvel. Henry Ford is said to have visited one such center and copied the assembly-line techniques it used for filling and shipping orders from its huge warehouses. Sears's efficiency lowered costs dramatically and provided a model for other industries.

If Sears stood for modern retailing in rural America in the late nineteenth century, the department stores played that role in the cities. Most of America's department stores had their beginnings in the nineteenth century, generally developing after the Civil War from small stores operated by Jewish merchant families. For the first three-quarters of the twentieth century, the department store—selling fashions, cosmetics, and household goods—was the retailing icon of the city-centered American culture.

Even small cities had a commercial "Main Street" with one or two department stores. The department store was the anchor for a block or two of smaller specialty shops around it, as well as movie theaters, restaurants, and other entertainment establishments.

After World War II, Bloomingdale's, Macy's, Gimbels, Saks, Kleins, Wanamaker's—nineteen department stores in all—fought for the huge New York City market. Filene's and Jordan Marsh were the two giants in Boston, but there were other competitors as well. Garfinkels, Hechts, and Woodward and Lothrop operated in Washington, D.C., all within a few blocks of the White House. Neiman Marcus had its roots in Dallas.

In the 1950s, a wave of change hit the department store sector, but the stores adapted reasonably well. Cities were becoming less dense. Americans began to move decisively to the suburbs, which were fast becoming the country's most rapidly growing and prosperous markets. The department stores responded by opening branches out in suburban areas to serve the expanding suburban middle class and their automobile culture. These branches did well, and the department stores themselves continued to look strong.[8]

The flagship department stores in their downtown locations survived a long time after the exodus from the cities. They had deep pockets and loyal customers; but it was a different story for the smaller businesses that had grouped around them in the cities. Most of them were too small to launch suburban branches, so the shopping streets around the department stores decayed well before the big stores began eventually to close.

In the 1970s, suburban shopping gradually became mall shopping. Malls were developed first to serve neighborhoods, and then larger regions. As in the downtown shopping districts, department stores usually anchored the mall, with the specialty shops that had once grouped around the urban stores now located around their suburban branches. Soon entertainment was added, replicating the mix of options once offered in the downtown shopping districts.

Suburban department stores were smaller than the ones in the big cities. Usually they did not carry less-expensive merchandise, and they rarely sold discontinued items in the basement the way the big stores in the cities often did. It was said that the suburban department stores had "left their basements behind," opting not to offer off-price merchandise, no doubt because at first the suburbs had few low-income residents. The differences created openings for the early discounters who sold products like TVs and refrigerators for less than the department stores did, as well as for fashion-oriented retailers. New specialized stores also moved into the malls to serve high-end customers, who also had less choice at the suburban stores.

The story of chain grocery stores was similar to that of department stores. Both developed at about the same time in the late nineteenth and early twentieth centuries. A&P (the Great Atlantic and Pacific Tea Company) had one hundred stores in the 1870s and was the country's first major grocery chain. By the 1930s, it had stores in thousands of neighborhoods, and was the target of a backlash quite like the one affecting Wal-Mart today.

Smaller retailers made repeated efforts to hold back A&P, much as they would try to hold back discounters and the mass-retailers decades later, but to little avail. By the 1990s, of course, A&P was being overtaken by new competitors: the Kroger Company, Albertson's, Safeway Stores, and the Dutch company, Ahold. These chains and many others started in the early twentieth century as smaller, local operations that to a significant extent followed the A&P model, but away from the Northeast where A&P was strongest. Today their principal challenge is not from other grocery chains, but from the expansion of Wal-Mart and similar retailers into the grocery field.

The Retail Competition Ripple Effect

Today's biggest and fastest-growing grocery chains are the result of mergers in the last two decades, prompted largely by the need to compete with Wal-Mart, Costco, and other giant mass-market retailers. Kroger's is now the leading American supermarket chain, with almost 2,500 stores and $50 billion in sales volume in 2001. Albertson's, Safeway, and Ahold all have at least 1,500 stores and sales volumes well over $30 billion each. The most startling recent development, however, has been Wal-Mart's competitive charge into the grocery business. Its supercenters, Sam's Clubs, and smaller local markets in 2001 sold $80 billion worth of grocery products, surpassing all other grocery chains.

To meet the challenge from Wal-Mart, grocery chains have had to consolidate, build larger stores, close smaller ones, improve their product offerings, strengthen their information-handling and logistics, add pharmacies and in-store banks, and experiment with convenience-store subsidiaries, prepared meals, and other innovations. All have become international, battling across the world for customers. American-owned grocery chains have stores in Canada and Mexico, as do Wal-Mart and the other mass-marketers, and are expected to join other American retailers in Europe and Asia in the near future.

Competition is driving innovation and technological change in the grocery business as it does in every industry. In the 1970s, for example, Ahold, a Dutch company active all over the world, began to acquire smaller American chains—such as Giant in the mid-Atlantic states, Stop & Shop in New England, and American Food Service. In 2001, the *Washington Post* noted that "faced with aggressive new competitors, such as Wal-Mart Stores Inc., that pared costs through the smart use of technology," Ahold "is introducing new cost-saving technology to deliver groceries faster and cheaper to neighborhood stores."[9] It is buying computer systems and software to bring order to warehouses that used to be large but unsophisticated. Information from the checkout lines is being fed increasingly to warehouses and suppliers, an approach pioneered by Wal-Mart and other mass-marketers. Truck deliveries and pickups are more carefully planned. Goods are stacked in preplanned locations, and computers choreograph the movement of forklifts through the huge spaces.

Competition from Wal-Mart and other mass-retailers was the driving force in retailing in the 1990s, and it still is today. It is now a fact of life rippling through most retail specialties, forcing changes in the business plans of pharmacies, home-remodeling suppliers and sellers of office supplies, marketers of toys and household furnishings, and even purveyors of fashion.

Pharmacy chains such as CVS, for example, that were driving modernization in their own sector, now have to adjust to the mass-retailers that are opening large pharmacies in their newer stores. CVS began as a New England chain in the 1980s. It grew explosively along the Atlantic seaboard in the 1990s in a process that paralleled events in the grocery area. Consolidation and mergers were necessary because wholesale-retail margins were being forced down by competition.

Working together, pharmacies have developed computer systems for prescription drugs so that almost all of them can communicate in real time with insurance companies to get approval for prescriptions.[10] More intense competition, however, also is forcing them to increase their efficiency in nondrug areas and to add new departments and services to keep up with grocery chains and mass-marketers. Small boutique pharmacies still exist and even thrive, but only by offering extraordinary service in a niche market.

Home Depot, Lowe's, and regional home-remodeling suppliers also are battling for customers, driven in part by competition from mass-marketers. In the office-supply market, Office Depot, Staples, and Office Max fight fiercely for clients, in Europe and Asia as well as in the United States, and face the same challenge from Wal-Mart, Costco, and others. Toys "R" Us, Circuit City, Best Buy, and other large, specialized chains also find themselves under pressure from the mass-marketers who are selling toys, electronics, and similar products.

Neiman Marcus, Nordstrom, Fresh Fields, and other high-end stores in every field continue to prosper by offering superior products and more and better services to affluent customers. At the same time, fashion specialty stores like Gap, The Limited, Banana Republic, Lands' End, and others have become powerful forces in American retailing by developing youth and leisure markets, although there is constant turmoil in the sector.

Chain specialty stores also have come along to sell merchandise such as books (Barnes & Noble, Borders), sports equipment (The Sports Authority), and even household linens and related goods (Linens 'n Things; Bed, Bath & Beyond). These stores are called "category-killers" because they create new groupings of merchandise in a big-box format and pull customers away from more traditional shops. All these retailers use computer technology, modern communications, knowledge of overseas manufacturing capabilities, and high-tech distribution centers to adjust to emerging customer preferences more quickly than the older stores. Outlet malls also have become shopping destinations, and they allow manufacturers to develop their own lower-priced outlets for name brands, competing with both the higher-priced department stores and the lower-priced mass-marketers and category-killers.

Wal-Mart, Target, Costco, and other mass-retailers face competition themselves, but they stand for a force that has sharply increased competition in American retailing over the past thirty years, pushed innovation in what would not otherwise seem to have been a high-tech industry, and made possible faster growth without inflation. Even if it is an exaggeration to say that Wal-Mart did more to fight inflation than the Federal Reserve, it is certainly not an exaggeration to say that the broader Wal-Mart phenomenon in retailing has done so.

Continuing Efforts to Limit Competition

Retailing has always been a competitive, modernizing, and evolving business in America, and that tradition continues. Most efforts to limit competition and preserve old retailing structures have failed, but the instinct to keep trying is very much alive.

The push and pull of politics in retail remains lively. Established retailers who fear competition from aggressive national chains and novel retail formats still develop alliances with other groups to hold back newcomers. Established retailers and environmentalists frequently organize to oppose the construction of a new mall, a Wal-Mart, a Home Depot, or a Starbucks. Few of these advocates say they are opposed to change or competition. They certainly do not think of themselves as champions of the status quo. To the contrary, most argue and certainly themselves believe that they favor fair competition, and are proponents of change within a less-commercial framework of values.

Many advocacy groups, however, argue that the newest crop of American retailers is a threat to the vitality of hometown businesses and old-fashioned neighborhood values.[11] Headlines featured on their websites tell the story: "Starbucks Not Welcome in Ocean Beach"; "Glendale Voters Reject Supercenter"; "Chain Store Complex Defeated in Petoskey"; "Madison Residents Say No to Walgreens"; "Home Depot Backs Out of Downtown Portland"; "Ikea Backs Out of New Rochelle." Many of the websites offer suggestions on the best tactics to stop the new retail invaders.

As these headlines attest, the prospect of new retailing competition nearby can cause bitter neighborhood fights and deep divisions within civic groups, such as the chamber of commerce. The local store owner, lunch-counter operator, or environmentalist is likely to say that the new development will bring too much traffic, change the character of the town, force local businesses to close, weaken the union, lead to a reduction in high-paying jobs, and damage the environment. Most of these arguments are perfectly consistent with those that were made against the industrialization that took place more than two hundred years ago in England.

The eager developer takes the other side, advising local residents to support new jobs and welcome an increase in the tax base. Developers also point out that dozens of storefronts have sat empty in the old downtown since the advent of the strip mall thirty years ago, and that the marginal businesses and not-for-profit organizations now operating there have barely any trade and pay little in taxes. Some towns have rejected major discounters or new malls, but most have welcomed the newcomers.

Most of these battles are resolved by local governments. Towns and cities adopt zoning standards that limit or expand parking, and let chains in or keep them out. Towns have also passed or revoked "blue laws" governing the hours a store can be open, and capped the size of new retail establishments. The federal government and the states may be pulled in and sometimes debate the issue, but there is little likelihood of serious state or federal legislation that would drastically limit the new retail stores. Even during the Great Depression, courts were skeptical of such efforts because they ran counter to America's antitrust traditions, and the legislation that did pass tended to be loose and relatively easy to evade, as we have seen. That continues to be the case.

California's Big-Box Battle. A 1999 political battle in California is an example of the politics of retail competition. This struggle pitted today's most potent competitors, big-box retailers like Wal-Mart, Target, and Costco, against an alliance of chain grocery and drugstores, their unionized employees, and assorted civic groups who saw a moral issue in this clash of large companies.

Wal-Mart, Target, and Costco are well-established in California and are expanding to sell groceries and drugstore items in addition to their usual mix of products. Costco, first called Price Club, is a native of the Golden State, the brainchild of retailing entrepreneur Sol Price, who started it in San Diego in 1976. Wal-Mart and its Sam's Club subsidiary, which compete with Costco, have hundreds of stores along the freeways of California. Target is the discount mass-market challenger developed by the upscale Dayton Hudson department store chain.

In the 1990s, the big-box retailers were closing their older stores and opening larger ones, and adding new product lines and components, including grocery and pharmacy departments, banks, and gasoline stations. The strategy behind this trend was clear. Profit margins are usually lower for groceries than for general merchandise, but customers come more often to buy them. Thus, adding new grocery lines brings more customer traffic to the store and exposes these shoppers to the merchandise from which the retailers make more money.

Concerned about this type of competition, unions representing workers at grocery and pharmacy chains such as the United Food and Commercial Workers in California sought state legislation in 1999[12] to place limitations on the size of new retail stores if they handled groceries ("non-sales-taxable" items). Older grocery and pharmacy chains joined with the unions in opposing the hard-charging big-box stores, but they were not themselves small operations. Two substantial California chains, Ralph's, which was part of the Kroger family of grocery stores, and Vons, part of the Safeway group, joined the unions in opposing Wal-Mart, Target, and Costco. The chains and the unions also made common cause with environmental and neighborhood groups, for whom the big-box retailers had become a particular target.

The grocery and pharmacy chains made a number of arguments: They were opposed to sprawl and wanted to protect existing jobs and neighborhoods. Their competitors, they said, were threatening neighborhoods, small businesses, and the aesthetics of American life. The big-box retailers, for their part, claimed to be fighting for middle-class consumers, who would benefit from lower prices for groceries and drugstore products, and for those who would find jobs in the new stores. None of these players could have passed for a "little guy" or a neighborhood store, but all invoked that term on their behalf.[13]

The anti-big-box alliance between the unions and grocery chains in California succeeded in the first round, pushing its measure through both houses of the California legislature at the end of its 1999 session. Ron Burkle, chairman of the Yucaipa Company, was an important business supporter of the measure. Burkle has many overlapping interests in the grocery field, and he and Yucaipa have a large stake in Ralph's. In 1999 Yucaipa played a key role in merging Ralph's and Fred Meyer (the Portland, Oregon-based grocery chain that had acquired Ralph's) into the Kroger group.[14] Burkle, who once worked as a bagger in a grocery store, is a billionaire financier and deal-maker, involved in many mergers in the grocery store industry. He is also a big contributor to the Democratic Party, with longstanding political ties to California's former governor Gray Davis and former president Bill Clinton.[15]

News reports recounting the "big box" battle with the grocery chains described Burkle's campaign contributions and political connections. Of the $6 million in political contributions that former governor Davis raised during his first six months in office, the Yucaipa companies were the fourth-largest source of funds.[16] Unions that had supported Davis with money and manpower during his various election campaigns urged him to sign the legislation, too. They had sworn to fight Wal-Mart's entry into the grocery business and were hostile to the aggressively nonunion company.

Yet in the face of conventional wisdom and pressures from big contributors like Burkle and the union, Gray Davis vetoed the bill. Wal-Mart, Costco, and the other big-box retailers won the fight in California. In his veto message, Davis explained that local land-use and zoning decisions should not be preempted by the states. Local governments in California, he declared, wanted to be able to attract new businesses and didn't want the state telling them what to do.[17] He was saying, in effect, that for every town in California that wanted to block a new mall or big-box store, there were many others eager to attract retail jobs and enlarge their tax bases, and he chose not to get into the middle of the fight.

Signing the bill, Davis said, would have meant caving in to special interests, and higher prices for consumers, and he noted that the legislation had been rushed through without the usual complement of hearings. Davis, no doubt, was also afraid that, had he signed the measure, he would have been vulnerable to charges of discouraging investment in California. In this battle, as we have seen so often in other areas, the conventional assumption that political decisions rest on campaign contributions was clearly wrong.

Political decisions that affect retail competition like those relating to manufacturing, utilities, and finance are far more nuanced than can be explained by simplistic pieties about the role of money.

That does not mean that the battle over the big-box retailers is over. Far from it. Shortly after the veto of AB 84, a new proposal was circulating in California that would have prevented local governments from providing incentives to any retailer with over 75,000 square feet of space to relocate from a nearby locality. In 2003, a grocery strike in California over efforts by grocery chains to contain wage and health care costs lasted several months, and was in part the result of efforts by the grocery chains to stay competitive with the mass-marketers. In 2004, a new version of AB 84, SB 1641, was circulating in California and the town of Inglewood decided not to allow a large Wal-Mart, and unions and groups across the country are mounting vigorous campaigns criticizing Wal-Mart's treatment of employees and its impact on communities and other businesses.

Clashes over what constitutes fair competition in retailing went on all through the twentieth century, and they are certain to continue in the twenty-first.

Besieging Manhattan. New York City since the late 1990s has provided examples of clashes between retail interests and civic groups and the gradual encroachment of new forms of retailing, even in areas where status quo forces are very strong. New mass-retailers are only beginning to gain footholds in New York City, but it is happening. New York has a hugely rich assortment of smaller boutiques, department stores, and other retailers, but far fewer of the larger mass-retailers and giant grocery chains that have grown up to serve middle-income working people in other parts of the country. This is one of the reasons that the cost of living in the city is high.

Retail in New York City is very different than in California or most suburban areas, where big-box retail formats are everywhere. It is more like Japan, where small retailers with old-fashioned business plans compete fiercely but work with wholesalers and other groups to keep out new competitors with new approaches. In New York City, department stores, drugstores, and smaller supermarket chains compete, but modern malls and big-box stores are far less prominent in the mix than in its suburbs and elsewhere in the country.

Some argue that the newer retail formats, dependent on the automobile and convenient parking, cannot work in the vertical metropolis. But, as in Japan, it is zoning—political obstacles, not parking constraints—that keeps them out. Experts have said for decades that rigid zoning rules impose high costs on New York City residents and drive many to shop outside the city whenever they can. Mayor Rudolph Giuliani tried to change the city's zoning rules in 1996 to allow stores of up to 200,000 square feet in former industrial areas, but the city council turned him down. Pointing out that "New York is a retail backwater" is not enough to quell opposition from unions, environmental groups, and "urban aesthetes" who have opposed zoning changes.[18]

Nevertheless, the long standoff may be ending because some new retailers are making inroads in New York City. The city council would not approve Giuliani's plan to give blanket approval to large retailers, but it has approved a number of specific projects, almost all of them in the boroughs outside Manhattan. Costco has opened two or three warehouse stores in the boroughs, and Home Depot, Target, and Ikea have opened stores in Queens, the Bronx, and Staten Island.[19]

One reason New York City may finally be opening up to new stores is that in America, much more so than in other countries, it is possible to evade local restrictions by going to a nearby community with different rules. Many New Yorkers, as we have seen, have always found ways to shop in stores outside the city where products are cheaper. These mostly middle- and upper-income city residents with automobiles do as much of their shopping as they can at malls in neighboring jurisdictions or on weekend or summer trips.

Other older cities also are torn between pressures to preserve the status quo in retailing and the recognition that new retail business plans are lower-cost and have many advantages for consumers. The mayor of Pittsburgh wanted to encourage the establishment of a new mall in a deteriorated downtown neighborhood and was willing to offer incentives to get Nordstrom as an anchor. But local retailers, neighborhood groups, and unions opposed the proposal, and the project collapsed.[20] Perhaps Pittsburgh will be better off for having blocked the development, but probably not. The effect, however, remains local. Pittsburgh's decision will not prevent new retail stores from opening elsewhere. Efforts to limit new retail competitors in various product lines and locales are a fact of life in America, and they sometimes succeed; but the decentralized nature of the American political system limits their impact.

The Vintners' Internet Wars. A fierce battle over the direct marketing of wines via the Internet is another example of the politics of retailing in America. New entrants are challenging incumbent interests, and the usual retinue of lawyers is involved. A number of interests and many states are joined in the political and legal battle, with most of the traditional arguments for and against competition being made at every level of government. There have been a half-dozen cases in state courts, and in May 2004, the Supreme Court agreed to review the constitutionality of state laws in Michigan and New York that restrict the interstate shipment of wine to consumers.[21]

The legal issues that frame the economic fight are complex. When Prohibition was repealed in 1933 by the Twenty-First Amendment, states were given the right to regulate sales of intoxicating beverages. On the other hand, the commerce clause of the Constitution makes the regulation of interstate commerce a federal responsibility. There is tension between state and federal authority, and the question in this case is whether a state's right to regulate intrastate sales of alcoholic beverages should limit the interstate sales of this particular product, wine.

When Prohibition ended, most states developed three-tiered distribution systems, with licensed wholesalers and retailers. Some even established systems of state-owned liquor stores, and several gave localities wide discretion to make their own arrangements. As of 2003, twenty-six states allowed direct shipments of wines that bypass wholesalers.[22] Several others have allowed intrastate shipments but not shipments from out of state, a position that has been challenged in the courts.

Direct sales of wine over the Internet have been growing in recent years and would grow significantly more if state rules were relaxed. Many wineries have been selling directly to consumers since the mid-1980s, not only via the Internet but by taking phone and mail orders. The Internet now, however, offers them a far larger market opportunity, and they have organized to challenge state restrictions. For their part, wine wholesalers and state governments, which tolerated direct sales when they were small, are more concerned now because they see the stakes increasing. Another issue is the tax money funneled by wine and liquor wholesalers to state coffers. One of the reasons some state legislatures oppose Internet sales is that they fear the loss of these large amounts of revenue.

Wholesalers have the most at stake. Wine producers, including even larger ones, have geared up to expand direct sales via the Internet, and wholesalers are leading the fight to stop them because they are worried that eventually this trend will allow producers to bypass them and sell directly to retailers. Larger, multistate liquor retailers have emerged, and smaller liquor stores have seen their margins squeezed. These large retail liquor chains want to do what Wal-Mart, Staples, and Home Depot do: buy their merchandise directly from producers in truckload lots, avoiding the wholesalers altogether.

The Wine and Spirits Wholesalers of America oppose Internet sales that bypass them. Southern Wine and Spirits of America, the biggest of the wholesalers, has led this fight, often arguing that direct Internet sales of wine will allow teenagers to get access to wine illegally.[23] The wholesalers have backed federal legislation that would allow states where direct shipments of wine are illegal to use the federal courts to prosecute winemakers who use the Internet to bypass wholesalers. The smaller vintners, organized as WineAmerica, are pushing to ease the state laws and stop federal legislation. Wine connoisseurs have joined with them. The smaller vintners argue that many of them cannot reach customers through the wholesalers. Big wholesalers, they say, are only interested in marketing the wines of the large-volume producers, and smaller wholesalers, who once might have been interested in small wineries, have been largely forced out of business.

Based on what has happened in other areas of the economy, it is likely that sooner or later larger retailers and small wine producers are going to be able to bypass middlemen. Internet sales will continue and expand, and efforts to get the federal government to limit competition will fail. Costs are going to be squeezed out of the system, and those who want to maintain the older arrangements are likely to lose faster in the United States than anywhere else.

Retail Battles in Japan and Europe

The changes in American retailing have taken place because political power is dispersed, and it is hard to prevent competitors, especially those with bases in other states, from challenging established local arrangements. There is fierce retail competition in Europe and Japan, but the centrally enforced rules of competition in both protect entrenched local retailers to a greater extent than they do in the United States.

U.S. retail spending in 1999 reached $6.5 trillion, while the comparable figures for Europe and Japan were $5.3 trillion and $2.7 trillion, respectively.[24] Retail competition in Europe and Japan, however, takes place within a less flexible framework that has handicapped new competitors. Laws designed to cushion the impact of competition on existing retailers have been far more effective than similar U.S. measures.[25]

The Well-Fortified Japanese Corner Store. The most important difference between retailing in the United States and Japan is the greater political power of established interests in Japan. New competitors in the United States play off one locality against another and have recourse to lawsuits and the courts. They invoke the antitrust laws and attack cozy arrangements at the local and state levels. In Japan, the process remains dominated by local interests who sometimes have the legal right to block out newcomers and are more difficult to challenge than their U.S. counterparts, perhaps because lawsuits play a lesser role.[26] Litigation-weary Americans may see some appeal in this situation, but it means that newcomers have to go up against the entrenched local establishments and their allies in government without the opportunities for legal challenge that almost always exist in the American system. In the United States, lawsuits have often softened up the entrenched interests and their allies, creating support in the bureaucracies and preparing the way for legislation. That seems to be less the case in other systems.

In Japan, swarms of inefficient wholesalers and "mom and pop" retailers have until recently made goods far more expensive than in the United States. There are chain and department stores in Japan, of course, but there have been no large domestic or foreign discounters in that country until recently, because established retailing interests were able to keep them out.

Corner stores are everywhere in Japan. They compete fiercely, but more in service and convenience than in price. They do what small stores used to do in the United States, letting recognized customers run tabs and delivering purchases to the home. In recent years, Japanese convenience stores have come together in large chains, but newcomers with new kinds of stores have not been able to break into the market and change the terms of competition.

During the 1990s, the only high-volume foreign retailer that caught on in Japan was Toys "R" Us. A few other foreign chains, like Tiffany, Gucci, and Starbucks, have done well by selling high-end brands with snob appeal, but this kind of boutique-like competition is not going to change the Japanese economy fundamentally. The kinds of competitors who could really change the status quo—U.S. and European retailers operating large stores all over the globe—have avoided Japan until recently because the resistance to them is so great.

For decades, the keystone of local resistance to changes in Japanese retailing was the Large Store Law. The law prevented large stores along American lines from opening unless they first obtained permission from local merchants with whom they wanted to compete. Needless to say, granting local merchants veto power over new competition is not in the interest of Japanese consumers.

The Large Store Law was revised in 1998 after years of pressure from the United States. The changes make it easier for foreign as well as domestic discounters to open modern stores. The law has somewhat loosened the grip of local Japanese shopkeepers over the permitting process. Costco, the French discounter Carrefour, and Wal-Mart began to test the Japanese market more actively after it passed. Some of these retailers, however, report that local groups are still able to block permits by demanding that new competitors accept less parking, adopt floor-plan changes, and make other adjustments that limit efficiency and the ability to lower costs. Even Japanese chains attempting to modernize and expand can be forced to make costly concessions to local associations of small shops. In some ways, the process is similar to negotiations that take place in the United States. A Home Depot or a Lowe's is often willing to make concessions to environmental, traffic, or similar concerns put forward by local communities. But in the United States, newcomers have legal rights and recourse and can often find allies in local governments who do not want to lose out to a neighboring jurisdiction. The balance of power is different in Japan.

Powerful wholesalers in Japan also stand in the way of more competition in the retail market. Of course, Sam Walton three decades ago fought to bypass wholesalers whenever he could. In response, wholesalers sometimes refused to sell to Wal-Mart and encouraged jeans makers and other manufacturers to continue to sell through them rather than directly to discounters. U.S. office-supply discounters had similar problems getting supplies from manufacturers and wholesalers in the 1970s and '80s, but they finally broke the wholesalers' grip. The power of the established wholesalers is greater in Japan, however. Even retailers with sales reaching $10 billion annually have had to purchase through the wholesalers.

The experience of Carrefour and Costco in Japan suggests the lay of the land. Carrefour is a French chain with hundreds of stores in Taiwan, Korea, China, and Latin America. It competes with giant U.S. retailers in China and Latin America, suggesting that it does not pull away from a competitive challenge. Costco also has stores all over the world. Even so, neither Carrefour nor Costco opened more than one or two stores in Japan during the 1990s. They hope to expand further but so far have been largely blocked from entering that market.[27]

In March 2002 Wal-Mart announced that it was acquiring a controlling share of the sixth-largest Japanese grocery chain, Seiyu, and that it had an option to buy more of that company. Like Costco and Carrefour, Wal-Mart has many stores in China, Indonesia, and other Asian countries, as well as in Latin America and Europe, but Wal-Mart has waited years before trying to break into Japan. This reticence and low level of penetration suggest how closed the Japanese retail market is to newcomers compared to the U.S. market and, indeed, to national markets all over the world.

The grip of wholesalers in Japan may be weakening, however. A surprising number of manufacturers have been willing to bypass them and sell to Carrefour and Costco directly.[28] Some probably see a major shakeout coming and want to be among the survivors. The change, if it materializes, will have come decades after it occurred in the United States, through a much slower process.

Restrictions on Competition in European Retailing. Like retailing regulation in Japan, European retailing regulation is oriented toward the interests of established retailers. In 2000, for example, the German government ordered Wal-Mart and other retailers to scale back their steep discounts on certain products because low prices were putting too much pressure on their competitors.[29] German laws also restrict the right of retailers to conduct sales. Imagine its surprise when the North American chain Speedy Muffler learned that, like other retailers in Germany, it could hold only one type of sale—an "end-of-season" sale—for a product where there is no season. Speedy Muffler must also obey Germany's blue laws, which prevent its shops from doing business for most of the weekend.[30] Many German consumers might benefit from more frequent sales or longer hours of operation, but until 2003 German law required that most stores close by 4 p.m. on Saturdays. Hours were then extended to 8 p.m. on Saturdays, and the government is likely to lengthen both weekend and weekday hours still further.

None of these restrictions, of course, is completely foreign to Americans. The United States still has many state and local blue laws that limit hours of operation. What makes America different is that the courts have usually backed antitrust rules that allow competition and made it difficult for local monopolies to hold their ground. It is natural for established interests to try to block new competitors, but the American system counters this by supporting the equally natural instinct to compete.

Balancing Interests

The vast American retail sector, like other sectors of the economy, has been transformed by new competitors since the 1970s. Customers flocked to the new retailers, mostly trying to get lower prices, like New Yorkers shopping outside of the city. Efforts by established retail interests to stop new competitors largely failed. Once the Depression came to an end, old retailers could never get much support at the national or state level in their effort to stop newcomers. The interests that supported restrictive laws were moved aside. The outsiders pushed in, driving down costs and consumer prices.

The most successful innovators survived and prospered by adopting new technology to lower costs and prices. In retail—as in manufacturing, the regulated industries, and finance—savvy entrepreneurs took advantage of emerging technology, the courts, and political divisions within communities to break in, and the courts and elected officials generally supported their right to compete.

We now return to a large, overarching question: why changes in the performance of the American economy have been credited less to our societal disposition toward competition than to changes in fiscal, tax, and monetary policy. Put another way, taxes and monetary policies had less to do with the economic transformation of retailing and the other sectors than did policies that protected new competitors, but this is rarely recognized.

7

Overlooking "the Plainest Truths"

It is astonishing [how] . . . ill-informed jealousy [or] too great abstraction and refinement can lead men astray from the plainest truths of reason and conviction.

—Alexander Hamilton[1]

The three decades at the end of the twentieth century were a period of change that ousted old elites, brought in new competitors, transformed whole sectors, and broadened and democratized the American economy. Ken Iverson, Jack Goeken, Michael Milken, and Sam Walton flourished in the more competitive environment that emerged gradually after the 1960s. The ripple effects of competition in autos, steel, utilities, communications, finance, and retailing spread across the economy and fostered the adoption of better technologies and management techniques, making faster growth possible in the 1990s.

This chapter focuses on questions raised much earlier in this book: Why do monetary and fiscal policy, the Federal Reserve, and taxes get so much credit for the prosperity of the 1990s—and so much more attention today—than issues relating to competition? Why the failure to recognize that changes in key industries have accumulated to the point that they have changed the way the whole economy can perform? And why did Democrats and Republicans spend the last thirty years fighting about government spending, monetary policy, and taxes, when plainly visible changes in various industries that were driven by competition had as much—if not more—impact on economic performance?

In the quotation that begins this chapter, Alexander Hamilton reflected on human nature and the frequency with which men overlook "the plainest truths." His timeless observation about the power of "ill-informed jealousy" and "too great abstraction and refinement" is the theme of this chapter.

Tools of the Economist's Trade

The economic theories that became the abstractions over which economists battled in the late twentieth century were shaped—like the postwar arrangements in all the key sectors we have reviewed—by the Great Depression. The economic calamity of the Depression led, as we have seen, to a great deal of economic regulation, but it also led to a different and larger role for government in the economy, a role solidified by World War II. The federal government for the first time became a large, direct buyer of goods and services, and after the war many thought that role would be a permanent one. Liberal academics, influenced by John Maynard Keynes, a British economist with a large American following, argued that to avoid another depression, governments would have to borrow and spend continually to maintain employment.

Other European ideas influenced American economic thinking, too. State-owned and private monopolies were the essence of the communist, socialist, and fascist economics. The idea of state ownership horrified most Americans, and few wanted to nationalize companies or permit outright monopolies even during the Depression; yet many on both the Left and Right thought that some borrowing from this pool of ideas might be useful. In any case, the U.S. government, like governments elsewhere in the world, certainly increased its influence over key industries and sectors.[2] And as we saw in chapter 1, economists like John Kenneth Galbraith thought this was almost the definition of a modern economy. So key industries such as autos, steel, transportation, and communications became intertwined with government, even in the United States.

Conservative Americans and business leaders after World War II were appalled by this development. They feared that a large, permanent role for government in the economy might lead to government ownership and socialism. Many business leaders had wanted to limit competition and even cartelize the American economy in the 1930s, but once they got their

nerve back these ideas had less appeal to them, and government ownership had never been part of their program. A conservative and libertarian
backlash developed in the business community and in academia against
the larger government role in the economy. The academics were led by the
University of Chicago Department of Economics and its future Nobel laureate, Milton Friedman. He and others of the Chicago School challenged
the leftist idea that the Depression was an indictment of the free enterprise
system and argued that if the Federal Reserve had managed monetary policy correctly in the early 1930s, the Depression could have been avoided.[3]
In effect, the Chicagoans said that good monetary policy would obviate
the need for New Deal– and socialist-type government intervention in the
economy, an argument that endeared these economists (who became
known as "monetarists") to the business community.

Friedman himself did not call for a powerful Federal Reserve Bank.
That would have been inconsistent with his profound distrust of the Fed,
whose bad decisions, he believed, had turned a manageable stock market
collapse into the Depression. His argument, however—that monetary policy could assure both adequate growth and low inflation—became a ral-
lying point for conservatives. Most of them preferred a powerful and
independent Fed that was strongly influenced by the financial community
over a government that would guide the economy by taxing and spending. Important differences with Friedman over how to conduct monetary
policy were largely ignored as these groups made common cause against
those who supported a larger government role.

Fundamentally, the issue between conservatives and New Deal liberals was how large a role government had to play as a spender and borrower to keep everyone employed. And because they were fighting over
this issue, both camps, in their analyses of the causes of growth and inflation, placed less importance on competition, which most favored, at least
in principle.

Nixon Lets the Private Sector Off the Hook

The argument between the advocates of reliance on monetary policy and
the liberals did not become a central one until the 1960s. As we saw in

chapter 1, Truman, Eisenhower, and Kennedy—two Democrats and a Republican—all agreed that weak competition was an important cause of inflation. Truman clashed with the Big Steel companies in the early 1950s because he thought they had used their power to raise prices. Dwight Eisenhower worried about the growing power of the "military-industrial complex." John Kennedy's administration blamed much of the inflationary pressure in the 1960s on the oligopolistic power of business and labor, especially in the steel and auto sectors.[4] By the same token, Democrat Lyndon Johnson's first Council of Economic Advisers' report in 1964 said that "the collective bargaining power of unions and the market power of large firms can interact to inject an inflationary bias to our price-wage performance."[5]

The big break came when Richard Nixon became president in 1969. He appeared to adopt the Chicago School view that inflation was a monetary phenomenon and threw his weight behind it. This shifted the economic debate from one centered on weak competition in the private sector—placing a share of responsibility for inflation on companies and unions—to one about monetary policy and the role of the government and the Fed. Nixon wanted a smaller government and no doubt agreed with the Chicagoans on its desirability, but he also saw political advantage in downplaying the issue of competition.

Unemployment was only 3.4 percent in 1968 when Nixon challenged Johnson's vice president, Hubert Humphrey, for the presidency, so Nixon wanted to find a way to weaken Humphrey's hold on labor. Knowing that, despite full employment, important labor leaders were unhappy about Johnson's pressure on them to limit their demands, he made political points during the hard-fought campaign by assuring labor that, if he were elected, he would not badger them to keep wages down the way Johnson had.[6] He would use monetary policy to control inflation instead.

Business interests also preferred this approach. They thought the Kennedy-Johnson price guidelines favored labor, and they had always liked the views of the Chicagoans, so this approach appealed both to Nixon's supporters and to labor leaders who were usually in the Democratic camp.

Nixon's approach, stripped to its essentials, was to blame the government for inflation while letting the private sector off the hook. He said, in effect, that the government and the Federal Reserve were chiefly responsible for inflation and, if that were so, then Big Steel, the Big Three automakers, and the unions could not be.

It was what business and the labor leaders wanted to hear. At his first presidential press conference in January 1969, Nixon told reporters that "the primary responsibility for controlling inflation rests with the national Administration and its handling of fiscal and monetary affairs." His administration, Nixon explained, would not attempt to control inflation by "exhorting labor and management and industry to follow certain [wage and price] guidelines."[7] In effect, he was assuring business and labor: *Don't worry—I won't pressure you to limit the use of your monopoly powers the way my predecessors did. Inflation is caused by poor monetary policy, and I will fix that.*

Nixon's shift reinforced a conservative effort to reassert the primacy of the Federal Reserve that had been building for two decades. The Fed had lost its independence in 1933, when Roosevelt had pushed it to the sidelines and used the Reconstruction Finance Corporation to replenish the reserves of the banks he had just reopened after the bank holiday that March. The objective of making the Fed independent again had been a conservative cause since the end of the war.

The struggle reached a first turning point in 1951. President Harry Truman, who did not want an independent Federal Reserve, was being pushed to negotiate a deal with the Fed but was dragging his feet. Truman's ally, William McChesney Martin, a Democrat and at that time a Treasury official with a long family connection to the Fed, took control of the negotiations and worked out an accord that restored its independence. Truman then appointed Martin chairman of the Federal Reserve Board, apparently expecting Martin, whom he must have trusted, to be subject to his influence.[8] Martin, it seems, had other ideas. When Truman asked the Federal Reserve to keep interest rates low to ease the financing of the Korean War, Martin, who believed as did Wall Street and most conservatives that low interest rates would lead to inflation, refused Truman's request: He raised rates, and Truman backed off.

Martin was still chairman of the Fed eighteen years later when Nixon came to power, although his last term had only about a year to run. Knowing Martin was not susceptible to presidential pressure, Nixon first tried to move him to the Treasury Department. Martin, however, knew where the power was and refused to give up his post at the Fed. Nixon bided his time. He was, in any case, in agreement with Martin at that time in 1969 that the Fed should raise interest rates to control inflation. But the results of the rate increases were disappointing. Inflation did not abate, and unemployment rose sharply during 1970, reaching 6 percent by January 1971.

Nixon no doubt believed in monetary policy—he was not just backing it because it had political advantages—but he had no intention of giving the Fed the power to make or break his administration. He was not going to let it raise interest rates and cause a recession, nor was he going to take his chances and wait until the policy worked to bring inflation down. He would have liked to rely on the Fed, but he was not going to do so at the cost of his reelection. So when higher interest rates failed to quell inflation, he changed tacks and went back to the "jawboning" tactics of Johnson and Kennedy.

In 1970, Nixon instructed his economic team to pressure the construction, copper, paper, and other industries the way Johnson had done to keep prices down.[9] In doing so, he was admitting that business and labor had the power to set prices—the very thing he had tried to move away from earlier by shifting the focus to monetary policy. He publicly criticized the rising cost of meat and groceries, suggesting that supermarkets were fixing prices.[10] He also began to talk about deregulating trucking, which would have meant ending the price-fixing arrangements that had spurred sharp increases in both wages and prices, and he appointed procompetition commissioners like Dean Burch and Richard Wiley to the Federal Communications Commission. Each action shows that Nixon understood, as other presidents had, that weak competition in the private sector was a major cause of inflation. He had chosen to emphasize monetary policy and budget deficits as a political expedient—indeed, he had turned this view into official orthodoxy—but he knew what the reality was. "The plainest truth" was that weak competition was a major cause of inflation, but Nixon did not want to focus on it.

Then, in 1971, Nixon made the conservative economists around him swallow hard. To assure his reelection, he not only threw the monetary approach out the window, but he went far beyond what Kennedy and Johnson had done in terms of direct interference with business. In August he imposed sweeping, across-the-board price controls on the American economy, just seven months after promising not to do so.[11] Again it was politically astute. Business interests opposed controls in principle but liked the idea that they would keep wages down. Union leaders, whom Nixon had been courting, hated the controls, but the rank and file, who always admired a strong hand, approved of what the president was doing. It was another well-considered political move.

With controls in place, Nixon urged Arthur F. Burns—the new chairman of the Federal Reserve who had just replaced Martin—to lower interest rates. Burns did as he was asked.[12] Nixon also increased federal spending to stimulate the economy. This was what Johnson had attempted in the late 1960s, but Nixon used price controls instead of jawboning to stop inflation. The new economic strategy worked for just long enough. Inflation fell, and employment rose. In the 1972 presidential election, Nixon easily beat the Democratic challenger, South Dakota Senator George McGovern, to win a second term.

But the triumph was short-lived. In 1973 and 1974, the economy deteriorated. Oil prices soared and price controls, which had lost popularity, were already being phased out in August 1974 when the Watergate scandal forced Nixon to resign.

Ford and Carter: Facing Economic Orthodoxy

Inflation had become a terrible problem by the mid-1970s. Oil prices, which had doubled quietly from 1968 to 1973 because of rising demand from expanding economies all over the world, suddenly quadrupled in 1974 as a result of the OPEC oil embargo, becoming a political hot potato. Because competition was weak, other industries could raise prices, too, and they did so. Inflation tripled in three years, rising from 4 percent—the level that had led Nixon to opt for price controls in August 1971—to over 12 percent when Ford took over. Unemployment surged to new postwar highs. Many industries and unions were poised to demand even larger wage and price increases. The Vietnam War added to the problems.

It was the worst economic situation since the Great Depression, and Americans were worried. The "new industrial state" with its weak competition and large, inflexible industries was staggering, and political leaders had to look for better ways to meet the demands of the voters. Johnson and Kennedy had tried to persuade powerful industries and unions to limit their price and wage demands. Nixon had wanted to rely on monetary and fiscal policy to control inflation and had made this approach a new economic orthodoxy, but the orthodoxy was not working.

In late September 1974, President Ford held the Summit Conference on Inflation with the backing of Democrats in Congress, who had called for such a summit before he took office. Surging inflation combined with slow growth, which gave birth to the neologism "stagflation," was a new economic phenomenon, but there were the same disagreements about how to deal with it. Some Democrats wanted Ford to extend price controls. Others wanted him to increase government spending to stimulate the economy and create jobs, and to live with any rise in inflation that would follow. Most Republicans wanted him to rely on the Fed and high interest rates to control inflation, even if this drove unemployment still higher.

Ford's old friend from Grand Rapids, Bill Seidman, a key member of his White House staff, quickly organized the summit.[13] It took a serious look at the country's problems, and Ford should have gotten more credit for holding it than he did.[14] Instead, what was remembered was the slogan, "Whip Inflation Now," which gave rise to "WIN" buttons that became a subject of ridicule. Ford, however, took his new responsibilities and the conference seriously. He attended almost the whole of it, even though his wife, Betty, had been operated on for breast cancer only a day before.

Monetary and fiscal orthodoxy, the "abstractions and refinements" of what had become the conventional wisdom, dominated the advice that Ford got at the conference. In lockstep, a dozen business leaders and economists solemnly read the catechism to the president. They told him he had to let the Fed raise interest rates and accept the high unemployment that would follow. Using a favorite phrase of the day, they told him to "bite the bullet"—do what Nixon had refused to do, and defer to the Fed. No speaker from the business community, which was well represented at the summit, mentioned the taboo topic of weak competition as a cause of inflation. Instead, they advised Ford to attack the problem with a combination of tighter money and cuts in government spending, even though they were aware that such a course would likely deepen the recession and further increase unemployment.

Only Otto Eckstein focused squarely on weak competition and blamed it for soaring prices.[15] A Harvard professor and successful businessman, Eckstein had started and eventually sold for a small fortune Data Resources Inc. (DRI), one of the first consulting firms to use computers to analyze the economy on an industry-by-industry basis for business clients. He had served on the Council of Economic Advisers from 1964 to 1966, when Johnson was concerned about oligopoly pricing. Earlier, in the 1950s, he had studied steel and other industries where competition was weak for the Joint Economic Committee of the Congress. At that time, he argued that rising steel prices were a driving force behind inflation in the whole industrial sector.

Eckstein certainly was not the only economist at the conference who thought weak competition was a problem—several others mentioned it—but he was the most systematic and outspoken. Others on the Council of Economic Advisers and at think tanks like the American Enterprise Institute and the Brookings Institution who were pushing at this time for deregulation and more competition were focused on specific industries. Eckstein made a much larger point: Weak competition generally was a primary cause of inflation and, because it led the Fed to keep interest rates high, it was inhibiting growth in the whole economy.

Instead of advising tight money and spending cuts like most at the conference, Eckstein called for an overhaul of regulatory policies which, he pointed out, prevented prices from falling and "create[d] cartel-like price increases." He recommended "a comprehensive program of structural reform of [the country's] many regulatory policies" and for the fuller use of antitrust powers. He also advised ending import quotas on steel, which, he said, were raising manufacturing prices and depriving the country of the benefits of international competition.[16]

Eckstein's program differed from both the approach taken by Kennedy and Johnson and that of Nixon and the conservatives. The former had treated oligopolies and powerful unions as a fact of life and had tried to live and deal with them. Nixon, on the other hand, had wanted to ignore their power and blame government. Eckstein advocated the restoration of competition, an approach that most who considered themselves political realists thought impossible.

Unlike the others at the summit who told Ford that the hard job politically would be to cut the federal budget and let the Fed raise interest rates, Eckstein said that the hardest but most rewarding political job would be to dislodge special interests that were benefiting from limited competition—the same position taken by Adam Smith two hundred years earlier.

Recommendations from economists like Eckstein and those at the think tanks had a real impact over the next two decades. As discussed in earlier chapters, Ford tried hard to open specific industries to competition. He started the deregulation of transportation, finance, and other sectors. Jimmy Carter pushed a similar agenda, even as talk about Federal Reserve policies and tax issues dominated the news.

President Carter when he came into office in January 1977 got the same generic advice—rely on the Fed and reduce government spending to fight inflation—that Ford got from most economists and the business community, and he tried to follow it. In 1978, when Burns's second four-year term expired, Carter appointed G. William Miller as chairman of the Federal Reserve Board. When inflation surged in the summer of 1979, however, and there were doubts about Miller's willingness to push interest rates up to stop it, Carter asked Miller to move to Treasury—the move that Martin had refused to make for Nixon in 1969. He then installed Paul Volcker, a former Treasury official and president of the powerful New York Federal Reserve Bank, as chairman of the Federal Reserve Board.

Carter certainly knew the political risks he was taking when he appointed Volcker. His staff told him that Volcker would change the Fed's approach to monetary policy, and that it probably would mean double-digit interest rates. Carter's response was that it would take painful measures to deal with inflation, and he would not shrink from them. Volcker tightened the monetary screws over and over again in late 1979 and all through 1980, forcing interest rates up sharply as the election approached. At election time in November 1980, the prime rate that banks charge their best customers was soaring. In January 1981, when Ronald Reagan took office, it stood at 21.5 percent.[17]

In this and other areas Carter, like Ford, showed great political courage. Nixon had not been willing to take the same kinds of political risks. He had been strong enough politically in 1971 to take power back from the Fed, impose price controls, get Arthur Burns to lower interest rates, and spend money on programs that fit his political agenda. Ford and Carter, the presidents who bore the brunt of responsibility for getting the economy back on an even keel after the oil crises and price controls, did not have the same control over their own political destinies. They had to do what the Founders expected of political leaders—to rise to their responsibilities and do what they thought was right for the country. They had to deal with a Fed that was more powerful than they were in many ways, and allow it to do things that they knew might cost them reelection.

The conventional view was that Volcker, Carter's appointee to the Fed, was the one who had the guts to deal with inflation. Politicians, the cynics told the public, were irresponsible, and only the Fed could be trusted. It is "the plainest truth" that Carter and Ford were the ones who took the political risks to restore the economy, but political "jealousies" denied them the credit.

Reagan and the Supply-Siders: Stressing Tax Cuts

Ronald Reagan defeated Carter in 1980. Like Carter and Ford, he supported liberal trade and deregulation—the end of government-sanctioned price-fixing—but these were not the issues he stressed or that defined his administration's economic policies. As president, Reagan had two central budgetary priorities: He wanted to cut taxes and increase spending on defense. Tax cuts were his signature political issue. Cutting them was the "abstraction" that drove his economic program, and, like Nixon, he found economists who supported his priorities.

Reagan's views on taxes and the economy were based on a set of ideas that has been called "supply-side economics." "Supply-siders" like George Gilder, Arthur Laffer, and Jude Wanniski believed that reducing tax rates would create incentives for people to work harder and give them the wherewithal to invest more, and therefore was the key to economic growth. Reagan's personal experiences made this seem right to him. As a movie star during World War II, he had seen that high tax rates made it hardly worthwhile to keep making films. It made sense to him, therefore, that lower taxes would lead to more work and investment, which would increase the supply of goods and services, lowering prices and halting inflation.

Reagan and the supply-siders shared with more orthodox conservatives a conviction that inflation was essentially a monetary issue—caused, as the saying went, by too much money chasing too few goods. Increasing the supply of goods by encouraging investment, they believed, would get inflation under control, if the Fed kept monetary policy steady. Competition was desirable, but the assumption was that it would essentially happen automatically if government would get out of the way. And, because supply-siders believed investment was driven by tax policies rather than by interest rates, they could take a hands-off attitude toward the Fed in that regard. The Fed's weekly figures on money supply got careful attention from the financial press during the Reagan administration, but the president's own attention was on taxes.

Reagan nevertheless supported the policies that Ford and Carter had put in place to increase competition in key industries. He also strongly supported liberal trade, despite a few transgressions, and initiated the Uruguay Round of international trade negotiations that was concluded by presidents George H. W. Bush and Clinton many years later. He sped up the scheduled decontrol of oil prices that Carter had initiated in 1978, and he rejected old-line business interests that pleaded with him and Don Regan, his treasury secretary, to protect them from corporate takeovers. He took the politically risky step of firing the air traffic controllers when they began an illegal strike, sending the unions another message that the old days were over.

These were not, however, the policies that drove his administration, or that Reagan emphasized when he talked about the economy. For him, the key to growth was always tax cuts. Reagan supported changes in American industries that were the result of foreign competition, antitrust, deregulation, and other procompetition policies, but he thought lower taxes would do much more to stimulate economic growth.

The rate of inflation fell in the 1980s during the Reagan years, principally because competition was becoming more intense. Imports of cars and other products forced U.S. manufacturers to control prices and costs. Increased competition in airlines, utilities, trucking, and railroads stopped prices and wages from rising in these areas as well. The decontrol of oil and natural gas prices contributed to their gradual erosion, which began in the early 1980s and continued for the rest of the decade. New lenders emerged to become sources of investment capital for new competitors. Retailing was changing and becoming more efficient. Reagan and subsequent presidents supported and contributed to these developments, but they had their origins in the '60s and '70s, as we have seen.

President Reagan's program to reduce regulation in areas such as the environment, health, and safety no doubt also reduced the costs of doing business in the United States.[18] More intense competition, however, was the key to declining inflation, and these other regulatory changes contributed little to that development. Reagan's supporters did not even claim that his support for less regulation had changed the inflation equation. For the most part, they said that his contribution in this area was that he (like Carter before him) had let Volcker have a free hand. The regulatory decisions made in the 1970s and phased in during the early 1980s that helped restore competition got little attention in the inflation debate.

Bush and Clinton: Cutting Deals with a Powerful Fed

George H. W. Bush, Reagan's vice president who succeeded him as president in 1989, was not a supply-sider like his former boss. He was essentially a conservative like William McChesney Martin, who believed in balanced budgets and the importance of monetary policy. While battling Reagan for the Republican presidential nomination in 1980, Bush had famously ridiculed the supply-side approach as "voodoo economics," a position he toned down when he became Reagan's vice president.

Bush tried to ingratiate himself with the supply-siders when he became president, but he found himself in a tough situation. Budget deficits had soared to between $200 billion and $300 billion a year during the Reagan years. The supply-siders said deficits were not so important, that the country could grow out of them, and that tax hikes as part of efforts to reduce them would be at the very least an economic mistake and, in political terms, close to apostasy. Traditional conservatives argued that the deficits had to be cut back. In his heart, Bush, who came from this school, agreed.

In 1986, with two years to go in the second Reagan administration, unemployment had dropped to 6 percent. Joblessness was the lowest it had been in eight years, and it was still coming down. In 1987, Reagan appointed Alan Greenspan to head the Federal Reserve Board. A man with connections to Wall Street as well as experience in Washington with both the Nixon and Ford administrations, Greenspan at the time of his appointment was one of those who believed that unemployment much below 6 percent would mean inflation. That was, as we saw in chapter 1, the conventional wisdom of the 1970s and '80s, and Greenspan had shared it with other economists since at least 1976, when he had been chairman of Ford's Council of Economic Advisers.

He did not believe that increased competition from imports and the reforms of the 1970s had changed the inflation-unemployment tradeoff since then. In 1988 and 1989, therefore, he tightened the money supply and raised interest rates from around 6 percent to over 9 percent as unemployment came down, to slow the economy and prevent inflation from reappearing.

The economy was still doing well when Bush took office, but the interest-rate increases Greenspan had put in place, combined with shocks from a collapsing real estate speculation involving the savings and loans and (later) the uncertainty caused by the Persian Gulf War, slowed it more than Greenspan intended. The Fed chairman began lowering rates in mid-1989, only six months into Bush's term. He did so over twenty times between 1989 and 1992. Unfortunately for Bush, investment stopped growing and actually declined between 1989 and 1991, and this pushed the economy into a recession like the ones that had hurt Ford and Carter before him.

The bitterness between the Bush White House and the Fed as the 1992 election approached was known all over Washington. A specific bone of contention was a 1990 agreement between the Fed and Treasury Secretary Nicholas Brady, which called for the Fed to lower interest rates if Bush would match and balance such a potentially inflationary move by raising taxes to reduce the budget deficits. Bush persuaded Congress to support that deal in the Omnibus Budget Reconciliation Act of 1990, which included significant tax increases as well as some painful spending cuts. The act, which also capped future government spending on many programs, was designed to reduce the budget deficit by $600 billion over five years, with about half the reductions coming from higher taxes.

The agreement with the Fed forced President Bush to break a very public promise, and the political fallout was terrible for him. During the 1988 campaign, Bush had boldly proclaimed, "Read my lips, no new taxes!"—a quip that made him more acceptable to the supply-siders and helped him patch up his problems with that wing of the Republican Party. Now the Omnibus Budget Reconciliation Act required him to break his pledge, reopening the wound.

Bush and Treasury Secretary Brady must have known they were stepping into a hornet's nest. They were betting that, with Greenspan's support, lower interest rates would get the economy moving before the next election, and that the president's breaking of the "no new taxes" pledge would be forgotten. Neither they nor the Fed foresaw that, in August 1990, Iraq would invade its neighbor Kuwait, initiating the Persian Gulf War—which probably tipped the country into recession. The war lasted just forty-five days, ending in February 1991, and the Bush Council of Economic Advisers predicted that the economy would improve that year. Instead, it got worse. The CEA assured the president that things would get better during 1992, but were wrong again: unemployment continued to rise. The economists called it a "mild" recession; unemployment had been higher during the Ford and Carter administrations and early in Ronald Reagan's term. Echoing a Reagan slogan, they told the president, and the president asked the voters, to "Stay the course."

Greenspan certainly wanted Bush to win in 1992. He miscalculated, however, as did the White House economists. The recession, as we have seen, ended in a technical sense late in 1991, when the GDP stopped declining and started to rebound. Unfortunately for Bush, voters were unimpressed by the economists' definition of the end of a recession. Unemployment continued to rise during the months leading up to the election, and they wanted jobs.

As the election approached, Treasury Secretary Brady and others around the president pushed Greenspan to drop interest rates further and faster. Greenspan had lowered them from well above 9 percent at their peak in 1989 to less than 4 percent by the summer of 1992, bringing them two to three points below where they had been during the middle years of Reagan's presidency. Despite this, the banks were feeling fearful because of the problems S&Ls were having in many areas and because the real estate boom was collapsing, and they hesitated to make loans to other borrowers.

It is not clear how much more Greenspan could have done. Nevertheless, Brady and Richard Darman, a key adviser to the president, became angry because they felt he had broken the spirit of their agreement. In March 1992, Brady stopped having lunch with Greenspan. Many in Washington knew the story. The media presented it as though the Bush administration were trying to improperly influence the Fed. The orthodoxy said the Fed was supposed to be independent, and presidents were supposed to grin and bear it. Nixon's elevation of the Fed for tactical political reasons in 1969 had more or less accidentally become a severe constraint on presidential power. The public held the president, not the Fed, responsible for unemployment, but powers once held by the president and his treasury secretary were now in the hands of a Fed chairman who was independent and apparently unmoved by presidential imperatives. The media and angry voters blamed unemployment on the president, but they also were critical of political leaders who had the temerity to challenge Fed policies thought to be above politics.

From 1989 to 1992, the Bush administration achieved some important economic milestones. It dealt efficiently and courageously with the savings and loan crisis, paying off the depositors of failed S&Ls, a cost that showed up on the nation's books as an increase in the deficit. The Bush team also handled a Latin American debt crisis in a businesslike way, and negotiated two major trade agreements that President Clinton would eventually conclude and sign. But it was hard to turn these issues into votes. The electorate, as we have seen, was unhappy because it wanted jobs—but the jobs that would materialize later in the decade were not there yet. Arcane arguments about monetary and tax policy—the 1990s version of Hamilton's "abstractions"—still dominated the debate, and no one pointed out that the economy had changed in concrete ways beneath the radar, and that the Fed's efforts to slow it were overkill because competition was preventing businesses from raising prices.

Clinton was caught up in the same debate about taxes and monetary policy when he became president in 1993. As a candidate, Clinton gambled that voters were more worried about their own problems than about opposition attacks on his character. He became president in 1992 principally because the economy was weak. Yet even as Clinton took office, most of the preconditions for an economic resurgence were in place and had been since early in the 1980s. Competition that had been weak in the 1970s was much stronger by the late '80s for the reasons discussed in earlier chapters, but Bush had not made much of it, nor indeed did Clinton's economists. The changes had gone largely unnoticed by the pundits who were talking about bad times and the fading American Dream. They lamented the inability of American politicians to confront special interests when, in fact, the politicians had already confronted and defeated some of the most powerful special interests and changed the fundamental structure of the economy. Mired in an abstract old debate, very like the one Hamilton was referring to in 1787, the critics ignored the plainest truths.

Clinton's principal economic advisers, like the Republicans they replaced, believed that the Federal Reserve and lower interest rates were the keys to economic recovery. Therefore, like his predecessors, Clinton focused on the supporting role of fiscal policy. And, like his predecessors, he set out to obtain the Fed's cooperation on monetary policy and interest rates by further reducing the budget deficits that Bush had already paid a high political price to bring down.

With unemployment still over 7 percent in 1993, Clinton's objective was to pass a series of measures to reduce the deficit by about $500 billion over six years by cutting programs and raising taxes. It was what Greenspan, the Federal Reserve, Wall Street, and most academic economists wanted and, indeed, had wanted since the 1970s when they gave similar advice to Ford and Carter. So Clinton's program focused on a fiscal policy that would support Fed monetary policy and allow Greenspan to bring interest rates down.

First, however, Clinton tried to meet the expectations of the unions and blue-collar workers who had supported him by proposing a quick stimulus package to boost employment. He already had given up the idea of a middle-class tax cut and wanted to have something to offer to his supporters. The idea was to bring forward into 1993 roughly $16 billion of federal spending that was already scheduled to take place in later years. It was not an ambitious program—the amount involved was less than 2 percent of annual federal spending, and one-hundredth the size of the

$1.6 trillion in tax cuts over ten years that George W. Bush, Clinton's successor, pushed through in 2001.

A Republican-led filibuster killed Clinton's stimulus program almost immediately, and the president's popularity ratings dropped below 40 percent. The public wanted results. Clinton, however, showed the same resolve he had demonstrated during the campaign. Minus the stimulus package, his proposals boiled down to a large increase in the Earned Income Tax Credit (EITC) for the working poor and various investment incentives for business. These were to be paid for by an across-the-board energy tax that would also encourage conservation, an increase in corporate tax rates, and an income tax increase targeted at high-income people. Disgruntled liberals in the president's party denigrated it as "Republican lite." Clinton himself raged that his remaining package was like something the Republicans would do.

Clinton, however, had to give still more in order to get a package that might induce Greenspan, whom he dared not challenge, to lower interest rates. He also had to reduce the investment incentives that he was pushing to court business support. These incentives might have been funded by a big energy tax, but the proposal was so unpopular that it had to be whittled down to a modest increase in the gasoline tax. The income tax increase that hit the top 1.2 percent of families survived, paying for the EITC, but it cost Clinton and the Democrats politically among the country's upper-income elites. In addition, Clinton got through Congress significant reductions in future spending on both military and civilian programs.[19]

Fundamentally, the Clinton program was an implicit deal with the Fed like the ones Ford, Carter, and Bush had felt forced to make before him: spending reductions plus tax increases in return for lower interest rates. The political costs of the deal were almost as high for Democrats in Congress as they had been for President Bush in 1990. In 1994, for the first time since the 1950s, Democrats lost control of the House of Representatives, in part because voters did not like tax increases even if they largely targeted upper-income people. What was really missing, however, from the whole debate over economic policy was a recognition that the economy had changed because of policies that encouraged competition, and taxes and monetary policy were less important than they seemed.

Conclusion

The battles fought by presidents George H. W. Bush and Bill Clinton to reduce budget deficits and appease the Fed in the early 1990s, as well as George W. Bush's focus on taxes from 2001 right into 2004, testify to the continuing power and political appeal of the idea that Richard Nixon endorsed on January 21, 1969. The line Nixon put forward on his first day in office—that "the primary responsibility for controlling inflation rests with the national Administration and its handling of fiscal and monetary affairs"—remains the conventional wisdom.[20] Even though inflation is dead in 2004 and will stay dead as long as competition remains intense, tax and (to a lesser extent) monetary policies dominate the 2004 debate about the economy. Analysts and pundits go about their business as if tax and monetary policies are the wellsprings of growth and prosperity, when the lessons of the recent past point in a different direction.

The central truth is that whole sectors of the economy have changed in fundamental ways, and tax and monetary policies did not cause the changes. The long debate centered on these issues, therefore, leads us to ignore the "plainest truths" about what is important. It has kept us from understanding the role more intense competition played in modernizing the economy during the last three decades of the twentieth century and from grasping the opportunities that a better understanding could open today.

8

The Competition Solution: "The Liberation of a People's Vital Energies"

All that we are going to ask the gentlemen who now enjoy monopolistic advantages to do is to match their brains against the brains of those who will then compete with them.

—Woodrow Wilson[1]

Circling Back

Like many other booms in American history, the 1990s boom ended when the stock speculation collapsed. The 9/11 terrorist attacks were a further blow, and a short recession followed. Even so, the preconditions for prosperity remained in place. Competition remained far stronger than it was in the 1970s, and it is still the central fact of the American economy. The question now is how to maintain it and apply the competition solution to additional areas of the economy.

The key to prosperity in the 1990s was the interaction between entrepreneurs and political leaders in both parties who prevented the established interests from blocking new competitors. American presidents, along with the regulators they appointed, legislators, and the legal system and the courts, supported the challengers who made competition more intense in whole sectors of the economy.

America's Founding Fathers designed our system to renew itself by preventing the permanent consolidation of power. Competition, which the Founders considered essential to development, became so intense that companies that had once been able to raise prices easily no longer could.

With investment and cost-cutting becoming a matter of survival, inflation stopped being a serious risk, job creation surged, and unemployment dropped to 4 percent.

Monetary and tax policies, while important, were not central to these changes; politicians from both parties encouraged competition from imports despite protectionist pressures that were always strong. Toyota, Honda, and Nissan got their chance here before they did in Europe. Presidential administrations of both parties also recognized that price and entry regulations affecting transportation, communications, and energy were holding the economy back, so they helped homegrown competitors—Southwest Airlines, MCI, Drexel Burnham—to overcome the opposition of established companies; ultimately, they got rid of this form of regulation. Antitrust policies and court cases also played a major role in opening up telecommunications, finance, and manufacturing to new competitors.

American politicians, it is said, are at the beck and call of powerful interests. The record from the 1970s through the 1990s shows something else. Jerry Ford shrugged off warnings from political advisers and lobbyists who tried to tell him that deregulation would turn Grand Rapids into a wasteland. Jimmy Carter told his staff to let him worry about the politics of airline, trucking, and energy deregulation—their job was to forge ahead. Presidents Reagan and Bush pushed for the Uruguay Round of trade liberalization and the North American Free Trade Agreement, and they accelerated deregulation that started in the 1970s, despite political pressures to roll it back. Bill Clinton overrode many of his political advisers who told him that supporting NAFTA and completing the Uruguay Round would alienate his union supporters.

The pundits who say that American political leaders will not take on special interests are equally wrong when they argue that the poor and middle classes are hurt by competition. More intense competition improved the fortunes of the less-prosperous regions of the country, allowing them to gain on the traditionally wealthier ones in the Northeast and Midwest. Many of the new competitors who got started in the 1970s began in parts of the country that had been lagging.

New competitors also tended to break in by serving lower-end customers, not the already well-served. The Japanese carmakers, MCI, the new financial institutions, and new retailers like Wal-Mart beat their established rivals by finding ways to make money serving less-affluent customers, whom the established companies tended to neglect.

Progrowth Policies for a New Century

Looking at today's challenges against the backdrop of this recent history tells us the kinds of policies that are crucial to prosperity. The key always, as the Founders understood, is to prevent incumbent interests from shutting out competitors and stifling change. Liberal trade, deregulation of prices and entry, antitrust, and related procompetition policies are the tools that prevent the economically powerful from strangling innovators. The difficult and never-ending task of political leaders is to support policies that prevent established private interests from shutting out challengers.

One of the most difficult parts of that political task is to recognize the various disguised arguments that the opponents of competition and change always use. Hardly anyone in the United States today argues directly against competition—but politicians and voters have to understand that many people are, in fact, opposed to policies that are needed to keep America economically competitive.

The Importance of Liberal Trade Policies. Trade policies made a vital contribution to the revitalization of the American manufacturing sector after the 1960s. The Big Three automakers and the manufacturing industries around them would never have modernized if imports had been severely restricted in the 1970s and '80s. Protected industries are—almost without exception—laggard, costly, and a burden on the countries that maintain them, so open-trade policies are a precondition for healthy economic growth.

There is proof of this proposition all around. The United States and a few other countries (such as the United Kingdom and Australia) that opened themselves up to imports during the past thirty years have done better than the countries—even the well-endowed ones—that followed more restrictive policies and sheltered their domestic industries from overseas competition.[2] The Eastern European and Latin American countries, for example, fell far behind because they were closed economies with a heavy mix of state-run or state-supported monopolies that did not have to compete against imports or domestic innovators.

Pressures for protection in the United States, however, are increasing, despite the experience of recent years here and abroad. Employment in manufacturing is declining, and unions and leaders in the affected businesses blame it on imports. Antiglobalist protesters and parts of the intellectual community support these status quo interests in the ahistoric belief that weak competition is better for poor people than the kind of competition that has vaulted the United States into its leading position. There is continuing political pressure to protect losing industries and maintain what exists rather than allowing the new and better to sweep it away.

In the United States, higher unemployment and a sharp decline in manufacturing jobs since 2000 are painful problems. Manufacturing industries here and in other developed countries, however, have been losing jobs for many reasons. The most important one is that manufacturing everywhere, like agriculture before it, is growing more efficient, producing more with fewer people. That is good, not bad.

In 2004, the focus of those in favor of protection has broadened to the "outsourcing" of white-collar "call-center" and programming jobs to places like India and Ireland. But the same issue arises. Limiting outsourcing forces U.S. consumers to pay more, and increases the risk that sheltered American industries will fall behind.

Unfortunately, there are always losers when industries have to become more efficient and productive, scrap old facilities, and change working arrangements. These painful adjustments always lead to complaints about "unfairness" and claims that workers are being hurt and that the country will be left without important capabilities. These arguments are understandable but hardly ever true. There will be far more working people hurt in the long run if old, inefficient, high-cost facilities are artificially kept afloat after newer ones are built at home and in other countries.[3]

History tells us that openness to trade and competition will need to find domestic support from segments of the business community. Gutsy car dealers played an important role in checking the influence of producers in the debate over auto imports in the late 1970s and early '80s. Steel wholesalers, steel-using manufacturers, the construction industry, and states that wanted a steel industry of their own played a similar role in supporting the growth of new steelmakers and backing the repeal of quotas on steel imports in the early 1990s. Similar groups will have to be mobilized in the future to preserve open-trade policies.

Steel users, retailers like Wal-Mart and Target, and similar companies are the most likely supporters of open-trade policies. American consumers are the primary beneficiaries of liberal trade, but it has been businesses like those above that have been its strongest advocates. Consumer advocacy groups, which might be expected to speak directly for consumers on trade issues, are often tied to organized labor; as labor has shifted toward a more protectionist stance in recent years, so have many consumer groups, sadly.

The Continuing Relevance of Antitrust. Antitrust also will continue to be important. In the 1960s, John Kenneth Galbraith thought it was outdated in the post–World War II world of industrial planning, and he poked fun at those who still believed it could be effective. Microsoft and others made similar arguments recently, saying that antitrust is out of date in today's fast-changing world. These arguments are simply false. The basic insights of the Founders about competition are insights about human nature, which so far is not susceptible to technological change. Established interests still try to prevent new challengers from competing for their customers, and as long as that is so antitrust will be relevant.

In the 1950s and '60s, antitrust cases, along with legislation like the Dealer's Day in Court Act (which was linked to antitrust statutes) prevented the big auto companies from limiting the ability of their dealers to sell rival domestic makes and foreign imports. A long-running antitrust case that was decided in 1982 was an important part of the effort to end the AT&T monopoly. Other antitrust cases contributed to the end of fixed brokerage rates in the mid-1970s, encouraging the development of money-market mutual funds and other innovations in financial markets. Antitrust cases and court decisions also prevented U.S. wholesalers and retailers from developing the restrictive relationships with manufacturers that their counterparts had in other countries, where the antitrust tradition was not as strong.

Microsoft and others continue to question the relevance of antitrust because it threatens their dominance. Two antitrust cases in the 1990s dealt with Microsoft's tactics in trying to prevent software distributors and original equipment manufacturers (OEMs) from using or selling products that might compete with its own. The first case ended in 1994 when Microsoft agreed to stop certain practices. In 1998, however, the Justice Department believed that Microsoft was not following the terms of the agreement, so Clinton's assistant attorney general for antitrust, Joel I. Klein, brought a second case. That case ended in 2001, when Microsoft was convicted of illegally preventing Netscape from marketing its Internet browser and of stifling other developers of applications software. Judge Penfield Jackson ordered that Microsoft be broken up, but that ruling was overturned. Ultimately, the Bush administration and several states' attorneys general agreed to a settlement under which Microsoft agreed to stop certain marketing practices.

Microsoft, founded in 1975, began as a creative innovator that developed a near-monopoly on computer-operating systems through the exercise of what legal experts call "skill, foresight and industry." Microsoft's legal woes came about because, as it became the dominant company in the industry, it used highhanded methods to maintain its position against Netscape, and caused the same kind of "backlash" among some of its customers that the old steel and auto companies created. It went quickly from underdog to top dog and abused the power it had developed along the way, as powerful companies often do.

Based on past experience, it seems likely that Microsoft will pay a price for its efforts to hold back its customers and competitors. Retailers who sell computer products and services have been emboldened and are experimenting with other operating systems, just as AT&T's angry customers eagerly shifted their business to MCI. Retailers do not want Microsoft to be their sole supplier, and they are less afraid than they might be in another country that Microsoft will punish them because they have a critical mass of political support in a number of states and in Washington. In the absence of antitrust, it is doubtful they would be so willing to risk Microsoft's wrath.

The antitrust battle is ongoing, like the Sisyphean struggles over trade policy. Well-established companies will try to limit competition from challengers in the new economy just as the oligopolistic industries did in the old, and the job of political leaders is to resist them in the name of consumers and the country's interest in innovation.

Regulation: Framework and Rules for Competition. Like trade policy and antitrust, the end of price and entry regulation in key industries helped make the prosperity of the 1990s possible. The Founders had recognized that setting rules for markets was a function of government. They were not for monopolies, government ownership, or laissez-faire economics any more than Adam Smith was. Article 1, section 8 of the Constitution made Congress responsible for regulating commerce with foreign countries and between the states, and for fixing "the standard of weights and measures." A succession of administrations at the end of the twentieth century increasingly took the position that the government's role was to encourage competition, not to supervise monopolistic industries.

The difference between economic regulation that facilitates trade and growth and regulation that stifles it is not always clear. The National Institute of Standards and Technology and other federal agencies set standards that define the rules of competition in literally tens of thousands of markets. These rules, which are meant to facilitate business, always are developed with the cooperation of the industries involved, and always involve political judgments and compromises.

The troubles that beset air transportation in the wake of 9/11 illustrate the kinds of problems that always accompany efforts to set standards for competition. The Federal Aviation Authority (FAA) is charged with setting standards for airline safety because no one wants airlines to compete in ways that endanger the flying public. Unfortunately, as the terrorist disaster made clear, there was a great deal of confusion in this process. The FAA apparently recommended that airlines bar box-cutters in 1994, but allowed passengers to carry blades up to four inches long onto the aircraft. To make matters worse, the FAA recommendations were not orders, and implementation was left up to the airlines.[4]

The airlines, represented by the Air Transport Association, and the airports did not want to charge passengers for adequate security measures before September 11, so security was lax.[5] As a result, the hijackers were able to seize control of four jetliners on September 11 using box-cutters with retractable blades. Apart from the appalling loss of life and cata-strophic damage caused by the attacks, the disaster shut down air travel for days, crippled it for weeks, and cost the industry far more than tougher security measures ever could have cost.

An important lesson for the future lies in the political response to this crisis. Congress was looking for a scapegoat to blame for the security breakdowns at the airports. It might have pointed a finger at the FAA because it had not assiduously enforced its security recommendations. It might have blamed the airlines or the public authorities who run the air-ports, who wanted to save money on security. These would have been legitimate targets. But instead, Congress took aim at the private security companies—the firms that had been providing security at airports. The assumption, which is questionable, is that they should have stopped the hijackers.

The FAA is politically powerful, with offices in many congressional districts with airports that provide jobs. It also has strong union support and cozy relationships with the airlines and airport authorities, who have their own political supporters. So rather than blame the FAA and others who were responsible for the security lapses, Congress federalized airport security operations, replacing the private security firms with the Trans-portation Security Administration (TSA). Congress also imposed tougher airport security standards and a timetable for achieving them—something the FAA should have done earlier under the old private structure of secu-rity. Those who recognized that the private security firms were being made scapegoats held out against these measures for a while but then settled for the possibility of some elements of private competition with the TSA in the future.

A better solution would have recognized that the breakdown that led to 9/11 was the result of the FAA's unwillingness to insist that airports, air-lines, and airline passengers pay for adequate security. It would have made the FAA set tougher standards even if passengers had to pay for them. This would have attracted better private security firms into the airport sector. The role of the government should have been to set standards for compe-tition, and to make sure those standards were being met. The FAA would have pushed security firms to upgrade their personnel, created incentives for cost-cutting and technological development, and kept costs down in this way. In short, it would have encouraged innovation and efficiency by encouraging competition the way other agencies did in other areas.

Security is better at airports since 2001; there is no question that TSA employees are trying to do a good job, and they are better trained and better paid than their predecessors. This proves little, though—every security firm, public or private, is much more acutely aware of the dangers we live with in the post-9/11 world. The country, however, is unlikely to get a flexible and innovative security service from a government agency that faces no competition. Money for the new agency is already being cut back because it depends on government budgets. Because of budget constraints, the technology will almost certainly lag behind what is available in the private sector.

The airport security experience underscores the political tensions that exist around government regulation of markets. A framework of rules is necessary to make markets work, but it cannot work well unless politicians appoint strong leaders to the regulatory agencies and give their support to difficult and politically unpopular decisions.

Policing Competition in Financial Markets. Financial markets are another area where the failure of government regulators to enforce adequate standards for competition contributed to a disaster. No one should have been surprised when the stock market boom of the late 1990s imploded in 2001. American history is full of such collapses. Nor should anyone have been surprised that greedy brokers and corporate executives hyped stocks, inflated profits, hid costs, and duped investors—such shady dealings are a permanent fault line in human nature that good government tries to mitigate.

The question is not why stock promoters and touts lured gullible investors into risky markets; the question is why the Federal Reserve and to a lesser extent the SEC did not more aggressively warn investors about the historic record of speculations. These agencies that were entirely familiar with Wall Street's long history of financial skullduggery did almost nothing during the long run-up to the crash. They should have known, based on historic experience, that rules were being broken everywhere. Just as the FAA set standards too low for airport security and failed to enforce the rules that existed, the government's financial regulators, led by the Fed, ducked their responsibilities when they failed to police the brokers, banks, corporations, and financial houses more vigorously in the years that led up to the collapse.

Alan Greenspan knew trouble was coming in the financial markets four years before the bottom fell out. In December 1996 he famously described the market's boom as "irrational exuberance" in a speech at the American Enterprise Institute that drew worldwide attention—but then he went quiet for the next five years.[6]

I hold Greenspan especially responsible because he was far and away the most influential economic expert of the 1980s and '90s, credited by some with being the engineer of the 1990s expansion. Yet he dallied and obfuscated rather than digging into the hype and insider dealings that were boosting the market. He did what Alexander Hamilton had warned against in *Federalist* 12—he turned the obvious problem of "irrational exuberance" that he recognized in 1996 into an abstraction. He should have relied on his knowledge of history and human nature to warn investors, and been willing to take the criticism that would have come. Instead, he had his staff look for economic models that would tell him with precision when a market might turn.[7]

Arthur Levitt, who headed the SEC during much of the Clinton administration, was more willing to speak out. He did warn Congress and investors that conflicts of interest were growing in the accounting profession. Greenspan met with Levitt regularly but never spoke out consistently to support his more courageous friend.

The Dow Jones Industrial Average was well below 7,000 when Greenspan spoke of irrational exuberance in December 1996, and the NASDAQ was even further below the peak it reached four years later. Strong and repeated cautions during those four years, especially with respect to high-tech stock prices, together with investigations by the respected Fed staff, might have prevented a great deal of the greedy misbehavior and held down the markets while doing little harm to the real economy. By the time the Dow reached 11,700 four years later, however, the bubble was much more swollen, and the disruption of its collapse was greater than it might have been.

The lessons of these regulatory mistakes are consistent with the lessons of deregulatory successes. Good regulatory agencies develop and enforce rules that encourage competition and prevent markets from being dominated by the narrow interests of any group of players. Their leaders have to take risks and political heat to do this. When the FAA and the Federal Reserve paid too much attention to the short-term concerns of those for whom they set the rules of competition, the country paid a high price.

New Sectors Where Competition Would Stimulate Growth

The American economy surged in the 1990s because companies had to invest and change to keep up with the competition. A growing share of the investment was in the form of new technology. In other sectors of the economy where competition is weak and distorted, investment and modernization have lagged. It is time to apply the competition solution to them.

Two large sectors stand out because they remain structured more or less as they were in the 1960s and '70s. They are elementary and secondary education and health care. These sectors stand apart from the rest of the American economy because of rising costs, increasing complaints about quality, and poor service to the lower end of the market. They also have top-heavy management structures, old capital plants, and labor arrangements that are reminiscent of the 1960s.

Both elementary and secondary education and health care are also essentially "local industries," like the electric utility industry discussed earlier. Nationwide competition does not exist in either as it does in most of the U.S. economy, and even at the local level, competition is weak.

Increasing Competition in Education. There are almost 90,000 public elementary and secondary schools in the United States in about 15,000 school districts with 50 million students.[8] Elementary and secondary education absorbs 7 percent of U.S. GDP today, and America's per-pupil expenditure of $7,000 to $8,000 a year is the highest in the world. Many American public schools are adequate if not spectacular, and public schools in many communities are excellent. The problem, however, is how to use these schools more effectively to help break the cycle of poverty that engulfs students in many central city schools, and raise U.S. student attainment levels more rapidly.

Elementary and secondary education is comprised essentially of 15,000 districts that are local monopolies, and which are funded primarily by local and state taxes. Local school boards direct 3 million teachers and (incredibly) roughly 3 million support staff who are local public employees. The uniquely local nature of primary and secondary education presents especially difficult problems when it comes to promoting reform by encouraging competition. In manufacturing and the other sectors, new challengers to the establishments could start in areas where they were welcome and develop the strength to "go national." Toyota, Honda, and Nissan did not have to locate in Detroit. Nucor Steel and the other mini-mills did not have to start in Pittsburgh. The North Carolina banks and Wal-Mart did not have to start out in a New York City dominated by incumbent rivals.

Challenging the local monopolies in education is different. Innovators have to challenge the teachers' unions, local school bureaucracies, state-chartered and favored teachers' colleges, and local school boards where their roots are deepest. They have to do this in the hard-pressed cities where the failing schools are concentrated, but where the entrenched interests that run them may be able to mobilize more voters and community support than any political party.

Efforts have been made for years to increase competition in primary and secondary education. Fifteen states have laws that require school districts to allow students to go to another public school within the district if there is room, and others permit districts to offer choice.[9] This is one sign that Americans are offended by the monopoly. Charter schools are another. There are now about 3,000 of these specially chartered public schools located in almost forty states with a total enrollment of about 700,000 students.[10]

School vouchers for individuals are another option meant to encourage competition in what most recognize as often dysfunctional school systems. Vouchers give public money to pupils who can use them at other public schools, or sometimes at private and parochial ones. There also have been efforts to contract out the management, operation, and even staffing of public schools to private companies.

Teachers' unions and local school boards in most areas have fought tooth and nail against competition on the grounds that it takes needed money away from public schools. They sometimes also portray their opposition to vouchers as a church-state issue in which they are preventing public money from going to religious schools. Fundamentally, however, this is a familiar effort to portray opposition to competition as a principled struggle to protect consumers—in this case students and their families. No monopolist in America has ever defended his position by unabashedly advocating his desire to protect his monopoly, and the debate over competition in education is no exception.

Cynicism aside, the challenge is to find ways to secure the benefits of competition for pupils who are falling behind, to bring innovation to bear in this vital area, and to prevent the incumbent teachers and school administrators from keeping potential challengers out.[11] New competitors in other markets pushed aside the underperforming establishments by doing things differently. The outsiders created better, less-expensive products and services by capturing the benefits of scale, eliminating layer upon layer of management, allocating resources and organizing workers differently, and employing better technologies. The incumbents either went out of business or had to change the way they behaved. Workers had to move around, some of them gaining and some losing. This has to be the pattern in education.

The problem is that public school choice within school districts, vouchers, charter schools, and other efforts to introduce competition cannot work if the existing public school systems and their personnel are held harmless. Would the trucking industry have provided a better product for less money after rate-bureau price-fixing was outlawed in 1980 if all the existing trucking companies had been guaranteed a fair living by the state and local governments, and all the old drivers kept in their old jobs on the old terms at public expense? Would the U.S. auto industry have pulled up its socks if all the companies and all their workers had been guaranteed the same incomes they had had before?

Yet this is what almost always happens in education when vouchers or charter schools are allowed to "compete." The established public school systems and their employees, in effect, are bribed to accept what is called competition by being held harmless financially and being fully protected in their jobs.[12] At the same time, the new competitors are often required to hire graduates of the same public teachers' colleges, organize education in similar ways, and carry much of the same overhead that the existing schools have built up.

The good news is that criticism of the current system of local monopolies in education is growing, and an intellectual climate is developing that recognizes that more competition would improve school performance. Think tanks are playing the role they played in other areas, for the most part criticizing the status quo and making opposition to it more acceptable. Ideas matter in America, and Americans think it is wrong to force pupils to forgo a tax-paid education if they do not attend the public school that the bureaucracy assigned them to. Americans are offended by this monopoly power even if they have a soft spot in their hearts for public schools and public school teachers, as many of us do.

My preference, based on what has happened in other sectors, is for private, for-profit management of local schools, perhaps by national companies, as well as local public school choice, vouchers, and charter schools. For-profit companies would bring investment and innovation to schools and make education less expensive as well as better. It is hard to believe that creative firms would not find ways to do a better job with poor students if they were paid the $7,284 per pupil ($145,000 per classroom of twenty students) that was going to educate students in the United States in 2001. And, in fact, per-pupil spending in many cities is much higher; Washington, D.C., for instance—one of the nation's most troubled school districts—spent an astonishing $10,852 per student for the school year ending in June 2001 (over $15,000 per pupil if equipment and capital outlays were included), more than the cost of many private schools.[13]

A few cities like Philadelphia have turned over school management to private companies like Edison Schools, but have so encumbered and handicapped these enterprises that the projects have flirted with disaster. The new companies have been forced to parachute into hostile environments and fight off or work out costly accommodations with the entrenched teachers' unions, school boards, and their allies. Imagine what would have happened to competition in America if Nucor, Southwest Airlines, the North Carolina banks, or Wal-Mart had been forced to pay off the established companies they challenged and work with their supporters as a condition of survival.

There is hope, however, even in this especially difficult area. No one ever thought that AT&T would lose, or that the truckers and Teamsters would be challenged and beaten. Moving toward competition took a long time in these areas. People knew that the Big Three auto companies were falling behind in the 1950s, but it took decades before real change happened. It may take longer to bring real competition to America's public schools, but policy is moving slowly in that direction.

It is also useful to recall that the steel and auto industries were changed by a combination of policies at different levels—by trade policy, by deregulation, by antitrust actions, and by competition among the states—which eventually got the job done. By the same token, vouchers, charter schools, and private management of public education may be slowly undermining the local monopolies. Most procompetitive changes in those other areas were uneven from state to state, even when strong federal support for more competition existed, and this is likely to be the pattern in education. A few states may lead the way, gaining economically as a result and slowly forcing others to follow, as was the case, for example, in intrastate trucking.

Increasing Competition in Health Care. Real competition in health care would stimulate the American economy even more than improvements in education. Today, rising health care costs are a heavy drag on American businesses and taxpayers, who together pay 80 percent of them. They are forcing companies to shift costs to their employees, pulling down the incomes of working people, and certainly encouraging companies to invest outside the United States, where the costs are both lower and paid for in other ways. A different approach to the business of health care could drive costs down and improve quality and safety, but only if innovators are able to make doctors and hospitals compete the way firms do in other parts of the economy.

The importance of the health care industry to future economic growth is hard to exaggerate. In 2002, U.S. health care expenditures were in the neighborhood of $1.4 trillion—14 percent of the country's GDP—and rising sharply. Other advanced countries like Canada, France, and Sweden pay only 8 or 9 percent of GDP for care that is quite comparable to that available in the United States, and even better in some areas.[14]

Health care costs in the United States are financed from three separate sources. American employers who provide insurance for their employees paid roughly 36 percent of the costs in 2002, or $474 billion.[15] The costs for federal, state, and local government employees, as well as Medicare and Medicaid, are paid by the taxpayers and come to 44 percent of the total national medical bill. Patients pay the last 20 percent "out of pocket." While costs are falling in almost every other area of the economy, they are rising at 7–8 percent a year in this one.[16]

Upward of 40 million Americans lack health insurance despite enormous and rising expenditures, and millions more have less protection than they would like.[17] A prescription drug program was added to Medicare in 2003 that will add about $500 billion to costs over the next ten years,[18] and health planners are worrying about how Medicare will be paid for when the baby boomers become eligible.

Health care in the United States has more problems than rising costs. The practice of medicine around the country is extraordinarily uneven. Researchers have known for years that more angioplasties, back operations, Caesarians, and hysterectomies are done in some regions and localities than in others, but these medically questionable variations in practice continue.[19]

These are only three of the problems of the U.S. health care system, and perhaps not the most serious ones. The industry also suffers from so-called "quality problems." This is a deceptively benign term that seeks to disguise an uglier reality: avoidable mistakes in hospitals and doctors' offices injure and kill tens of thousands of patients each year.

The Institute of Medicine of the National Academy of Sciences (IOM) reported in 1999 that between 44,000 and 98,000 patients die in American hospitals each year from medical errors, such as mistaken prescriptions and drug interactions, many of which are avoidable.[20] Other estimates are twice as high, but the data for all these estimates are so bad that precision is impossible. Nonfatal injuries in hospitals, however, certainly total in the hundreds of thousands, and no doubt tens of thousands of patients are killed or injured by mistakes in nonhospital settings, where they are even harder to document. Doctors complain about the cost of malpractice lawsuits, but there is no doubt that there is an epidemic of avoidable accidental deaths and injuries. Unfortunately, the medical establishment has been slower to take steps to reduce them or even to report them than the country would tolerate if they were taking place on the highways or in coal mines. If people were dying this way on a factory floor it would be called something much more graphic than a "quality" problem, but Americans for some reason give doctors more leeway.

A principal problem in health care that contributes to rising costs, mistakes, and uneven treatment is its archaic business model. There are hundreds of thousands of small medical practices and doctors who, in the words of the Institute of Medicine, "practice in isolation," and five thousand or so hospitals, mostly independent and local, that operate largely without knowledge of one another. In this fragmented organizational structure, doctors don't communicate easily or work as team players with specialists, labs and pharmacies, hospitals, sources of advice, or outside expertise to keep a patient well or cure a disease or condition. As almost anyone who has experience with this system will tell you, the patient or the patient's family has to coordinate care because it is unusual for a doctor or any part of the medical team to do so.

Coordination of patient care is rare even within small practices, where doctors share office space and support personnel. Doctors rarely know much about the patients of other doctors in the practice. This is made worse by the fact that health care remains an oral and paper culture in which it is difficult to know what is going on in the next office, let alone in the rest of a patient's medical world.

One way to think about the organization of health care is to see it as large numbers of dispersed and unconnected small stores like those that were predominant in this country in the 1920s, when chains like A&P were just developing. Local customers then had no good way of comparing their small store with others. If the storekeeper was reasonably personable he was likely to keep their business. Of course, some patrons of these stores had an idea of what was available in other places, but many depended on their local stores just as most of us depend on our doctors. Choosing a doctor remains largely a matter of convenience, word-of-mouth, insurance coverage, and, most of all, faith. Patients have no way to compare the quality of care, its appropriateness, or its cost, so faith and friendship drive all.

Hospitals, like doctors, are also similar in some respects to the department stores of fifty or eighty years ago. Most small cities and towns have one. They are important institutions and major employers, but patients' ability to compare them is limited. Most patients lack the information to choose such facilities, and many medical plans limit their choices. In large cities, several hospitals can coexist, but most people cannot choose which one to patronize. Wealthier people may go to hospitals or specialized clinics with better reputations in other cities—just as wealthy people used to go shopping in New York or Chicago—but middle-class people do not have such options.

The department store analogy works within hospitals, too. Even doctors will tell you that most departments in most hospitals operate separately, and coordination of care is informal and loose, although billing is usually centralized. Even large, new hospital corporations follow this model. The for-profit conglomerates try to coordinate the purchasing of supplies and the billing of insurance carriers, but it is difficult to change the culture of care within the hospitals. Informed comparisons of doctors and hospitals based on who gives the best care for the least money simply cannot be made by patients, or even by businesses that may pay to insure hundreds or even tens of thousands of employees and retirees.

The question is, where does competition fit into the picture? Experts have talked and written about weak competition in health care for years. The focus, however, has been on competition between insurance plans, and that focus has been further narrowed to what is covered and how much the plans cost, not who produces the best outcomes for the least money, which is what competition should be about.

This is where the role of government as a standard-setter and facilitator of competition comes in. Information is crucial to making comparisons and therefore to making markets work. Requiring doctors and hospitals to adopt computerized patient records (with appropriate privacy protections) would, over time, allow patients and insurers to compare doctors, hospitals, and approaches to treatment. The Securities and Exchange Commission requires companies to make information available to protect the investing public; health care would benefit from similar disclosures.

Unfortunately, according to a 1994 report, only 13 percent of U.S. hospitals and 14–28 percent of medical practices use electronic health records.[21] My experience tells me that the second number is almost certainly an exaggeration. The Institute of Medicine of the National Academy of Sciences said in 1991 that computerized records that could be shared by all the personnel treating a patient were an "essential technology for health care today and in the future."[22] But they have not been widely adopted in the United States. A decade after the original IOM report, the organization lamented that only a handful of hospitals and medical practices were using computerized records; neither state governments nor a succession of administrations in Washington had done much to promote this life- and cost-saving technology.[23]

This is changing. In 2004, both President Bush and challenger John Kerry have committed themselves to a national system of computerized records within the next decade. Senate Majority Leader Bill Frist (a doctor) and Senator Hillary Rodham Clinton also have called for such a system to improve care, spur competition and innovation, and lower costs, so bipartisan support is building.[24]

Competition among doctors and hospitals based on who provides the best health outcomes depends on computerized records' becoming widespread. In the current pen, paper, and telephone world of medicine, even the government, with all the information it has from Medicare and Medicaid, has difficulty identifying the doctors and hospitals that are safer, better, and less expensive because the information is hidden in rooms full of manila folders and almost impossible to get. We cannot have competition in health care until medical providers invest in the technology that could allow such comparisons; government must force them to do so.

The lack of computerized information also drives the costs of research sky-high because of the expense of combing through those manila folders. Instead of easily finding a sample of 50,000 fifty-year-old diabetics who smoke and whose blood-type is O-positive, it takes months to put together the records of just a few hundred.

Because only a few doctors use computerized records, most patients have never seen what they are missing, so they don't demand that their doctors modernize. Imagine going to a doctor, giving him permission to open your medical record, and seeing on the first computer screen all the information you have given to him and other doctors over the years. On the same page is a list of the doctors you are seeing, the conditions for which you are being treated, the medicines you are taking, and the follow-ups that are on order.

Now compare this with the real world. You arrive at the doctor and fill out the same three-page form you have filled out countless times before. You can't remember the name of the blood-pressure pill you are taking, or you forget about the malaria shots you had two years ago. Or you arrive at a neurologist with your elderly mother because her internist thinks she may have experienced a minor stroke. Without a hint of embarrassment, the neurologist greets you with, "Your doctor and I have been playing telephone tag for two weeks. Tell me why you are here." He has not seen your mother's records, and you wonder how he would have known why she was there if you had not been present, and what quality of care he could have given if he had had to rely on the responses of a ninety-two-year-old with a failing memory.

Anecdotes like this are legion. An acquaintance of mine whose young son is hearing-impaired carries around reports of his latest hearing test with her at all times, because otherwise the doctors would test him over and over again. These needless tests are traumatizing for the boy, not to mention costly to the insurance company and a waste of time. A Clinton cabinet member told me that doctors lost his MRI—twice.

But experience makes it clear that doctors and hospitals will not invest in computerized records unless they are required to do so, or until some competitor threatens to put them out of business if they fall behind. So government has to set standards for this market that will require doctors and hospitals to invest in information technology the way other industries have.

Doctors know that medical information systems are inadequate, but unpressured by the current system and a lack of competition, they make excuses for the system and for themselves. Like the auto companies, AT&T, Big Steel, and the workers in all those cultures of weak competition, doctors believe they are doing their best, and that outsiders who criticize them just do not understand.

The doctors remind me of the auto industry leaders at the hearings back in January 1958. They thought the people who wanted them to build small cars did not understand their industry, that it was impossible to build small cars profitably in America, and that the outsiders should leave them alone. Even the auto industries' critics, like critics of today's American health care system, parroted the comforting idea that the

American industry was the best and most advanced in the world—until Toyota, Honda, and Nissan proved them wrong.

The same faith exists among Americans about today's health care system. Many think that health care in this country is modern and perhaps the best it can be. But it is not, because of the fragmented, archaic nature of the industry. And the government regulators at Centers for Medicare and Medicaid Services (CMS), which pays most of the government's huge share of the bills, have not until recently stepped in to make this market work better by requiring computerization. Similarly, the American Medical Association, while saying it wants to see computerized information systems, makes it clear that doctors and hospitals are likely to resist "unfunded mandates" requiring doctors to adopt the new technology.[25]

A hopeful development is that private payers have been pushing the industry to modernize.[26] They will welcome the increase in government support that seems to be coming. Over one hundred large companies, including the Big Three auto companies, GE, and Caterpillar, have formed an organization called the Leapfrog Group, whose short-term aim is to reduce deadly and expensive medical errors in hospitals.[27] As one of a few opening steps, the group is trying to get the employees they insure to take their business to hospitals that use computerized systems for ordering prescriptions. In the longer run, the group wants doctors and hospitals to adopt full-fledged computerized information systems that will vastly improve the coordination of care and help doctors and patients with timely reminders for flu or pneumonia shots or specific examinations, keep them abreast of the latest developments in medicine relevant to particular patients, and—it is rarely said but well understood—provide the information needed for real competition. Government support for these private-sector customers may finally break the logjam.

An important problem for the businesses that pay for health care is that their employees tend to trust doctors and suspect the motives of the employers. The businesses have been afraid to push the medical establishment hard, therefore, because they know that the doctors will impugn their motives and push back. CMS for its part now is committed to encouraging computerized information systems in health care, but these efforts until very recently have been too timid. So far, procompetitive change in the structure of health care has gotten nowhere near the kind of support that, for example, competition in the airlines got from John Robson and Fred Kahn.

Why so timid? One reason is that government agencies have been afraid of the firestorm they could stir up if they try to force doctors and hospitals to modernize their information systems and compete on the basis of performance. The health care establishment intimidates the government more effectively than the truckers and Teamsters did thirty years ago.

In a sense, the unsavory reputation of the Teamsters made it easier for presidents Ford and Carter to deal with them. Closing a hospital, no matter how bad it is, is not easy. The medical establishment usually holds the moral high ground when it deals with cost-conscious Medicare and Medicaid bureaucrats, insurance companies, and businesses. The private and government organizations that pay for health care feel they must be careful and avoid making political waves.[28]

Political ideologies—the kinds of jealousies that Alexander Hamilton talked about in *The Federalist*—also stand in the way of competition, better care, and lower costs. Liberals are reflexively committed to Medicare and Medicaid as government programs, and would like to expand them to cover the uninsured. They are suspicious of efforts to cut costs by changing the business structures of the industry, and have not always recognized that runaway health care costs make covering more of the uninsured almost impossible.

Conservatives would like to see patients pay more of their own costs through mechanisms like health savings accounts. They believe that having people pay more of their own health insurance costs would lead to less waste. But this assumes that a significant fraction of the high costs in health care are the result of overuse by patients who aren't paying for their own care rather than the result of an archaic system of local monopolies in an industry where almost everything could be done more efficiently.

What happened in other industries should be a model for health care. Setting higher standards for information technology and requiring they be met are first steps toward making this market work. Federal law should require modern information technology in hospitals and doctors' offices because it will save lives and allow patients, governments, and businesses that pay for health care to compare doctors, hospitals, and treatments, and give them a better idea of whether a given treatment is likely to be cost-effective.

The states can play a role in promoting competition as they did in other areas. Hospitals and other medical institutions in California, Colorado, Indiana, Massachusetts, New York, North Carolina, and Utah all have reputations for being particularly advanced in the application of information technology. They are models to carry to other areas. In any case, a critical mass of support is slowly forming that will gradually make the political job of supporting competition easier. If payers and patients in large numbers begin to find ways to patronize modern hospitals—even if they are in other states—and take their business away from the laggards, others will be forced to follow their examples. Care will improve and costs will fall.

Concessions may have to be made to the medical establishment, as they have been to other interest groups. They would be worthwhile if they created the preconditions for competition. Hospitals and doctors, for instance, want assistance with the cost of computerized data systems and information technology, and there are good reasons to concede them this. Modern information systems in 5,000 hospitals and 500,000 doctors' offices might cost $150 billion—a lot of money. The cost in the form of tax deductions, tax credits, or direct subsidies to fund these investments could be spread out over several years, and the payoff in reduced health care costs would be huge. One year's worth of health care inflation, for example, costs consumers $75 billion.[29]

Businesses and taxpayers would do well to subsidize modernization in this industry because it would be a shot in the arm for the whole economy. My bet, based on what happened in other industries between the 1970s and the '90s, is that competition in a health care industry with modern information technology could save the country 30 percent of current costs—or $300 billion to $400 billion a year—improve care, give wage earners more money to spend on other things, and turn an industry with an outdated business model into one that the rest of the world will want to emulate.

Conclusion

Competition made the prosperity of the 1990s possible, and political leaders played a vital role in preventing the established interests from crushing the innovators. The power of established interests that had previously slowed progress in key sectors was broken. Credit has to go to all the political leaders who kept trade open, used the antitrust laws, and ended price and entry regulation in key sectors. It was never easy, and the politicians of both parties have gotten far too little credit for this tough work.

New competition spurred a surge in investment and innovation that made faster growth possible without inflation. To borrow a phrase, it did more to fight inflation than the Federal Reserve. It also helped America resolve temporarily the problem that troubles almost every country and civilization—the tendency of powerful establishments to shut out energetic and ambitious challengers.

The American political system was deliberately designed to encourage economic as well as political competition, and Americans still have this approach ingrained deeply in their character. The Founders wanted to prevent special interests from gaining so much power that the country could not renew itself, and they set up political and economic institutions that could prevent that from happening. It is a task that never ends. Innovators who succeed become part of the new establishment. Working people fight to get new opportunities, then fight to prevent the next wave of working people from displacing them. While the country focuses on weak competition in some areas, it overlooks it in others.

Competition is what matters most. As Adam Smith understood perfectly, it is what drives innovation and creates wealth. When we look at the American economy today and compare it to the economy of the 1960s, we have to marvel. Whole sectors and industries were opened up one at a time, by different policies, at different speeds, and to different degrees. Monetary policy played a helpful role at times. So did efforts in the 1990s to get budget deficits under control. But the most important changes were in sectors where competition became more intense, and where monetary and tax policies had little to do with the transformations.

Believers in competition fought for it, and politicians took political risks to restore it. Americans of both parties should be proud of this. If we continue to recognize the importance of competition, it will—as it always has—release the energies of the people and assure prosperity.

Notes

Introduction

1. "Woodrow Wilson's Progressive Program: The New Freedom from His Campaign Speeches, 1912," http://www.nv.cc.va.us/home/nvsageh/Hist122/WWNewFreedom.htm.

2. The first surplus of $69.2 billion was achieved in 1998. Four years of surpluses (1998–2001) peaked at $236.4 billion in 2000. Deficits reappeared in 2002 (–$157.8 billion) and grew in 2003 and 2004. See Council of Economic Advisers, *Economic Indicators* (Washington, D.C.: Government Printing Office, May 2004), 32, chart entitled Federal Finance.

3. Bureau of Labor Statistics, "Historical Monthly Labor Force for the United States, 1994–current," www.BLS.gov/CPS/home.htm (accessed October 5, 2004).

4. Quoted by Jonathan Weisberg, "Keeping the Boom from Busting," *New York Times Magazine*, July 19, 1998. Regarding the strength of the economy, Rubin said, "It's a combination of factors. It's some things we've done, some things other people have done, what the private sector has done. It's good fortune. It's all of this coming together, plus some elements I'm sure that no one recognizes today. Economic historians twenty-five or thirty years from now will identify factors you can't see sitting where we're sitting."

5. W. James Antle III, "Is Supply Side Economics Returning?" December 2, 2002, www.enterstageright.com/archives/articles/1202/1202supplysidetax.htm (accessed September 8, 2004).

6. A *Business Week* editorial in December 2002 captures the sense of adulation. It says that Greenspan "broke . . . the principle that inflation automatically rises when unemployment falls," and had "the courage to act on his convictions against strong criticism among conservative economists both within and outside the Fed, allow[ing] the economy to grow faster than they thought possible." Editorial, "Lessons of the Greenspan Era," *Business Week Online*, http://www.businessweek.com/magazine/content/02_50/b3812152.htm (accessed October 12, 2004).

7. See for example, *Federalist* 51, which discusses the "structure of government" and says, "This policy of supplying, by opposite and rival interests, the

defect of better motives, might be traced through the whole system of human affairs, private as well as public." This shows the Founders understood that "opposite and rival interests" were meant to operate in the private (that is, economic) sphere, as well as in the public (that is, political) sphere.

Chapter 1: A Tale of Two Economies

1. Council of Economic Advisers, *Economic Report of the President* (Washington, D.C.: Government Printing Office, 1962), 16–17.

2. Stephen B. Shepard, "The New Economy: What It Really Means," *Business Week,* November 17, 1997, 38.

3. Council of Economic Advisers, *Economic Report of the President* (Washington, D.C.: Government Printing Office, 1993); *Economic Report of the President* (Washington, D.C.: Government Printing Office, 1994). The important comparison is between the projections in tables 2.3 and 2.4, 66–69 in the 1993 report, and table 2.2, 92 in the 1994 report. The tables from the 1993 report show that President Bush's council believed pushing unemployment down from 5.3 percent to 5 percent in 1998 would make inflation jump two full percentage points (from 3 percent to 5 percent).

4. Author's luncheon conversation with Alan Blinder at the Brookings Institution, summer 2000.

5. Council of Economic Advisers, *Economic Report of the President,* 1993, tables 2.3 and 2.4, 66 and 69; and 1999, tables B-42 and B-64.

6. Phillips's formulation was basically a refinement of the law of supply and demand with respect to labor. When unemployment is very low, we know that wages will rise. It is also reasonable to assume that some of the wage increases will show up later as price increases, especially in areas of the economy where it is hard to reduce the use of labor. What Phillips noted is that in the postwar economy, areas with falling wages and prices did not compensate for areas where they were rising. The general price level rose instead.

7. Paul Krugman, "Stable Prices and Fast Growth: Just Say No," *The Economist,* August 31, 1996, 19.

8. See "The Phillips Curve and the Natural Rate Hypothesis," The Inflation Acceleration Controversy, cepa.newschool.edu/het/essays/monetarism/acceleration.htm#top (accessed November 1, 2004).

9. N. Gregory Mankiw, "Alan Greenspan's Tradeoff," *Fortune,* December 8, 1997.

10. David A. Stockman, *The Triumph of Politics: Why the Reagan Revolution Failed* (New York: Harper & Row, 1986), 12.

11. Kevin Phillips, *Boiling Point: Democrats, Republicans, and the Decline of Middle-Class Prosperity* (New York: Random House, 1993), xxv.

12. Jonathan Rauch, *Government's End: Why Washington Stopped Working* (New York: Public Affairs, 1999).

13. The Gallup Organization, "Poll Trends—Rating the Economy," Gallup News Service, January 4, 2001, www.gallup.com/poll/trends/strateecon.asp (accessed April 8, 2003). Other polls had similar results. In November 2000, 72 percent thought conditions were good or excellent.

14. See Stanley B. Greenberg, "The Economy Project," draft report prepared by Greenberg Research Inc. for the Service Employees International Union (Washington, D.C., January 16, 1995). The author was part of a briefing on the paper conducted at the Department of Commerce, and the draft copy comes from that meeting.

15. U.S. Bureau of the Census, *Statistical Abstract of the United States 2001* (Washington, D.C.: Government Printing Office, 2001), table 643.

16. Ibid.; *Statistical Abstract 1987*, table 700; *Statistical Abstract 1992*, table 675.

17. D'Vera Cohn, "Poverty Declines to 20-Year Low; Central Cities Account for Most of Drop; Incomes Hit Record," *Washington Post*, September 27, 2000.

18. Karlyn Bowman, "The Clinton Legacy: A Poll Compilation," AEI Studies in Public Opinion (Washington, D.C.: American Enterprise Institute, February 6, 2002), 6. Bowman is citing an NBC News/*Wall Street Journal* poll, December 2000.

19. See John Kenneth Galbraith, *The New Industrial State* (New York: Signet, 1967).

20. Ibid., 206.

21. Dwight D. Eisenhower, "Military-Industrial Complex Speech," in *Public Papers of the Presidents* (Washington, D.C.: Government Printing Office, 1960), 1035–40.

22. Congress later lowered it to 70 percent.

23. Herbert Stein, "Why JFK Cut Taxes," *Wall Street Journal*, May 30, 1996, A14; David Shreve, "President John F. Kennedy and the 1964 Tax Cut," *Miller Center Report* 17, no. 2 (Spring 2001): 30–34.

24. In recent years, the Kennedy tax cuts have been cited often, principally by conservatives, as the most important cause of the powerful economic surge during the mid-1960s, but that clearly was not the case. While they may have contributed to it, Stein's history lesson makes it clear that they did not cause it.

25. Council of Economic Advisers, *Economic Report of the President*, 1962, 16.

26. Ibid., 171.

27. Ibid., 184.

28. See Joseph A. Califano, Jr., *The Triumph and Tragedy of Lyndon Johnson: The White House Years* (New York: Simon & Schuster, 1991), especially chapter 5, 86–105.

29. Ibid., 146.

30. Shepard, "The New Economy."

31. See, for example, Otto Eckstein and Gary Fromm, "Steel and the Postwar Inflation: Materials Prepared in Connection with the Study of Employment,

Growth and Price Levels for Consideration by that Joint Economic Committee," Study Papers Nos. 2 and 3, Congress of the United States, 86th Cong., 1st Sess., Committee Print, November 6, 1959, pp. ix–81.

32. Robert V. Delaney, "11th Annual State of Logistics Report: Logistics and the Internet" (research sponsored by Cass Information Systems and Prologis, National Press Club, Washington, D.C., June 5, 2000), 38, figure 12. Note that the ICC's regulatory powers were largely eliminated by the Motor Carriers Act and the Staggers Rail Act, both of which passed in 1980 in the last months before Jimmy Carter left office.

33. Phil McManus (president, Maryland Industrial Inc.), in conversation with the author, July 6, 2000, and April 10, 2003.

34. Mortimer B. Zuckerman, "A Second American Century," *Foreign Affairs* 77, no. 3 (May/June 1998): 18–31.

35. The index to my copy of *The Wealth of Nations* makes reference to more than eighty industries that Smith must have observed. Adam Smith, *An Inquiry into the Nature and Causes of the Wealth of Nations* (New York: The Modern Library, 1937).

Chapter 2: The Passing of "Generous Motors"

1. Smith, *Wealth of Nations*, 438.

2. Senate Committee on the Judiciary, Subcommittee on Antitrust and Monopoly, *Study of Administered Prices in the Automobile Industry*, 85th Cong., 2nd Sess., January 28, 1958, part 6 of the hearing transcript.

3. U.S. Bureau of the Census, *Historical Statistics of the United States: Colonial Times to 1970* (Washington, D.C.: Government Printing Office, 1975), 224, series F 1-5, and 200, series E 40-5.

4. Weaker companies that depended on outside financing, like the Auburn Automobile Company of Indiana, which produced the ultrastylish and technologically daring front-wheel-drive Cord, went out of business or had to let themselves be acquired by GM, Ford, or Chrysler, who together held 90 percent of the car market by 1939. Five other American makers divided up the remaining 10 percent.

5. Frigidaire was the GM brand of appliances.

6. *U.S. v. Du Pont (General Motors)*, 353 U.S. 586 (1957).

7. The American companies did not completely ignore Volkswagen. They offered U.S. car buyers stripped-down models of their large cars and, in the 1960s and '70s, developed several midsized cars in their usual lockstep fashion. GM came out with Vega, Corvair, Chevette, and other similar models. Ford built the Falcon and Pinto, and Chrysler tried the Dart, Valiant, and Horizon. Some of these cars sold well, but they were uniformly undistinguished and never came close to matching Volkswagen's reputation among consumers for quality and

value. They usually took more sales from other American makes than from VW or the Japanese imports that followed.

8. Norman Macrae, "Banks, Steel, and Cars," *The Economist*, June 3, 1967, 21.

9. See http://www.forbes.com/2002/05/08/0508iacocca.html (accessed October 12, 2004).

10. Tom Paxton, "I'm Changing My Name to Chrysler," from *My Downtown Fun Zone, Music of Tom Paxton*, http://www.kramerskorners.com/Paxton/lyrics/iacmntc.htm (accessed April 7, 2003).

11. The ITC, where the UAW filed its petition, is a quasi-judicial body set up by Congress, originally as the Tariff Commission, to determine whether industries are being hurt by imports and recommend "remedies" to the president.

12. In the 1980s, GM President Roger Smith actively encouraged Japanese carmakers to bring their auto plants to the United States, sure that he could beat them if they faced the same labor demands that he did.

13. Section 201 of the *Trade Act of 1974*, P.L. 93-618, 93rd Cong., 1st Sess., the so-called "escape clause" provision.

14. See U.S. International Trade Commission, *Certain Motor Vehicles and Certain Chassis and Bodies Therefore*, Publication 1110 (Washington, D.C.: Government Printing Office, December 1980). In 1979, after the second oil shock, U.S. industry sales fell by more than 700,000 cars. Import sales, though, could not have caused most of that decline, the commission reasoned, because imports went up by only 100,000 cars in 1979 compared to 1978, and could not have caused the loss of 700,000 domestic sales. Most of the decline in domestic sales had to be due to the drop-off in economic activity due to the recession, and the shift to small cars.

15. See David A. Stockman, *The Triumph of Politics: Why The Reagan Administration Failed* (New York: Harper & Row, 1986), 154–55; William A. Niskanen, *Reaganomics: An Insider's Account of the Politics and the People* (New York: Oxford University Press, 1988), 139.

16. GM warned that numerical quotas would lead the Japanese to produce more high-priced cars, which they would use to attack the Big Three's most lucrative markets; they were right. One result of the VERs was that the Japanese automakers speeded the development of higher-priced cars like Acura, Lexus, and Infinity, a shift that allowed them to make more money selling the fixed number of cars allowed them. These new models eventually created even more serious problems for the Big Three than the smaller, low-priced ones.

17. Henry Misisco, in telephone conversation with the author, 2001.

18. Honda began by building motorcycles in Japan and expanded into automobiles despite opposition from the Japanese government, which wanted only three or four companies to make cars.

19. It already was part owner of a joint venture plant in Fremont, California, with GM.

20. Author's conversation with George Eads in Washington, D.C., in 2000.

21. Bill Abernathy and Bob Hayes, "Managing Our Way to Economic Decline," *Harvard Business Review* 58 (July/August 1980): 67–77.

22. Paul Ingrassia and Joseph White, *Comeback: The Fall & Rise of the American Automobile Industry* (New York: Simon & Schuster, 1994), 95.

Chapter 3: Steel

1. *Metal Bulletin*, "GM Buying Switch Could Shake-Up Steel," March 26, 1982.

2. The terms Voluntary Restraint Agreement (VRA) and Voluntary Export Restraint (VER) are often used interchangeably. There is no consistently definable technical difference between a VER and a VRA. Agreements of this kind were negotiated on an ad hoc basis, so they varied in content.

3. Michael O. Moore, "The Waning Influence of Big Steel," in *The Political Economy of American Trade Policy*, ed. Anne O. Krueger (Chicago: University of Chicago Press, 1996), 75, table 2.1.

4. *Metal Bulletin*, "GM Buying Switch Could Shake-Up Steel."

5. Kempton Jenkins, in conversation with the author, April 15, 2003.

6. Ibid.

7. Ingrassia and White, *Comeback*, chapter 17, 391–414.

8. American Iron and Steel Institute, "Comments of the American Iron and Steel Institute and the Ad Hoc Committee for a Competitive Energy Supply System," FERC docket number RM88-5-000 concerning Regulations Governing Independent Power Producers, Washington, D.C., draft dated July 11, 1988, submitted by the law firm of Sutherland, Asbill and Brennan.

9. For a full discussion of how the Japanese government directs and shapes the Japanese steel industry, see a paper by Dr. Mark Tilton, chair of the Asian Studies Program at Purdue University, entitled *Japan's Steel Cartel and the 1998 Export Surge*. The paper is available through the Japan Information Access Project in Washington, D.C.

10. Smith, *Wealth of Nations*, 438.

Chapter 4: The Demise of the Government-Supported Oligopolies

1. Arthur M. Schlesinger Jr., *The Politics of Upheaval* (Boston: Houghton Mifflin, 1960), 289.

2. Philip L. Cantelon, *The History of MCI* (Dallas: Heritage Press, 1993), 23.

3. *Hush-A-Phone Corp. v. AT&T*, 22 FCC 112, 114 (1957).

4. Adam L. Gruen, "Net Gain: The Use of Satellites at MCI," http://nasa.gov/SP-4217/ch22.htm (accessed October 5, 2004).

5. U.S. Department of Commerce, Bureau of the Census, *Historical Statistics of the United States: Colonial Times to 1970*, Bicentennial Edition (Washington, D.C.: U.S. Government Printing Office, 1976), 135, 236, 912.

6. Franklin Delano Roosevelt, "Statement by the President of the United States of America Outlining Policies of the National Recovery Administration, June 16, 1933," appendix to *The Blue Eagle from Egg to Earth*, by Hugh S. Johnson (New York: Doubleday, 1935), 441.

7. See Johnson, *The Blue Eagle from Egg to Earth*.

8. *Schechter Poultry Corp. v. the United States*, 295 U.S. 495 (1935).

9. Schlesinger, *The Politics of Upheaval*, 281.

10. Truckers were given shelter from price competition by the Motor Carrier Act of 1935, which put them under the aegis of the old Interstate Commerce Commission (ICC).The Federal Reserve Board, the Office of the Comptroller of the Currency, and several new organizations, like the Federal Deposit Insurance Corporation (FDIC) and the Securities and Exchange Commission (SEC), regulated the financial markets. The Federal Communications Commission (FCC) regulated interstate telephone rates and entry provisions, radio, and eventually TV, cable, and related industries. The Federal Power Commission was charged with regulating electricity and natural gas prices.

11. Schlesinger, *The Politics of Upheaval*, 289.

12. Johnson, *The Blue Eagle from Egg to Earth*, 440.

13. See James M. Landis, "Report on the Regulatory Agencies to the President-Elect" (December 27, 1960). This report is available at the John F. Kennedy Library.

14. Council of Economic Advisers, *Economic Report of the President* (Washington, D.C.: Government Printing Office, 1969), 106–13. Roger Noll, who wrote this section during the last days of the Johnson administration, was working at the time on easing the entry of competitors into the communications area, an interest he is still following more than thirty years later. Noll's work was passed on in 1969 to Thomas Gale Moore and Sam Peltzman, who came to the White House in the Nixon administration.

15. Sam Peltzman (professor of economics, University of Chicago), in telephone conversation with the author, April 2000.

16. Louis M. Kohlmeier, "The Politics of Deregulation," *National Journal Reports*, May 10, 1975, 703. Kohlmeier wrote that John F. Kennedy, Lyndon B. Johnson, and Richard M. Nixon "all supported deregulation" but "took the weight and measure of the political opposition . . . and retreated instead of fighting for what looked like hopeless causes." They appointed people who supported competition to some of the regulatory agencies, but they did not make competition a central focus of their administrations. It was Gerald Ford who, as president, moved the process of restoring price competition to a higher level.

17. L. William Seidman, unpublished handwritten note to Roderick Hills, May 30, 1975 (from the files of Roderick Hills).

18. Edwin M. Zimmerman, "The Legal Framework of Competitive Policies toward Regulated Industries," in *Promoting Competition in Regulated Markets: Studies in the Regulation of Economic Activity*, ed. Almarin Phillips (Washington, D.C.: The Brookings Institution, 1975), 371. This book is a collection of essays, most of them written for a Brookings conference held in 1971. Excellent in itself, the book also is a useful source for references to earlier literature on regulatory issues dating back to the 1950s.

19. Paul MacAvoy, "The Existing Condition of Regulation and Regulatory Reform," in *Regulating Business: The Search for an Optimum*, ed. Chris Argyris et al. (San Francisco: Institute for Contemporary Studies, 1978), 3–13.

20. McGowan came up with the approach of franchising groups all over the country to build systems that would be linked together. Eventually, in 1974, he and Goeken would fall out over strategy and Goeken would leave MCI, but Goeken was always a successful entrepreneur; he developed FTD, the telephone system that links florists, and Airphone, which he sold to GTE.

21. Cantelon, *The History of MCI*, 101.

22. Richard E. Cohen, "Ma Bell, Meet Your Competition," *National Journal*, October 29, 1977, 1697.

23. See Stephen Breyer, *Regulation and Its Reform* (Cambridge, Mass.: Harvard University Press, 1982), 317–18; and Michael E. Levine, "Is Regulation Necessary? California Air Transportation and National Regulatory Policy," *Yale Law Journal* 74 (July 1965).

24. Frederick Smith (CEO and founder of Federal Express), in conversation with the author, March 26, 2002.

25. Phillips, ed., *Promoting Competition in Regulated Markets*, list of conference participants, 385.

26. Author's conversations with Simon Lazarus, 2001.

27. Borman had good reason to oppose deregulation. Eastern could not make it in a competitive environment. Its high costs quickly forced it to sell off its profitable shuttle routes between Washington, New York City, and Boston. It was eventually acquired and then liquidated in 1991.

28. Author's conversations with Lazarus.

29. Alfred E. Kahn, "Regulation of Airlines," in *The Political Economy of Deregulation*, eds. Roger Noll and Bruce Owen (Washington, D.C.: AEI Press, 1983), 137–38, tables.

30. Richard E. Cohen, "Airline Deregulation Is Not Yet Cleared for Take-Off," *National Journal*, July 30, 1977, 1193.

31. Today, in a competitive environment, Manchester, New Hampshire, a bigger city that is closer to other population centers in New England, has developed as the regional hub north of Boston.

32. Cohen, "Airline Deregulation Is Not Yet Cleared," 1193.

33. Ibid.

34. This is the central point in an excellent book by Martha Derthick and Paul Quirk, *The Politics of Deregulation* (Washington, D.C.: The Brookings Institution, 1985).

35. Nixon had tested the waters of trucking deregulation in 1971. As part of the process he sent Henrik Houthakker, a member of his Council of Economic Advisers, up to Capitol Hill to present the economic arguments that were summarized in the *Economic Report* and see how key representatives reacted. One of the members Houthakker talked to was New Hampshire Senator Cotton, who, as a member of the Commerce Committee, would have to take up any legislation that affected trucking. Nixon knew that Cotton could advise him of prospects in the Senate. Houthakker laid out the arguments. Cotton listened and said he would be disposed to support the president if he decided to support competition. Then suddenly, to Houthakker's surprise, the New Hampshire senator asked if Nixon could let Teamster leader Jimmy Hoffa out of jail, where he was serving time for fraud and jury tampering. The economists thought they were there to answer economic questions, not political ones. But Cotton was saying that this was also a political issue, and that freeing Hoffa would make it easier to get the Teamsters to go along with the change. (Nixon pardoned Hoffa soon after this conversation.)

Sam Peltzman said in a telephone conversation during the summer of 2000 that he recalls hearing that Fitzsimmons had visited the White House to warn Nixon away from the trucking issue. The Teamsters were the only large union that historically had tended to back the Republicans. Rumor had it that Fitzsimmons promised to support Nixon in the 1972 election on the condition that he back away from any move to restore competition. For whatever reason, Nixon pulled back. His key assistant on economic matters, Peter M. Flanigan, a former investment banker from Dillon, Read, and Co., announced that the idea of proposing trucking deregulation before the 1972 election was dead. The economists were not surprised. They knew there was a lot of pressure from both the truckers and the union. Flanigan had been a strong supporter of competition, and the economists appreciated the backing he had given the idea within the White House. They knew he was with them, even if he was dropping the idea temporarily for political reasons. They had the same feeling about Nixon himself.

36. Author's conversation with Paul MacAvoy (Yale University) at AEI in Washington, D.C., 2000.

37. Ibid.

38. Ibid.

39. Paul MacAvoy and John Osborne, *White House Watch: The Ford Years* (New York: New Republic Books, 1977), 193.

40. Derthick and Quirk, *The Politics of Deregulation*, 148–49.

41. Lawrence Mosher, "Trucking Deregulation—An Idea Whose Time Has Come and Almost Gone?" *National Journal*, May 19, 1979, 820.

42. Stu Eizenstat, in conversation with the author at the White House ceremony for the fiftieth anniversary of NATO, April 25, 1999.

43. Section 601 of the Airport Improvement Act of 1994. Freight trucking was added to a bill to expand competition in intrastate airfreight.

44. Jeff Westcott (vice chairman of Guardsmark), in a telephone interview with the author, April 10, 2003.

45. Laurence Zuckerman and Matthew L. Wald, "Gridlock in the Skies: A Special Report—Crisis for Air Traffic System: More Passengers, More Delays," *New York Times,* September 5, 2000, C12.

46. Kirstin Downey, "Dreamers Find Themselves Grounded," *Washington Post,* April 13, 2003.

47. News Batch, "Electricity Deregulation," updated May 28, 2002, www.newsbatch.com/electric.htm (accessed June 17, 2004).

48. S. David Freeman, "California Consumer Power and Conservation Chairman, S. David Freeman," speech to the International Convention of the International Brotherhood of Electrical Workers, *IBEW Journal on Line,* October/November 2001, http://ibew.org/stories/01journal/0110/speeches/Freeman.htm (accessed April 16, 2003).

49. Smith, *Wealth of Nations,* 437–38.

Chapter 5: Opening Up American Finance

1. Zuckerman, "A Second American Century," 24.

2. Frank Cruz (chairman of the Corporation for Public Broadcasting), in conversation with the author, July 2000.

3. Zuckerman, "A Second American Century," 24.

4. U.S. Bureau of the Census, "Flow of Funds Accounts—Assets of Financial and Non-Financial Institutions by Holder Sector," *Statistical Abstract of the United States 1978,* table 849; *Statistical Abstract 2001,* table 1163.

5. See Robert Litan, *American Finance for the 21st Century* (Washington, D.C.: Brookings Institution Press, 1998).

6. See Milton Friedman and Anna Jacobson Schwartz, "The Great Contraction," chap. 7, sec. 7 in *A Monetary History of the United States, 1857–1960* (Princeton, N.J.: Princeton University Press, 1963), 407–19.

7. Glenn Yago, *Junk Bonds: How High Yield Securities Restructured Corporate America* (New York: Oxford University Press, 1991), 20.

8. Drexel's management had no idea how lucrative creating a market for the bonds of smaller firms would become, so in 1974 it cut a deal with Milken. Milken would keep one dollar for every three he made for the firm. That seemed reasonable then; nobody else wanted to deal in these kinds of bonds. In the 1980s, when the market grew beyond anyone's wildest dreams, the deal

Milken had made right out of college in the 1970s made him fabulously rich. Ibid., 21.

9. Lorraine Spurge, *Failure Is Not an Option: How MCI Invented Competition in Telecommunications* (Encino, Calif.: Spurge, Ink!, 1998), 88–92.

10. Michael Bader (MCI's long-serving general counsel), in conversation with the author, May 29, 2001.

11. Yago, *Junk Bonds*, 187.

12. Ibid., 181–83.

13. Ibid., 27.

14. Similar markets operate all over the world. As a doctoral student in 1970, I visited rural merchants in India who received hundreds of postcards from merchants in other cities every day with quoted prices for grains, butter, sugar, fertilizer, and other products.

15. The pink sheets and OTC market continue to exist and function today. The changes in the 1970s, which created a new stock market for smaller, riskier companies, reduced the need for pink sheets but did not eliminate it.

16. Greg Schneider, "A Man of Many Epiphanies," *Washington Post*, March 5, 2001, E-1. Also, Sidney Harman, in conversation with the author, July 2003.

17. Alexis de Tocqueville Institute, "NASDAQ Fast Facts," www.adti.net/html_tax/nasdaqtrib (accessed May 29, 2001).

18. Today, a similar OTC market with pink sheets and quite similar problems operates for thousands of firms that cannot or do not want to trade on the NASDAQ, although trading in these stocks is becoming more computerized, too.

19. The NYSE's rules sometimes irritate its competitors at NASDAQ, but they do not seem to be a serious problem. NASDAQ spokespeople point out, for example, that NYSE rules make it hard to leave the NYSE and go to the NASDAQ. For years the NYSE's rule 500 required firms leaving the exchange to get the approval of their stockholders and jump through other hoops. In a conversation with the author in the summer of 2002, Dick Syron, who once headed the American Stock Exchange and in 2004 is the chairman and CEO of the Federal Home Loan Mortgage Corporation (Freddie Mac), recalled with a laugh that when he headed the American exchange, he called the NYSE the "Hotel California," a reference to the popular song by the Eagles about a hotel where "you can check out any time you like, but you can never leave." It is still harder to leave the NYSE than the NASDAQ, but investors and those who want to sell stock have real choices now that they did not have in the 1970s and that are just now coming to other parts of the world.

20. Richard R. West and Seha M. Tinic, "Minimum Commission Rates on the New York Stock Exchange," *RAND Journal of Economics* 2, no. 2 (Autumn 1971): 577–605. Abstract available from www.rje.org/abstracts/abstracts/1971/Autumn_1971._pp._577_605.html.

21. Louis M. Kohlmeier, "Reform is Racing Ahead Slowly," *National Journal*, June 28, 1975, 973.

22. The Federal Reserve Bank of Minneapolis, "The Federal Reserve System: An Overview of Times and Events—Regulatory Policy Environment," http://minneapolisfed.org/pubs/region/88-08/reg888b5.cfm (accessed September 1, 2004).

23. Paul A. Gompers, "The Rise and Fall of Venture Capital," *Business and Economic History* 23, no. 2 (1992): 1.

24. U.S. Census Bureau, *Statistical Abstract 1985*, 495, table 826; *Statistical Abstract 2000*, 514, table 806.

25. Richard Tilghman, in telephone conversation with the author, summer 2001.

26. Ibid.

27. *Northeast Bancorp v. Board of Governors, FRS*, 472 US 159 (1985).

28. There have been numerous other mergers involving North Carolina banks and financial institutions, including the merger of Wachovia and First Union, which was announced in 2001 and completed in 2003.

29. The North Carolina banks all acquired other financial institutions as well. First Union, one of the major North Carolina banks even before its merger with Wachovia, acquired Wheat First Securities and Montgomery Securities. Bank of America-NationsBank bought Robertson Stephens. BB&T of Winston-Salem acquired Scott and Stringfellow, a broker-dealer, and Craigie Inc., an investment bank.

30. For a discussion of the gradual change in banking regulation, see Laurence H. Meyer, "The Federal Reserve and Bank Supervision and Regulation" (lecture, Widener University, Chester, Pa., April 16, 1998), http://www.federalreserve.gov/boarddocs/speeches/1998/.

31. See Lonny E. Carlile and Mark C. Tilton, eds., *Is Japan Really Changing Its Ways? Regulatory Reform and the Japanese Economy* (Washington, D.C.: Brookings Institution Press, 1998).

32. See Eugene R. Dattel, *The Sun That Never Rose* (Chicago: Probus Publishing, 1994), especially 4–22.

33. For an entertaining description of all the reasons people can conjure up for making irrational investments in a boom, see John Kenneth Galbraith, *A Short History of Financial Euphoria: Financial Genius Is before the Fall* (Knoxville, Tenn.: Whittle Communications, 1990).

34. Elizabeth Norville, "The 'Illiberal' Roots of Japanese Financial Regulatory Reform," in ibid., 129. It took fourteen years, until 2004, for the Japanese economy to show solid signs of recovery from this blow.

35. Schroder Salomon Smith, "Mezzanine Capital and High Yield Bonds," www.privateequityonline.com/ch7_14.html (accessed May 14, 2001).

36. There is, for example, an over-the-counter market in France that is called—charmingly—the "*Coulisse*," or backstage. It is ancient, but it is a narrower market than the OTC is in the United States and, not surprisingly, more directly under the control of the main French stock exchange, the Bourse.

37. See Galbraith, *A Short History of Financial Euphoria*.

Chapter 6: The Revolution in Retailing

1. Daniel Akst, "On the Contrary: Why Chain Stores Aren't the Big Bad Wolf," *New York Times*, June 3, 2001.

2. Not including automobiles.

3. Leslie Kaufman, "As Biggest Business Wal-Mart Propels Changes Elsewhere," *New York Times*, October 22, 2000, A1 and A24.

4. Akst, "On the Contrary."

5. Sam Walton with John Huey, *Sam Walton, Made in America: My Story* (New York: Doubleday, 1992), 183.

6. Leslie Kaufman, "The Real Retail Revolution: It's Wal-Mart, Not the Internet," *New York Times*, December 20, 1999.

7. *Schwegmann Bros. v. Calvert Corp.*, 341 U.S. 384 (1951).

8. "Emerging Trends in U.S. Retailing," http//www.hawaii.gov/dbedt/he8-98/emerge.htm (accessed October 6, 2004).

9. Martha McNeil Hamilton, "Super Strides for Supermarket Industry," *Washington Post*, June 20, 2001, G8.

10. Of course, communications between doctors and pharmacies remain primitive—dependent almost entirely on slips of paper, fax, and telephone—but that is due to the backwardness of the business models in health care, not to the failure of the pharmacies. This issue is discussed in more detail in chapter 8.

11. See *Hometown Advantage Bulletin*, May 2001, http://www.plannersweb.com/sprawl/reports/rep-hometown-advantage.html and http://www.newrules.org (accessed April 30, 2003).

12. The bill, called AB 84 in its 1999 incarnation, would have blocked local governments in California from approving construction of any store of more than 100,000 square feet, if the store devoted more than 15,000 square feet of selling space to food and drugs, which are nontaxable in California.

13. A survey of the highly competitive Atlanta-area grocery market suggests how problematic the new big-box competition is for grocery and pharmacy chains. Kroger had long been the strongest grocery chain around Atlanta. Publix, a successful, somewhat more upscale, Florida grocery chain, came into the market in the mid-1990s to challenge it. More recently, Target and Wal-Mart have begun selling groceries in the area at new supercenters. The Atlanta market-basket survey shows supercenters underselling Kroger and Publix by 12–30 percent on almost every one of forty items chosen at random. These are wide disparities, although the survey may somewhat exaggerate the price advantage of the supercenters. (The prices of brand-name items were compared in the market basket used in the survey because these lend themselves to comparison. Customers, however, can save money at grocery chains by buying sale items and "house brands" that are harder to compare.) There is no doubt, however, that the supercenters are driving prices down and giving consumers low-cost options, and this is clearly worrying the grocery and drug

chains. Laura Heller, "Wal-Mart Outprices Atlanta Competition," *DSN Retailing Today*, June 18, 2001, 18.

14. Greg Brouwer, "Big Box Blow Up," September 24–30, 1999, www.laweekly.com/ink/99/44/offbeat.shtml.

15. "The Power Broker Nobody Knows: California Billionaire Ron Burkle," *Talk Magazine*, April 2001, www.talkmagazine.com/talkmedia/april (accessed in 2002).

16. Dan Smith, "Davis Casts Broad Net to Pull in $6 Million," *Sacramento Bee*, August 5, 1999, www.fairvote2000.org/9908/080599a.html.

17. See www.sprawl-busters.com/search.php?readstory=306 (accessed October 6, 2004).

18. Rita Kramer, "New York's Missing Megastores," *City Journal* 6, no. 4 (Autumn 1996): 68–73.

19. Richard Lipsky Associates, "Hell's Kitchen on Line—Focus on Costco," September 8, 1999, www.tenant.net/pipermail/hkonline. Lipsky Associates was representing the Food and Commercial Workers Union. See also Empire State Development, "Governor, Mayor Announce Major Development in East Harlem," March 29, 1998, www.empire.state.ny (accessed June 12, 2001).

20. Jeff Stacklin, "City Courting Nordstrom," *Pittsburgh New Tribune-Review*, June 20, 1999, 3.

21. Jonathan Bick, "Legality of Interstate Wine Sales in Flux," *New Jersey Law Journal*, July 19, 2004, http://www.bicklaw.com/index_files/Page1269.htm (accessed October 6, 2004).

22. Edward Epstein, "Battle Royal Over Wine Shipped Interstate: Winemakers Want Direct Internet Sales; Distributors Say No," *San Francisco Chronicle*, December 8, 2003.

23. R. W. Apple Jr., "Zinfandel by Mail? Well, Yes and No; Strict Laws May Get Stricter," Dining In, Dining Out/Style Desk, *New York Times*, May 19, 1999.

24. Hedehiko Aoki, "New Moves on the Global Chessboard: Big-Box Retailers Enter Japan," report from Goldman Sachs Global Equity Research, *Retail Global*, April 25, 2001, exhibits 3, 4.

25. Yuko Aoyama, "Structural Foundations for E-Commerce Adoption: A Comparative Organization of Retail Trade Between Japan and the United States," *Urban Geography* 22, no. 2 (2001): 130.

26. Mark C. Tilton, "Market Opening in Japan," in Carlile and Tilton, *Is Japan Really Changing Its Ways?* 166–68.

27. Aoki, "New Moves on the Global Chessboard." The Goldman Sachs report contains an exhibit showing the penetration of mass merchandisers in Asia. See exhibit 30 (last item in first three columns), 25.

28. Ibid., 14

29. Ernest Beck, "Stores Told to Lift Prices in Germany," *Wall Street Journal*, September 11, 2000, A27, A30.

30. Author's conversation with Hershel Ezrin, February 2002.

Chapter 7: Overlooking "the Plainest Truths"

1. Hamilton, *Federalist* 12.

2. Daniel Yergin and Joseph Stanislaw, *The Commanding Heights: The Battle between Government and the Marketplace That Is Remaking the Modern World* (New York: Simon & Schuster, 1998), see especially 12. This very important and much-cited book, which was turned into a television documentary, describes the forces that led countries after World War II to seek control of most key industries, and then relax this control in later years.

3. Friedman and Schwartz, *A Monetary History*.

4. Council of Economic Advisers, *Economic Report of the President*, 1962, 171.

5. Ibid., 1964, 114.

6. Many working-class union members were also angry at the Democrats because they hesitated to crack down on the protests against the Vietnam War and over civil rights that were sweeping the country.

7. "National Affairs," *Facts on File* 29, no. 1474 (January 23–29, 1969): 39C.

8. "Biography of William McChesney Martin Jr. (1906–1998)," in *The Fiftieth Anniversary of the Treasury-Federal Reserve Accord 1951–2001*, http://www.rich.frb.org/research/specialtopics/treasury/bios/martin.html (accessed September 11, 2004).

9. Council of Economic Advisers, *Economic Report of the President* (Washington, D.C.: Government Printing Office, 1972), 73–74

10. See Richard Reeves, *President Nixon: Alone in the White House* (New York: Simon & Schuster, 2001), 263–64.

11. Council of Economic Advisers, *Economic Report of the President* (Washington, D.C.: Government Printing Office, 1971), 7.

12. See William Greider, *Secrets of the Temple* (New York: Touchstone, 1987), 342–43.

13. Seidman later played an important role in cleaning up the S&L mess during the administration of George H. W. Bush.

14. See *Summit Conference on Inflation Transcript*, O-559-102, September 27–28 (Washington, D.C.: Government Printing Office, 1974).

15. Ibid., 30–32.

16. Ibid., 31.

17. See Council of Economic Advisers, *Economic Report of the President* (Washington, D.C.: Government Printing Office, 1983), table B-67. This table tells an interesting story. It shows that all of the increases in interest rates engineered by Volcker in 1979 and 1980 took place while Carter was in office. Volcker let rates fall 5–7 percent from their Carter-era highs by the end of Reagan's first year, despite the prospect of unprecedented deficits, and he let them

fall further in 1982, despite these deficits' having actually come about. Interest rates already were 8–9 percent below late-Carter levels by September 1982.

18. Presidential Task Force on Regulatory Relief, "Reagan Administration Achievements in Regulatory Relief, A Progress Report" (unpublished report, Washington, D.C., August 1982).

19. Council of Economic Advisers, *Economic Report of the President*, 1994, 30.

20. "National Affairs," *Facts on File*, 39C.

Chapter 8: The Competition Solution: "The Liberation of a People's Vital Energies"

1. Woodrow Wilson, *The New Freedom* (New York and Garden City: Doubleday, Page & Co., 1918), 257. The Wilson quotation in the chapter title appears on page 277.

2. Australia unilaterally reduced tariffs on imports in the 1970s and then embarked on a major program of deregulation and "antitrust" in the 1980s. In the process, it went from having a sleepy, inflation-prone economy, in danger of becoming a backwater, to a vibrant, forward-looking one, with many world-class industries.

3. One of the most important insights in *The Wealth of Nations* is that management and labor in most industries are on the same side when it comes to limits on competition. Smith said that "the same increase of competition reduces the profits of the masters as well as the wages of the workmen. The trades, the crafts . . . would all be losers. But the public would be a gainer." Smith, *Wealth of Nations*, 123. Marx adopted the contrary and very ancient populist view that workers and owners have fundamentally different interests, and this view of the world continues to be widely held in the United States and certainly in Western Europe. Smith understood that the workers and the bosses in most industries share a powerful interest in maintaining a monopoly, even if it means raising costs for other working people, and in keeping new competitors out.

4. Jonathan D. Salant, "The Airline Industry and Self-Regulation: Pre-9/11 Rules Barred Box Cutters," *The Associated Press*, November 11, 2002, http://archives.californiaaviation.org/airport/msg31262/html (accessed September 8, 2004).

5. Ibid.

6. Alan Greenspan, remarks at the Annual Dinner and Francis Boyer Lecture of the American Enterprise Institute for Public Policy Research, Washington, D.C., December 5, 1996; Louis Uchitelle, "He Didn't Say It. But He Knew It," Money and Business, *New York Times*, April 30, 2000, http://cowles.econ.yale.edu/news/shiller/rjs_00-03-30_nyt_knew.htm (accessed September 8, 2004). Just before the stock market broke, Uchitelle said:

An irony is that Mr. Greenspan, despite having introduced the notion of over exuberance into the national dialogue, increasingly sees high stock prices—a lot higher than they were in 1996—as a rational appraisal of corporate America's profitability and prospects.

Technology is transforming the American economy, he says in his speeches and Congressional testimony. Productivity is rising, along with profits. And so investors are logically investing with enthusiasm in companies that are likely to grow in value. What's more, Mr. Greenspan notes, computer technology has increased the amount of information available to investors, and has thus reduced their risk of overpaying for stocks. "Because knowledge once gained is irreversible, so too are the lowered risk premiums," he declared in one recent speech.

7. Bob Woodward, *Maestro: Greenspan's Fed and the American Boom* (New York: Simon & Schuster, 2000), 218.

8. U.S. Bureau of the Census, *Statistical Abstract 1999*, tables 274, 276, 175, 176.

9. The Heritage Foundation, "School Choice 2003," overview and introduction, http://www.heritage.org/Research/Education/Schools/schoolchoice_introduction.cfm (accessed September 8, 2004).

10. U.S. Department of Education, "U.S. Charter Schools," overview, http://www.uscharterschools.org/pub/uscs_docs/o/index.htm#national (accessed September 8, 2004).

11. For excellent discussions of the potential benefits of competition in elementary and secondary education see Caroline M. Hoxby, "School Choice and School Competition: Evidence from the United States," *Swedish Economic Policy Review* 10 (2003): 11–67; and *Frontline*, "The Battle over School Choice," interview with Caroline M. Hoxby, 2000, http://www.pbs.org/wgbh/pages/frontline/shows/vouchers/interviews/hoxby.html (accessed September 8, 2004).

12. Frederick M. Hess, "Without Competition, School Choice Is Not Enough," American Enterprise Institute, On the Issues, May 1, 2004, http://www.aei.org/publications/filter.,pubID.20491/pub_detail.asp.

13. *Washington Times*, "Per Pupil Spending," editorial, March 13, 2003, http://www.childrenfirstamerica.org/DailyNews/03Mar/0313038.htm (accessed September 8, 2004).

14. National Coalition on Health Care, "Health Insurance Cost," http://www.nchc.org/facts/cost.shtml (accessed September 8, 2004).

15. One painful effect of rising health care costs is that they often prevent employers from paying higher wages.

16. U.S. Bureau of the Census, *Statistical Abstract 2003*, table 132, 105.

17. Ibid., table 153, 114.

18. Daniel J. Mitchell, "A Ticking Time Bomb for Tax Increases," The Heritage Foundation WebMemo no. 462, March 31, 2004, http://www.heritage.org/Research/HealthCare/wm462.cfm (accessed September 8, 2004).

19. Amitabh Chandra and Jonathan Skinner, "Geography and Racial Health Disparities," National Bureau of Economic Research (NBER) working paper no. 9513, February 2003, http://www.nber.org/aginghealth/winter03/w9513.html (accessed September 8, 2004). The synopsis uses angioplasties as an example: In 1996, it notes, "There was an average of 7.5 angioplasty procedures performed per 1000 Medicare enrollees in the US, but the rate varied from 2.6 to 22.3 per 1000 across the 306 'hospital referral regions' (HRR) in the country. The authors find that substantial differences persist even after adjusting for differences in patient characteristics, and that large disparities exist not only across regions of the country but also within states and even cities."

20. Institute of Medicine, introduction to To Err Is Human: Building a Safer Health System, ed. Linda T. Kohn, Janet M. Corrigan, and Molla S. Donaldson (Washington, D.C.: National Academy Press, 2000). Also available online at http://books.nap.edu/books/0309068371/html/1.html#pagetop.

21. Amanda Gardner, "U.S. Sets Sights on Electronic Health Records," July 26, 2004, http://www.klkntv.com/Global/story.asp?S=2089854 (accessed October 7, 2004).

22. Institute of Medicine, The Computer-Based Patient Record: An Essential Technology for Health Care (Washington, D.C.: National Academy Press, 1991), 51.

23. Institute of Medicine, To Err Is Human.

24. Bill Frist and Hillary Clinton, "How to Heal Health Care," Washington Post, August 25, 2004, A17.

25. Markian Hawryluk, "President Launches Push for Electronic Records; Funds for Project Still in Question," AMNews.com, May 17, 2004, http://www.ama-assn.org/amednews/2004/05/17/gvsa0517.htm (accessed September 8, 2004).

26. Rod Winslow, "Employer Group Creates Institute to Brainstorm about Health Costs," Wall Street Journal, December 19, 2001, B-17; Tyler Chin, "Electronic Medical Records: Mastering the Maze," AMNews, December 24 and 31, 2001; and David Brown, "The End of Error: Big Business in an Era of Reform Is Pressuring Hospitals to Cut Mistakes—and Costs," Health section, Washington Post, March 26, 2002.

27. Bob Brewin, "Health Care IT Plans Get a Renewed Push; Bush, Industry Groups Try to Jump-Start Adoption of New Medical Technologies," Computerworld, May 3, 2004, http://www.computerworld.com/industrytopics/healthcare/story/0,10801,92822,00.html.

28. See, for example, Susan Okie, "Building an Electronic Network of Care," Washington Post, December 12, 2001.

29. Assuming an inflation rate of just 5 percent.

Index

About the Author

Paul A. London served as deputy under secretary of commerce for economics and statistics in the Clinton administration from 1993 to 1997. He wrote *The Competition Solution* while a visiting fellow at the American Enterprise Institute. Previously, he worked on European economic integration for the Department of State, and spent three years working in Vietnam in the 1960s. Mr. London is the author of *The Role of Merchants in Economic Development* (Praeger, 1975), a study of privatization in India. Subsequently, Mr. London served as an economic adviser for Senator Walter Mondale on the Senate Banking Committee in the 1970s, working on tax, banking, energy, and transportation issues. He later served as director of the New England Economic Research Office and executive director of the Coalition of Northeastern Governors. In the 1980s and early 1990s he did consulting work on international trade, natural gas, electric, and airline deregulation, and pharmaceuticals.

Mr. London is the author of numerous articles that have appeared in the *New York Times, Washington Post, Newsday, The New Republic, National Journal,* and other publications. London has an AB from Harvard University and a PhD in political economy from the John F. Kennedy School of Government.